Landmark

Upper Intermediate **Student's Book**

Simon Haines & Barbara Stewart

OXFORD
UNIVERSITY PRESS

7 Survival

Pages 64–73

Preview	Listening	Reading
Reading: Aborigines *can, could, be able to* review Weak forms	Personal survival stories Ability and inability	One of the world's greenest cities? Articles

Vocabulary	Language in action		
Connotations Distinctions between verbs	Persuading / advising someone not to do something	Making generalizations The use of *you know* Unfinished statements	Writing: Radio scripts

8 In the family

Pages 74–83

Preview	Reading	Listening
Reading: The Fonda and the Kennedy Families Relative clauses review	Benetton family business Relative clauses	Children in families Emphasizing words and structures Sentence stress

Vocabulary	Language in action		
Informal words, *nice* and *get*	Making and responding to requests	Preparing the listener for a difficult request The use of *OK, The thing is …*	Writing: A letter of request

9 On the move

Pages 84–93

Preview	Reading	Listening
Reading: Travellers Time and reason clauses review	Tourists move into cities as locals move out Participle clauses	Young people's driving habits Cause and effect

Vocabulary	Language in action		
Synonyms	Making, accepting, and rejecting suggestions	Ending conversations The use of *just* and *actually*	Writing: A letter of suggestion

10 Playing with reality

Pages 94–103

Preview	Reading	Listening
Listening and reading: Brandon Lee Passives review	Virtual pets Passive constructions	Optical illusions and perception The pronoun *it*

Vocabulary	Language in action		
Metaphorical language The verbs *look* and *see*	Announcing / confirming decisions Questioning decisions	Missing words Asking negative questions Sentence stress	Writing: Announcing decisions in writing

11 Followers

Pages 104–113

Preview	Reading	Listening
Reading: Paparazzi Causatives review	Tornado followers Causative verbs and the passive; non-causative use of *have something done*	Fans Question tags Intonation of question tags

Vocabulary	Language in action		
Word-building: prefixes Word stress American and British English	Expressing likes, dislikes, and preferences	Giving examples Uses of the pronoun *You*	Writing: A review

12 Communication

Pages 114–123

Preview	Listening	Reading
Reading: Types of communication Reported speech review	Interpreting Reported speech: reporting verbs	Gossip Infinitives or gerunds after verbs

Vocabulary	Language in action		
Compound nouns Stress on compound nouns	Expressions for answering and making telephone calls	Expressions to use when you can't think of what to say Instructions using *if*	Writing: Telephone messages

1 Why do they do it?

Preview

Your thoughts

1 Can you imagine doing any of the things shown in the photographs? Which of these reactions matches your own feelings most closely? Compare your ideas in pairs or groups.

You wouldn't catch me doing that!
They must be crazy!
I'd quite like to try that, but I'd be too scared!
I'd love to try that!

2 What is your opinion of the people in the photographs? For example, do you think they are brave, stupid, talented?

Of the thousands of large snakes kept as pets, only a handful have ever attacked their owner.

Spacewalks have become a routine part of an astronaut's life.

People have walked on fire for thousands of years.

Listening

1 **1.1** Listen to people talking about the activities and match them to three of the photographs.

2 Listen again.
   a What are the speakers' attitudes or feelings towards the activities they are describing?
   b Which speaker is:
      • giving advice?
      • explaining a process?
      • describing personal reactions?

Standing up in front of a large audience can be a terrifying experience.

Reading

1 Read about some of the dangers of working in space.

  a Why do you think people want to become astronauts?

  b What kind of dangers do they face?

Defying danger – a way of life for astronauts

In the next few days, spacewalking astronauts will attempt to enter a damaged part of their space station to connect power cables to the batteries inside. It will be a difficult and dangerous operation.

'It's going to be an extremely challenging task,' said one of the crew, 'but it's not as bad as it sounds. We are well trained, and this job is no more dangerous than many others in the past.'

It is quite true that astronauts have faced dangerous spacewalks before. In one of the earliest spacewalks, two Russian astronauts used a knife to cut through metal to fix a leaking fuel tank. To prevent their spacesuits from being torn, which almost certainly would have meant instant death, they put blankets over the sharp edges of the hole before climbing through. It took five spacewalks to fix the leak.

On another occasion, astronauts had to go out to repair the insulation on their space station. They did not realize, however, that the outer door was damaged while they were opening it. They finished their exhausting work, and re-entered the station, but they couldn't close the damaged door. They almost ran out of air while they were trying to close it. Eventually they closed the inner door and hoped for the best. It worked.

2 What abilities, skills, and qualities do you think astronauts need? Discuss your ideas with a partner and compile a list of five essential skills and qualities.

Person to person

1 What do you do, or what have you done in the past, that is (was) risky or dangerous? Describe your feelings.

2 Is there anything you would like to do, but haven't yet found the opportunity or the courage to do?

Grammar – Present tenses review

1 When do we use present tenses? Match the extracts **a**–**d** with the different uses of the two present tenses **1**–**4**.

  a *He's staring at me and his tongue is going in and out.*

  b *I always feel nervous for several days in advance.*

  c *More and more people are taking it up as a regular activity.*

  d *… wood does not conduct heat well.*

  1 something that is always true

  2 a temporary action that is happening now

  3 a situation or trend that is true at the present time

  4 a regular action or experience (habit)

2 In what other ways are the two present tenses used?

  a I *fly* to New York on Sunday.

  b He's always *losing* his keys.

  c We're *meeting* our friends in Paris next Tuesday.

▶ **Language commentary p.124**

Pronunciation

3 The third person singular ending of Present simple verbs is pronounced in three different ways.

  a Read these words aloud and sort them into three groups.

rises	catches	buys	washes	types	rides	writes	asks
damages	runs	kisses					

  b **1.2** Listen and check your ideas. What rules of pronunciation and spelling can you work out?

Check

4 Put the verbs in brackets into the correct form of the Present simple or the Present continuous.

  a Today young men on Pentecost Island in the South Pacific still .... from treetops as part of a traditional ceremony. (dive)

  b Adrenalin .... the heart rate. (speed up)

  c What an amazing sight. The man .... out of the window. Now he .... I don't think he .... a parachute. (climb, jump, wear)

  d At the moment, more and more young people .... dangerous sports or hobbies. (take up)

  e I .... my first parachute jump next Saturday. It's all arranged. (do)

  f I'm leaving tomorrow morning. My plane .... at eleven o'clock. (take off)

▶ Aspect   p.7
▶ Action verbs and state verbs   p.9

Reading

1 Look at these titles of magazine articles.

> The dangerous games our children play
>
> An easy, risky way to get around
>
> A restaurant dish to die for

a Predict what you think each article is about.

b Match these words to the right article title.

> chef   fell off   injuries   lift   meal
> motorist   poisonous   road   speed
> taste   thumb   train

As you read

2 Work in groups of three. Each read a different article.

a Match your article to one of the titles.

b Check your answers for **1a** and **b**.

c Underline four or five of the most important words in the article to help you remember the main points.

Close up

Article 1

1.8 Think of a one-word alternative for *getting around*.

1.21 What does *pick up* mean here? Do you know any other meanings of *pick up*?

Article 2

1.6 What does the word *Apparently* tell you about the writer of this article?

1.10 What does *numbness* mean? What is the adjective related to it? How are the noun and the adjective pronounced?

Article 3

1.4 What does *pick up* mean here? Do you know any other meanings of *pick up*?

1.4 + 1.19 What are the different meanings of *rock*? *The carriages started to rock violently … children leap off rocks and cliff tops into the sea.*

---

1 It's easy, it's cheap, it's convenient, and it's a good way of meeting people. It simply involves standing by a road and
5 sticking out your thumb. Every day hundreds of people in Ireland hitch lifts. It is a frequent method of getting around, especially in rural areas, where there is little
10 danger, since people often know those offering them a lift.

But hitch-hiking can be risky. Leave any city or town on a Friday evening and the main roads out are lined with hitch-hikers, mainly young people, seeking lifts from strangers. Last month a 21-year-old girl accepted a lift late at night on the
15 outskirts of a large town and has not been seen since.

A Dublin Tourist Authority spokeswoman said recently, 'We never advise tourists to hitch. If they are stuck, we suggest that they ask in a local hotel or pub whether anyone is going in their direction.'

Motorists too are being warned. The spokesman for a motoring organization
20 said, 'We are now recommending that, for their own personal safety, motorists should not pick up hitch-hikers.'

The Irish Times

---

2 You won't find Fugu fish in many Japanese restaurants. Firstly, it is very expensive – over £100 per person. And secondly, one fish contains enough poison to kill an entire restaurant.

Restaurants who want to offer Fugu must get
5 permission and only chefs who have had special training can prepare the fish. Apparently, it has very little taste but what makes Fugu so appealing to its fans is precisely what makes it so dangerous – its poison. If eaten in small
10 amounts, it produces a pleasant numbness. In larger amounts, it results in death. On average five people a year die from Fugu poisoning in Japan.

The most famous case occurred in 1975 when Goru
15 Mitsu, an actor, went for a Fugu meal with friends. At his request some of the poisonous parts were presented on a plate. Mitsu dared his friends to eat some poison, but they refused. So he ate more than his share. He went back to his hotel and told his wife that he felt like he was flying. He became so numb he could no longer stand and eventually died the following morning.

The Independent

---

3 It was 4.30 on a Friday afternoon at a busy London station – a teenage boy watched a train arrive. When the passengers had got on and the train began to move off, the boy ran forward, jumped up and grabbed one of the train doors. The train picked up speed. At 45 kph the carriages started to rock violently.
5 The boy was shouting with excitement, but suddenly he lost his grip and fell off. He was the first known victim of the craze of train surfing, riding on the side or roof of trains. Since then there have been more
10 deaths and many injuries.

It's not just on trains that boys risk death for fun, however. Lift surfing – riding on the top of lifts in tall buildings – was first suspected when council
15 inspectors discovered drink cans on lift tops. Tables and armchairs have also been found. Then there is bonnet surfing – standing on the bonnet of a fast-moving car as the driver skids and zig-zags, imitating the movement of waves in the sea; and tombstoning, which is sweeping the west coast, where children leap off rocks and cliff tops into the sea.

The Independent

Interpretation

1 Answer the questions on the article you read.

Article 1
a Why do you think hitch-hiking is popular in rural areas?
b Why do you think so many people leave cities on Friday evenings?

Article 2
c Why do you think Fugu fish is so expensive?
d Why do you think people want to eat Fugu poison?

Article 3
e Why do you think only boys are mentioned in this article?
f Why do you think tables and chairs were found on lift tops?

2 a Using some of the most important words you underlined, complete this sentence in ten words or less. 'The article I read is about …'
b Let others in your group read your sentence.
c Discuss what the three articles have in common.

Speaking personally

1 What is your opinion of hitch-hiking? Have you ever hitch-hiked?

2 Why do young people take more risks than older people? Think of examples.

Class survey

3 Work in groups. Make a list of questions about taking risks, then conduct a class survey.

Example
Would you eat or drink something that you knew might be dangerous?
Which dangerous sports might you be prepared to try?
Have you ever … ?

— Grammar —

Aspect

Exploring concepts

Aspect describes the way we think about the action of a verb. There are two aspects in English: the continuous (or progressive) aspect and the perfect aspect.

1 Sort the verbs in these sentences into three groups: continuous, perfect, and other.
a … a 21-year-old girl **accepted** a lift late at night …
b … (she) **has not been seen** since.
c We never **advise** tourists to hitch.
d We **are** now **recommending** that motorists should not pick up hitch-hikers.
e … only chefs who **have had** special training can prepare the fish.
f … five people a year **die** from Fugu poisoning in Japan.
g The boy **was shouting** with excitement …
h … suddenly he **lost** his grip and **fell off**.
i Since then there **have been** more deaths …

2 Which group of verbs, continuous or perfect, describes actions which:
a are finished but are still relevant now?
b are/were temporary or in progress?

3 How could you describe the verbs in the other group?

▶ **Language commentary p.124**

Pronunciation

4 a ▐ 1.3 ▐ When we ask someone about their personal life, it is important to sound interested. Listen to two people asking the same question. Which speaker sounds more interested?
b Listen and repeat the remaining questions. Then practise saying them with a partner.

Exploitation

1 For each of the following topics, make up three sentences, one for each of the verb types: continuous, perfect, and simple.

• reading books • holidays • television
• sports and other interests

Example
• (continuous) *At the moment I'm reading a book of short stories.*
• (perfect) *I've read about thirty books so far this year.*
• (simple) *I read three books last week.*

2 You are going to interview your partner. Prepare some questions about these kinds of actions or situations.
• temporary or in progress
  Where are you working at the moment?
• completed but still relevant
  What have you done this week?
• permanent or completed
  Where do you live/work/study?

Free speech

3 Work in groups. Talk about the current situation in your country. Choose two of these subjects to talk about:
• economics: prices/taxes/jobs
• society: family life/education/crime
• the latest gossip involving famous people

Listening

1 a Make a list of as many dangerous jobs as you can think of. What are the dangers of each job?

Example
racing-driver – high-speed car crashes

b Compare your list with a partner.

c You are going to listen to four people talking about the dangers involved in their jobs. Here are some of the words and phrases the speakers use. With a partner, work out what each job is. Use a dictionary to check meanings you are uncertain of.

Speaker 1	risky business, life-and-death situation, smoke and flames
Speaker 2	obsessed with kicking, international level, operations
Speaker 3	spell in the Middle East, arrested, lens missing
Speaker 4	speed limit, minor accidents, dual control cars

As you listen

2 ▣ **1.4** What are the jobs? Listen and check your ideas.

3 Work in pairs or groups. Listen to the speakers again.

a Rank the four jobs in order of danger from the most to the least dangerous. Add four of the dangerous jobs you listed in **1a**.

b Discuss which jobs on your list you would most and least like to do. Why?

Interpretation

1 The first speaker says that she doesn't think about the danger while she's doing her job but *afterwards* **it hits you** – *when you get home and relax*. What kinds of feelings do you think she is talking about?

2 The second speaker talks about the *mental* and *physical risks* that sports people take. Can you think of examples of these different kinds of risks?

3 The third speaker mentions *calculated risks*. What are these? Why does he continue to take them?

4 The fourth speaker says *The most important thing is to keep a cool head*. Why do you think she needs to do this?

Vocabulary

1 Which of these verbs commonly go with the nouns? Match a verb from **A** with a noun from **B**. Use a dictionary to check your ideas.

A keep   play   run   waste

B (a) cassette   football   (a) trick on someone   (a) business   (the) guitar   time   control   (your) head   ten kilometres   energy   (your) job   (your) temper   (a) race   (a) risk   (a) secret   money

2 a Make up four sentences about yourself using some of the verb-noun combinations.

Example
*I've never **run ten kilometres** in my life.*

b Compare your sentences with a partner.

3 What is the difference in meaning between these pairs of words? Compare your ideas with a partner and then check in a dictionary.

a job / work   **c** mental / physical
b smoke / flames **d** obsessed with / interested in

4 Now discuss these questions.

a Is it possible to like your *job* but not enjoy the *work* you do?

b What are the different harmful effects of *smoke* and *flames*?

c Give an example of when you might be *physically* exhausted but *mentally* alert.

d Is there anything that you were once *obsessed with* but are now just *interested in*, or the other way round?

Action verbs and state verbs

Exploring concepts

Action verbs refer to something which happens or which causes a change.
*Smoke **was pouring** from the building, people **were jumping** from the windows.
He **ran** inside and **brought** out three children.*

State verbs refer to something which usually stays the same.
*She **seems** much happier now that she **owns** her own business. She **prefers** working
for herself.*

1 Read the following text.
   a Sort the verbs in *italics* into action verbs and state verbs. Make two lists.
   b What grammatical difference is there between the two types of verb?

I *belong* to the police force and I *love* my job, though I *wish* it was less dangerous. Last Thursday was typical. *I'm working* nights at the moment and I *left* the police station at ten o'clock and *walked* towards the town centre. I *was approaching* the Metropolitan Hotel when a fight *broke out*. A gang of youths *attacked* a middle-aged man as he *was getting on* to his motorbike. They *dragged* him onto the pavement, then *kicked* and *punched* him. I *thought* about trying to stop them but I *knew* there were too many of them. So I *radioed* the station and *said*, 'I'm outside the Metropolitan, there's a fight *going on* and I *need* assistance.' While I *was waiting* for help to arrive someone *threw* a bottle which *hit* me on the back of the head. I *woke up* in hospital three hours later with a dreadful headache. The motorcyclist was quite badly hurt. I *hope* he's OK – I *believe* he's off the danger list. Unfortunately, this is partly what being a policeman *involves*. I *doubt* if they *will* ever catch the people concerned. That's the worst thing.

2 Look at your list of state verbs. A number express feelings or emotions: *love*, *hope*, *doubt*. What other kinds of meaning do state verbs express?

▶ Language commentary p.124

Exploitation

1 Work in pairs. Take turns to be Student A.

Student A
You are researching an article on people's feelings and attitudes towards their jobs. Make up questions to interview a partner about:
- their responsibilities
- their likes and dislikes
- the challenges of the job
- what they would like to change about their job and why.

Make notes of their answers.

Student B
Think of the questions based on the topics above that your partner might ask you about your job. Prepare what you are going to say, then answer your partner's questions.

2 Use your notes to write an article based on your partner's answers. Write what they think and how they feel in general about the work they do. Show your partner your article and discuss any improvements.

Vocabulary development

Each unit of this book covers important general vocabulary topics. Look at the definitions and examples related to some of these topics and then do the short activity which follows. Check any words you are uncertain of in a dictionary.

Collocations

These are pairs or groups of words commonly used together.
play a trick *(on someone)* – NOT *do a trick*
keep a **cool** *head* – NOT *keep a* **cold** *head*

1 Work with a partner. Make a list of all the verbs you can think of that collocate with *money*.
Example
earn money

2 Each talk for one minute about the subject 'Me and my money' using the verbs you listed in **1**.

Connotations

These are extra meanings associated with words in addition to their normal meanings.
routine = *regular* or *normal* with the added idea of being *boring*. (*The work is very* **routine**.)
chuck = *throw*, with the added idea of *casually, with contempt, without caring*. (*They* **chuck** *you in a cell overnight*.)

You receive references for two applicants for a job in your organization. Here are some of the words used to describe the two people. Who would you prefer to employ, Sue or Dave? Why?
Sue is *serious, inexperienced, ambitious*.
Dave is *humourless, immature, pushy*.

Word-building

This is adding prefixes or suffixes to the roots of words to make new words.
organize *organizer organization organized disorganized*
nation *national nationalistic international internationally*
Work in pairs. Make as many words as you can by adding prefixes and suffixes to these root words.

use believe advise

The office disorganizer

Formality

This is the difference between formal and informal language.
release *somebody* (formal) / **let** *somebody* **go** (informal)
in **rural areas** (formal) / *in* **the country** (informal)
Rewrite these sentences using informal English.

I am most grateful for your help.

Do you mean 'Thanks'?

a May I introduce you to my mother and father?
b I apologize for my lateness.
c Do you have any objection to my opening the window?

Homonyms

These are words which are the same in sound or spelling but are different in meaning.
I have been feeling **weak** *all* **week**. (homophones)
The couple in the front **row** *of the cinema were having a* **row**. (homographs)

I've been feeling weak all week.

1 Make a list of other words that sound like these.

two right wait wear

2 Choose two pairs of words on your list and make up sentences that show the difference in meaning.

Metaphorical language

This is language used in non-literal ways.
When I asked where he'd been he looked rather **sheepish**.
(= like a sheep / embarrassed or ashamed)

1 What would it mean if a person was described as: *mousy, a dinosaur, a rat,* or *catty*?

2 What would a person be doing if they *buried their head in the sand*?

He looked sheepish but said nothing.

Language in action

Agreeing and disagreeing

Eavesdrop!

Look at the picture and guess the answer to this question.

- Where are the people?
  Think of a country, place, and type of building.

Listening 1

1 **1.5** Listen, check your ideas and think about these questions.

  a Who are the speakers?

  b What is the subject of their conversation?

2 Work in groups of four. Listen to the conversation again.

Student A Listen and note down expressions the speakers use to agree with each other.

Student B Listen and note down expressions the speakers use to disagree with each other.

Student C Listen and note down expressions one speaker uses to try and get into the conversation.

Student D Listen and note down expressions that other speakers use to prevent someone from getting into the conversation.

Tell each other the expressions you heard. Make lists with the following headings:

- agreeing with someone
- disagreeing with someone
- getting into the conversation
- preventing someone from getting into the conversation.

Listening 2

1 **1.6** You are going to listen to two more conversations in which people agree and disagree with each other. As you listen, answer these questions.

  a What is the subject of the conversation?

  b What is the relationship between the speakers? Are they friends, acquaintances, or colleagues?

2 **1.7** Read and listen to the extracts from the conversations on the next page.

  a Mark any expressions used to:

- agree
- disagree
- get into the conversation
- prevent someone from getting into the conversation.

  b Add the marked expressions to the lists you have already made.

Extract 1

J It might look a bit strange if you've just ... got one sort of colour, don't you think?

R Not necessarily.

J I think it could be like a little rich gem in here with all sorts of deep vibrant colours, like a fruit cake.

K Oh, I don't know about that. I don't know that I could live in it.

J Don't you like that?

K Ooh ...

R Well, as you say, a room this size.

J Right. What would you do?

R Well, ... I'd ...

S I'd ... Sorry.

R I tend to go along with the neutrals, but with a splash of ... strong ... strong ...

J Something bright ...

R ... strong ... but not make that the overall theme ... you know ...

J Mmm – I see your point. Mmm ...

S Yeah, I agree with you, I think, I think. The other thing I think about is, strong colours is they're likely to date.

J Mmm ...

S I mean I wouldn't ...

R Yeah, that's a good point ...

Extract 2

T Yes, I know, but the point the point is we work our guts out for this place and they're just constantly leaning on us all the time. It's more work, it's more money, it's more hours, it's more admin.

J Oh Tony, Tony, be reasonable.

T This is getting ridiculous.

R Wait a minute, wait a minute. You know, I mean if everyone could bring their car in, nobody could park in there anyway because ...

J Exactly!

R ... there'd be too, too many cars.

J Absolutely. Absolutely right! Absolutely! So that's going to give you a great opportunity of a guaranteed place to park.

T Where's the money going to go to? What's it going to be used for?

J Well, I suppose they're going to have a security man there so that your car at least it'll be safe – it's not on the road, Tony.

T Oh come on, I mean, ... it's, the, there're gates, the gates are normally closed – that's no particular problem anyway, is it?

R But that can be decided later.

T This is just one way of ripping off the staff.

J Oh no, that's not true.

T It is!

J No, I don't agree. Oh come on Roger, you know you're nearly there. It is ...

T Twenty quid a year, well all right, but a hundred, a hundred is absurd.

J Oh twenty's nothing. What's that going to do?

T Yes, but think how many people there are. If everybody's chipping in twenty quid, that's plenty of money to pay a security man or one or two people to run round with walky-talkies and this sort of silly equipment.

J A hundred is nothing if you work out how much that is a quarter. What do you pay in the multi-storey?

R It's really nothing for over a year, I mean what is it? Two pounds a week?

J Exactly! How much do the meters cost?

R Yeah, what is it? Two pounds an hour or something in a meter?

J You're right, you're right.

T Well that's, all right, yes ...

R I understand why they're charging ...

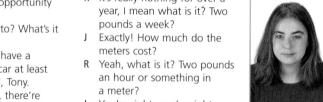

Features of natural conversation

1 Underline all the examples of these exclamation words or sounds in the two conversations: *Mmm, Ooh,* (Extract **1**), *Oh* (Extract **2**). What ideas are they used to express?

2 Listen to the conversations again and check your ideas.

Practice

1 a **1.8** Listen and repeat these expressions of agreement.

  1 I agree with you.   5 Absolutely!
  2 You're right.   6 Exactly!
  3 I'd go along with that. 7 Absolutely right!
  4 That's a good point.

  b Listen and say the expressions again, this time showing strong agreement.

2 a **1.9** Listen and repeat these expressions of disagreement.

  1 That's not true.   3 I'm not so sure.
  2 I don't agree.   4 I don't know about that.

  b Listen and say the expressions again showing stronger disagreement.

3 Work in pairs. Respond to these statements. Use any of the expressions in **1** or **2**.

  a It's always cheaper and safer to travel by car.
  b Green's a very restful colour.
  c You're only as old as you feel.
  d 99 per cent of television programmes are boring.

4 **1.10** Listen and repeat these expressions which are used to get into a conversation. What do they all have in common?

  a Excuse me, could I just say (what I think)?
  b Can I just say (what my opinion is)?
  c I'd just like to say (I'm not happy about this).
  d Can I just get a word in, (please)?

Exploitation

Work in groups. Discuss one of these situations.

Situation 1

Your company has made much larger profits than anyone expected. You have to decide how to spend this extra money. The basic choices are:

  a to improve the social facilities for the employees
  b to give all staff a three per cent bonus.

Situation 2

You want to try to raise money for charity and you are meeting to decide on the best way of doing this.

Writing

1 You are going to write a letter expressing agreement and disagreement.

a First, think about the main differences between spoken language and formal writing.

Spoken language

R I tend to go along with the neutrals, but with a splash of …
   … strong … strong …
J Something bright …
R … strong … but not make that the overall theme … you know …
J Mmm – I see your point. Mmm …
S Yeah, I agree with you, I think, I think. The other thing I think about is, strong colours is they're likely to date.
J Mmm …
S I mean I wouldn't …
R Yeah, that's a good point …

Writing

I completely agree with Mr Forsyth that people should decide for themselves whether or not to take part in dangerous sports. On the other hand, I do not accept that anyone has the right to endanger the lives of others. I have nothing against the activities themselves. I am sure many people get a lot of pleasure from parachuting, hang-gliding, and bungee jumping. However, I entirely disagree with Mr Forsyth when he says that these activities should be allowed in public places. This is unacceptable in any situation where there is a risk that ordinary people may be injured or even killed.

b Underline all the examples of formal language used in the extract from the letter.

c Make two lists: expressions of agreement and expressions of disagreement.

d Which two words does the writer use to show how strongly he agrees or disagrees?

e Which two words and phrases does the writer use to link points of agreement and points of disagreement?

▶ **Writing guidelines p.155**

2 You are going to write a formal letter to the authorities in your town or city.

Your town or city has serious traffic problems especially during rush hours, causing delays, congestion, and pollution problems. Several suggestions have been made to improve the situation:

- a ring road
- a fast lane for cars with three or more passengers to encourage fewer cars
- a new subsidized rail / bus link
- making the town centre a pedestrian area, to encourage people to leave their cars at home
- increased tax on local roads.

In a TV broadcast an important local politician has called for action. He wants people to write giving their opinions and saying which suggestions they agree or disagree with.

Follow this paragraph plan.

1 Say why you are writing.
2 Say which suggestions you agree and disagree with, using expressions from your list.
3 Finish by making any different suggestions of your own.

3 Exchange your letter with a partner.

a Read each other's letters. Is the language appropriate for a formal letter? Is it clear what the writer wants to happen and what they agree and disagree with? Make any suggestions for improvements.

b Rewrite your letter, including any improvements you discussed.

Unit 1 Summary

In this unit you have worked on the following language points.

☐ Present simple, Present continuous
☐ Aspect
☐ Action verbs and state verbs
☐ Vocabulary development
☐ Agreeing and disagreeing

☐ Getting into a conversation
☐ Preventing someone from getting into the conversation
☐ Writing a formal letter

Tick ✓ the points you are confident about and cross ✗ the ones you need to revise.

2 First person singular

Preview

Your thoughts

Look at the magazine cover. What kind of competition is it? Think about something naughty you, or someone you know, did as a child. Tell another student the story.

True **Confessions**

I let down the tyres of all the cars in our road.

I locked my parents out of the house

Childhood confessions **COMPETITION**

Win a first prize of **£250** for your story.

Reading

1 You are going to read three entries to the 'Childhood confessions competition'. First make sure you understand the meanings of the words in the list below. Then use the titles and words to help you guess what the stories are about.

Sorry grandad	doze snore scissors
	moustache tiptoe
I was a ten-year-old hoaxer	church siren fire-engine
My first lie	medicine bitter hide

2 Read the stories and check your ideas. Make a note of how the storytellers felt immediately after their actions.

Sorry grandad

I was about six or seven at the time. I was at home with my grandad. He looked after me during the week whenever my mother was at work. He was dozing in an armchair while I was playing with my toys. When I asked him what time Mum was coming home, he didn't answer. I asked him again but there was still no reply. You can probably guess – he was asleep. Anyway, while I was playing, I found some old scissors in my doll's house. I don't know what gave me the idea, but I just couldn't resist it. I picked up the scissors and tiptoed across the room till I was next to grandad's chair – he was snoring loudly. Really quickly I cut off the ends of his moustache. Then I just stood there and stared at him – he looked completely different. I felt so guilty I burst into tears. Of course he woke up and wondered what was happening. When I told him, he felt his moustache, leapt out of his chair and looked in the mirror. Then, amazingly, he just laughed.

I was a ten-year-old hoaxer

One Friday morning I went into a phone box, rang the fire brigade and said that the local church, the one I actually went to, was on fire. You often do things like that because your friends persuade you to, but I just did this on my own. I remember, as I was walking home through the park five minutes later, I heard the sirens and saw the fire engine arriving at the church. I ran home as fast as I could, went up to my bedroom and peered through the curtains, but I couldn't see anything. I was expecting someone to knock on the door at any minute and take me off to the police station. I was only ten years old and I was absolutely terrified – I don't know why I did it. I never did anything like it again.

My first lie

I can't have been more than four when this happened. I can't remember what was wrong with me, but I was taking medicine twice a day. It had such a bitter taste that I took it mixed in a glass of sweet orange juice. The problem was I could still taste the medicine in the orange juice. One particular afternoon I was watching television and my mother brought the horrible drink in. As she gave it to me, the phone rang and she went to answer it. I looked at the orange drink and decided I couldn't face it, so I hid the glass behind a pile of magazines. Of course, when my mother said, 'Have you taken your medicine?' I said, 'Yes.' I felt very pleased with myself.

She found the drink the next day when she was doing the housework. She looked at me very seriously and said, 'It's very naughty to tell lies!'

3 Which of these three entries to the 'Childhood confessions competition' do you think should win the first prize? Think of reasons for your choice. Compare your ideas with other students'.

4 Look at the two main stories mentioned on the magazine cover.

  a Work in pairs. Decide what one of these stories is about.

  b Make up the story. How old was the person? Who else was involved? What did they do? How did they feel? What were the consequences?

  c Tell your version of the story to another pair.

Person to person

1 At what age do children know they are being naughty?

2 Why do they do things they know will make their parents or other adults upset?

Grammar – Past simple and Past continuous review

1 How are the Past simple and the Past continuous used?

  a Which form do we use to emphasize that an action or event took place over a period of time in the past?

  b Which form do we use to refer to a completed action or event which took place at one or more particular times in the past?

  c Which form is more often used for temporary situations?

2 Match sentences a–f with the descriptions 1–6. Compare your ideas with a partner.

  a *He **was dozing** in an armchair while I **was playing** with my toys.*

  b *He **looked** after me during the week whenever my mother was at work.*

  c *She **found** the drink the next day when she **was doing** the housework.*

  d *I **worked** in New York from January to May last year.*

  e *One Friday morning I **went** into a phone box, **rang** the fire brigade …*

  f *One particular afternoon I **was watching** television and …*

  1 a specific action which took place while a longer action was in progress

  2 an action in progress which forms the background to a story

  3 a number of completed actions which took place one after the other

  4 a repeated action that took place at certain specified times

  5 two actions in progress over the same period of time

  6 a completed action which took place over a specified length of time

▶ **Language commentary p.125**

Check

3 Choose the correct form of the verb for these sentences.

  a While I *had / was having* breakfast, someone knocked on the door.

  b I *often phoned / was often phoning* my friends when my parents were out.

  c While he was talking on the phone, the meal *burned / was burning* in the oven.

  d The sun *shone / was shining* and the birds *sang / were singing*. Suddenly …

  e I *left / was leaving* the house at 6 o'clock, *got / was getting* into my car and *drove / was driving* off.

  f He *played / was playing* tennis for Australia between 1988 and 1997.

Pronunciation

4 a The past tense *-ed* ending of these regular verbs is pronounced in three ways. Practise saying them with a partner and then put them into three groups.

need	long	want	laugh	knock	add	love	gaze	kiss	watch	stop
wait	judge	try	wash							

  b ▮2.1▮ Listen and check your ideas. What rules of pronunciation and spelling can you work out?

▶ Past perfect   p.16
▶ *used to, would*   p.19

Listening

1 Work in pairs. Look at the two pictures and discuss these questions.
  a What sort of people live in these rooms? What sort of characters do you think they have?
  b Which of the two rooms would you feel more comfortable in? Why?

You are going to listen to an extract from a radio programme called *Hidden Talents*, where people talk about an aspect of their character.

As you listen

2 **2.2** Answer these questions.
  a What is the speaker's particular 'talent' or 'secret power'? Listen for examples. How does the speaker feel about her talent?
  b Which of these words describe the tone of her talk?

  amusing   heavy   humorous   ironic   light-hearted   serious

Interpretation

Listeners often have to interpret things they hear in order to get the full meaning. You have to 'listen between the lines' to understand what the speaker is really saying.

1 a How do you interpret these extracts from the programme?
    1 … *I spent a whole day looking for an important document that I knew I'd left … on the table. **Although I could not see the document, it was there.***
    2 … *I feel the **unusual combinations of objects** in my house might have made the burglar think that my house had already been broken into.*
    3 … *the object will not be staying for long.*
  b What advantages and disadvantages of her 'hidden talent' does the speaker mention?

2 a Which of these negative qualities could be used to describe the personality of the speaker you have just heard? Discuss your choices with a partner.

  untidy   disorganized   inefficient   careless   impatient

  b What are the opposites of these five qualities?

Speaking personally

1 Have you ever put something in a safe place and been unable to find it again?

2 Which of your things do you never have to look for because you always know where they are?

3 Do you have any 'hidden talents'? What are they?

— Grammar —

Past perfect

Exploring concepts

1 Underline all the verbs in these extracts from the programme.
  a *I spent a whole day looking for an important document that I knew I'd left in an obvious place on the table.*
  b *… as I was unpacking the food I had just bought at the local supermarket, I discovered the missing key under a bag of potatoes.*
  c *… while I was looking for my glasses, I came across a sandwich I'd lost the previous weekend.*

2 Now answer these questions for each of the three extracts.
  a What is the main action or event in each sentence? What tense is used?
  b Which of the actions or events mentioned in each extract took place first? What tense is used?
  c Why does the speaker mention these other events or actions?

3 Here are some more sentences referring to past actions or events. What is the purpose of the Past perfect verbs in these sentences? Choose one or more of the uses **1–4**.

  a By seven o'clock this morning, I'*d done* three hours' work.

  b After I'*d finished* working, I had breakfast.

  c I'*d eaten* hardly anything the day before so I was really hungry.

  d It *had been* a tiring day. I *hadn't* slept well the night before. By mid-afternoon I was almost asleep.

  1 to show a particular sequence of actions or events in the past

  2 to give background information to a story

  3 to explain a past action, event, or state

  4 to give information about an action, event, or state which preceded a particular time in the past

4 How does the use of the continuous aspect change the meaning? What is the difference between these sentences?

  a While I was looking for a screwdriver recently, I found my daughter's birth certificate, which I'*d been searching for* for months.

  b I'*d searched* for months for my passport. Then, the day after I got a replacement passport, the old one turned up.

▶ **Language commentary p.125**

Pronunciation

5 **a** How is *had* pronounced in natural speech?

    1 After John *had* finished he left.

    2 What *had* he done to deserve that?

    3 *Had* the party finished by two?

    4 No, I don't think it *had*. No, it *hadn't*.

    5 I **had** thought of that, you know.

  b **2.3** Listen and check your ideas. What rules of pronunciation can you work out?

Exploitation

1 Make a list of five interesting things you had done by the age of fifteen. Then ask other students questions based on your own experiences.

Example
By the age of fifteen I'd visited Australia, Portugal, and Japan. Which countries had you visited by the age of fifteen?

You could think about some of these things:

• places you'd lived in or visited
• events you'd attended or watched
• people you'd met.

Agree on the most interesting or unusual experiences.

2 Imagine you arrived at work after the weekend and found your office in a terrible mess. What had happened?

Example
There were small, round, burn marks on your chair.
Someone had been smoking and had put out their cigarette on the chair.

  a The door lock was broken.

  b There were red stains on the floor and bottles in the bin.

  c There was a half-eaten sandwich on one of the desks.

  d There was a broken window and a football on the floor.

  e There were opened letters on the floor.

  f The desk drawers and filing cabinets were open.

3 Work in groups. Use your imagination to explain the background to these events.

  a Last weekend your favourite singer or sporting personality collapsed and was taken to hospital.

  b Quite suddenly, your best friend got married and emigrated.

4 A mini-saga is a very short story with a title, a beginning, a middle, and an end. It must be exactly 50 words long, not including the title. Read this example.

┌─ **Learner driver** ─────────────────┐
It was the first time I'd driven alone, although I'd often been out with my parents. I knew what to do and was driving carefully. When the policeman stopped me and asked me why I was driving so slowly, I said I didn't think children under ten should drive fast.
└──────────────────────────────────────┘

Work in pairs. Make up an entry for a mini-saga competition. Start in one of these ways.

• I'd spent the whole morning waiting for my friend to arrive.

• I couldn't remember where I'd seen her before.

Reading

1 Think about a particularly happy day in your life. Compare your ideas with a partner.

2 You are going to read about the happiest day in someone's life. Read the first paragraph of the article.

a What happened on that day?

b Which words and phrases tell us the writer was happy?

As you read

3 Find out whether the writer remained happy after the excitement of the happiest day.

Economy Single

Geelong to **Melbourne**

001098 51

Close up

1.3 What does *but* mean in this sentence? (It is used twice.)

1.11 What do you do if you *keep something under your hat*?

1.13 What does *house-sit* mean? Which verb ending in *-sit* means 'to look after young children'?

1.33 What does the phrase *let alone* mean here?

My single ticket to freedom
The happiest day of my life

The day I left home was the happiest day of my life. I walked away from my parents' house, along narrow suburban pavements to the railway station, and into the brightest afternoon I had ever lived. I had no baggage but a briefcase,
5 and in it nothing but a nightshirt, a paperback book, a hairbrush, and a sample bottle of 'Shocking' by Schiaparelli. 'A single ticket,' I sang at the man in the ticket office. Even now, whenever I travel, I feel the warm afterglow of that afternoon.

If I was entitled to housing I had no knowledge of the fact. I didn't even know if I was eligible for the dole, and it never occurred to me to ask. I don't
10 suppose I thought of a home of my own so much as somewhere to live. For years I lived in other people's houses. Sometimes I would keep the fact that I was at university under my hat, so as to work as a housekeeper. Sometimes, I'd house-sit in properties that were to be pulled down or done up and sold. More than once I came 'home' to find my few belongings dumped unceremoniously
15 on the pavement and the locks changed. But one day I found an empty hay loft at the back of a Victorian house near the university. The tenants in the house didn't mind whether I lived there or not.

My loft was only 15 feet by 11, the sole access was a trap
20 door in the floor, and the ventilation was a half-door that opened into a tree. It was freezing, it was insecure, it was perfect.

I bought an old cast-iron wood stove and used to burn the hardwood blocks that were removed as the streets of Melbourne were macadamized; being impregnated with tar,
25 they'd burn a treat. On the stove I kept a pot of stew, bunged in the least battered vegetables I could find after the market closed and scrag ends of this or that fowl or sheep, and a few bones. Dozens of people survived on stew out of that pot, probably because of the antiseptic action of the red wine that
30 we used to drink by the demijohn.

Whatever my abode was, it was not fixed. The owner could have thrown me out at any time. With no running water, no electricity but a single 40-watt bulb hanging from a rafter, bare brick walls, no ceiling, let alone insulation, my home was unfit for human habitation. I was living in a shed and I liked it fine.

35 From the outside you would never have known that anyone lived there, which is why I was not turfed out as a fire risk or a health hazard or a lunatic. If I'd been gathered up and forced to return to my parents' clean, warm house, I would have gone berserk, beaten up my warders, and thrown myself under a truck. I needed that space just as it was. Perhaps I felt I had proved I could
40 survive in a crack in the consumer society. It didn't matter to me whether people classified me as a beatnik or a loony as long as I could sit with my feet in the oven of the old stove reading my book until I felt sleepy, and sleeping until I felt like waking up.

My parents made no attempt to find out what had become of me. I was both
45 glad and bitter. I told myself that I didn't need to feel any remorse about running away and not letting them know where I was. If they'd wanted to know, the university could have told them. What I didn't realize (because like all teenagers I was totally self-absorbed) was that when a child does not fit in at home, the tension is felt by everyone. It was probably better for the rest of
50 the family that I had taken myself off. It was certainly better for me. In my parents' house I was sleepless and nervous and used to suffer from repeated bouts of bronchitis; in my loft I had to develop a resistance to respiratory and gut infections.

The Guardian

Interpretation

1 What is the opposite of a *single ticket*? Why does the writer use this expression about leaving home? (l.5)

2 Why were the writer's belongings *dumped unceremoniously on the pavement*? (l.14)

3 Why does the writer say her *freezing, insecure* home *was perfect*? (l.21)

4 What does this extract from the text tell you: *Dozens of people survived on stew out of that pot …* ? (l.28)

Speaking personally

Do you agree or disagree with these opinions?

1 The writer is the kind of strong-minded, independent person I admire.

2 The writer was cruel towards her parents, and selfish and irresponsible towards other people.

3 The writer must be a strange person to enjoy living in a cold, insecure hay loft.

4 It's better for children over 18 to live independently of their parents.

—————————————————————————————— Grammar ——

used to, would

Exploring concepts

1 Read these extracts from the text and underline all the past verbs.
   a *I walked away from my parents' house, …*
   b *Sometimes I would keep the fact that I was at university under my hat …*
   c *But one day I found an empty hay loft at the back of a Victorian house …*
   d *I used to burn hardwood blocks …*
   e *… they'd burn a treat.*
   f *… the red wine that we used to drink …*
   g *… (I) used to suffer from repeated bouts of bronchitis …*

2 Work in pairs. Discuss these questions.
   a Which of the extracts refer to a past habit or typical behaviour?
   b Which of the extracts refer to a single past action?

3 *Used to* and *would* can both refer to past actions and habits. *I **used to / would smoke** whenever I felt nervous.*
   a Which form can also refer to past states? Which of these sentences is correct?
      1 I *used to have* long hair and a beard in my twenties.
      2 I *would have* long hair and a beard in my twenties.
   b Which form do we use to compare the past with the present? Which sentence suggests that the speaker no longer smokes when they feel nervous?
      1 I *used to smoke* whenever I felt nervous.
      2 I *would smoke* whenever I felt nervous.

   ▶ Language commentary p.125

Pronunciation

4 a How is *used to* pronounced in natural speech?
      1 I *used to* go out more.
      2 I *used to* eat meat.
      3 No, but I *used to*.
      4 Yes, but I didn't *use to*.
   b **2.4** Listen and check your ideas. What rules of pronunciation can you work out?

Exploitation

1 Work in pairs. Talk about what life used to be like in your country 100 years ago. Make positive and negative sentences using *used to* and *would*. Use these topics and verbs.
   • jobs and work (work, start, finish, be paid)
   • health and illness (die, suffer from, pay)
   • families and children (have, work)
   Example
   forms of entertainment (play, do)
   *People **used to make** their own entertainment. For example, on Sunday afternoons, my great grandmother **would play** the piano.*

2 A popular magazine is running a series of articles called *The Good Old Days* to which readers are invited to send contributions. Write a short description of one or two of the most interesting aspects of life you have just been talking about.

3 Work in pairs. What is your life like now compared with five or ten years ago? Talk about some of these aspects:
   • your daily routine
   • your appearance
   • hobbies, sports, and interests
   • holidays.

Free speech

4 Work in groups. Discuss any of these subjects that you find interesting. Don't spend more than about two minutes on any subject.
   • My first school
   • My first girlfriend / boyfriend
   • Favourite TV programmes from my early teenage years
   • Favourite or least favourite kinds of food when I was very young

Collocations

Collocations are pairs or groups of words which are commonly used together. Often there is no logical reason for these word groups so it is easier to learn combinations of words rather than single items. Here are some different kinds of collocation, with examples from this unit.

a   verbs and nouns
*I felt so guilty I **burst into tears**.*

b   adjectives and nouns
*My house had no **running water**.*

c   verbs and adverbs
*It was **raining heavily**.*

Verbs and nouns

1 Match a verb from list **A** with an appropriate noun from list **B**. Some of the verbs collocate with more than one noun.

A	answer do lock make play
	suffer (from) take tell watch

B	the door the housework an illness
	a lie a loss medicine the piano
	the telephone television

2 Work in groups. Spend about two minutes on each of these questions.

a   What musical instruments would you like to play?
b   What's the worst medicine you've ever had to take?
c   How much housework do you do each week?
d   What illnesses did you suffer from as a child?
e   What do you say when you answer the phone?

3 Which ten of these nouns collocate with *do* and which ten collocate with *make*? Make word webs.

a job

aerobics   your best   a complaint   the cooking
a crossword   a decision   an effort   an excuse
an exercise   someone a favour   friends
your homework   ~~a job~~   a living   a mistake
money   a noise   notes   research   the shopping

4 Now make word webs with these verbs. Check your ideas in a dictionary.

answer   play   take

Adjectives and nouns

1 Match an adjective from list **A** with an appropriate noun from list **B**. Some of the adjectives collocate with more than one noun.

A	bare bitter hard rich single strong sweet

B	bed beer chocolate country exercise facts feelings feet person
	potato room sauce taste ticket town walls wind wine

2 Some adjectives have different meanings in different collocations. Compare the following uses of the same adjectives. What is the difference in meaning?

a   a *hard* exercise / a *hard* bed
b   a *rich* person / a *rich* sauce
c   a *single* person / a *single* room / a *single* ticket
d   *strong* coffee / a *strong* wind
e   a *sweet* apple / *sweet* wine

3 What are the opposites of the adjectives in 2a–e?

Verbs and adverbs

1 Think of three verbs which each of these adverbs can be used with.
Example
carefully: drive, speak, write

~~carefully~~   dangerously   honestly   loudly   neatly   quickly   seriously   simply
slowly   strongly

2 Work in groups. Take turns to talk for 20 seconds about some of these subjects.

·   single beds
·   rich people
·   the best way to make friends

·   people who snore loudly
·   people who drive dangerously
·   people who never do anything neatly

Language in action

Expressing opinions

Eavesdrop!

Look at the picture and guess the answers to these questions.

* Who are the people?
* Where are they?
* What are they discussing?

Listening 1

1 **2.5** Listen, check your ideas and think about these questions.
 a What is the relationship between the speakers?
 b One of the speakers is unwilling to express an opinion. Who do you think it is and why?

2 Work in groups of three. Listen to the conversation again.

Student A Listen and note down expressions used to express opinions.

Student B Listen and note down expressions used to ask someone's opinion.

Student C Listen and note down expressions Charlie uses to avoid expressing an opinion.

Tell each other the expressions you heard. Make lists with the following headings:

* expressing opinions
* asking someone's opinion
* avoiding expressing an opinion.

Listening 2

1 **2.6** You are going to listen to two more conversations in which people express opinions. As you listen, answer these questions.

 a Who are the speakers?
 b What is their relationship?
 c What are they talking about?

2 **2.7** Read and listen to the extracts from the conversations on the next page.

 a Mark any expressions used to:
  * express opinions
  * ask someone's opinion
  * avoid expressing an opinion.

 b Add the marked expressions to the lists you have already made.

Extract 1

T About seventy quid, wasn't it?
J Is it? Have you any ideas, Roger?
R No, nothing, no, nothing springs to mind, no.
T I think we ought to get a picture or a print, something, you know, something she can actually put on the wall – it'll be there to remember us by.
B Well, she's keen on art. I mean she went to that art course this, this year, so …
T That would work, yeah. What sort of things does she like, then?
B Well, I don't know. It'd be nice to get something original, but I don't know if we've got enough money for that.
T No, seventy quid's not much for an original, is it?
R No, it's not much for that.

J I suppose so. Might be able to get a nice piece of pottery, though, or glass, or something like that.
T Yeah, there's quite a good place down, is it down the end of … the High Street somewhere …?
J That's right, that's right, they're lovely.

T … that's very often got some stuff there.
B She's got quite a lot of pottery already, I mean …

T Oh, has she?
B Well, she's … it's quite a small house – a bit limited space really.
J Roger, come on, what do you think?
R No, I can't really think.
B You know her well, you know her well, I mean.
R I really don't have any strong ideas on it, I mean … I don't think pottery or glass, as you say, she's got a lot already.

Extract 2

K What, going to the health farm?
J No, no. I think if you want something relaxing, perhaps we ought to do something a bit more active, but relaxing.
B Yeah, but with the health club you can do both, I mean you can do exercises in the gym, you can do aerobics, or you can do swimming, or you can just lounge around and do nothing.
K Mmm, sounds all right.
B What do you think?

K Well, you know, it's … we're going away. I don't mind really where we go or what we do.
J Well, don't you think you might waste your weekend if you were just lazing around?
K Well, I don't know. It's difficult to say, I mean once we get there we might find that, you know, there's all sorts of things we could do.
B Well, in the end, I mean, I don't suppose I really mind, I mean, you know, whatever you two decide, I mean, if we can all decide … if two of us decide on something …
K Yeah, fine, that's OK with me.
J Well, how about … Well, I think perhaps then we ought to then choose a neutral erm … one that we all …
B Karen, can you suggest something?
K Well, I'm quite happy with any of these suggestions really, I mean the health, the health club, that sounds fine.
B Yeah, but Julie's not keen on that, so …

Features of natural conversation

Vague language

The term *vague language* refers to words or phrases which do not give precise information. People use vague language for different reasons:

- they don't know the exact facts
- the precise facts are not important
- they don't want to express their real opinions

Read Extracts **1** and **2** again, and note the highlighted examples of vague language. Decide what the vague terms could mean and why they are being used.

Example
About seventy quid …
Which amounts could this mean? £65, £69, £72, or £78? The speaker doesn't know the exact amount.

Practice

1 **2.8** Listen and repeat these expressions asking someone for their opinion. Underline the syllable in each expression which carries the main stress.

a What do you think?
b How do you feel about it?
c Have you any ideas?
d What do you reckon?
e Don't you think we should discuss it?

2 a Say these expressions of opinion (or lack of opinion), and underline the syllable which carries the main stress in each clause.
   1 I'd say (it's a good idea).
   2 If you ask me, I think (it's fantastic).
   3 I don't really mind.
   4 I don't have any very strong feelings.
   5 I think we ought to (stay in).
   6 It's not up to me (to decide, is it)?
   7 I don't think (we should).
b **2.9** Listen and check your ideas.

Exploitation

Work in groups. Choose one of these situations. Discuss the people in the photographs opposite. You do not need to reach agreement, but simply to express opinions.

Situation 1

You are the personnel committee of a small business. You are looking to recruit two new members of staff to work in your team. Agree what your business is, then decide who you want in your team. All the candidates have similar qualifications and experience.

Situation 2

Your group is going on a two-month adventure holiday. One of the original members of the group has dropped out and you are looking for a replacement. Which of the four applicants would you choose?

Max

24, unmarried, confident public speaker, tolerant, sense of humour, good at mending things, useless at housework, TV addict, good with figures, smoker.

Isabel

28, engaged to be married, practical, good listener, non-smoker, can't cook, lazy, diplomatic, good with money.

Neil

26, divorced, has experience of running successful business, good cook, good with children, always goes to bed late, workaholic, can't keep a secret, excellent report writer.

Kate

35, widow (has a five-year-old child), trained first aider, honest, untidy, independent, hard-working, bossy, talks a lot, punctual.

Writing

1 You are going to write notes that you could refer to when having a serious conversation using semi-formal language. These are the kind of notes you would make to remind yourself about important ideas and opinions you wanted to express.

a First, think about the similarities and differences between normal conversation and more formal spoken language.

Spoken language

J   Personally, I wouldn't even consider Jackie or Rachel – they just wouldn't fit in, but I quite like the look of Christina and I'd say Robin sounds OK from his letter.
A   Charlie?
C   It's difficult to say. Several of them sound OK from their letters.

Semi-formal spoken language

My own view is that Jackie's too young. She's got hardly any experience of living with other people. It seems to me that Rachel is rather shy and quiet. I don't think she'd feel comfortable with older people. In my opinion, Robin's better and I feel sure he'd fit in well. I must say, I found him a bit talkative on the phone – I imagine this might be rather irritating. From my point of view, Christina would be ideal. She seems mature and, as far as I can tell, she'd get on well with all of us.

b Read these notes that the speech above was based on.

Writing

Jackie	*too young, little experience of sharing*
Rachel	*rather shy and quiet, not very comfortable with older people*
Robin	*talkative but OK, could be irritating but would probably fit in*
Christina	*my first choice, quite mature, think she'd get on with us all*

c What has been added to the notes to turn them into semi-formal language?

▶ **Writing guidelines p.155**

2 Choose one of these situations.

Situation 1

Write notes in preparation for a telephone call you are going to make to one of the managers of your business. Your notes should summarize your opinions about the kind of person you would like to join your department to work with you on a new project.

Situation 2

Write notes in preparation for a meeting, summarizing your opinions about the kind of person you are looking for to join your group on an adventure holiday.

3 Work with someone who chose the other situation. Explain your situation and give your opinions. Refer to your notes to make sure you cover your points.

Unit 2 Summary

In this unit you have worked on the following language points.

☐ Past simple and Past continuous
☐ Past perfect
☐ *used to*, *would*
☐ Collocations

☐ Asking about, expressing, and avoiding expressing opinions
☐ Writing notes

Tick ✓ the points you are confident about and cross ✗ the ones you need to revise.

3 It'll never happen

Preview

Your thoughts

1 In 1890 the cartoonist Albert Rabida predicted that by the year 2000 the skies above Paris would be busy with aerotaxis. Look at these pictures of how previous generations imagined life in the future. How accurate were their predictions?

2 Here are some pictures showing recent predictions about life in the future. Do they seem realistic to you?

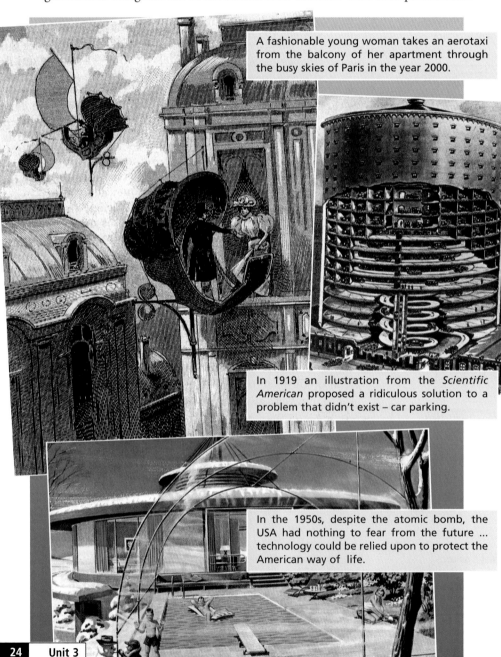

A fashionable young woman takes an aerotaxi from the balcony of her apartment through the busy skies of Paris in the year 2000.

In 1919 an illustration from the *Scientific American* proposed a ridiculous solution to a problem that didn't exist – car parking.

In the 1950s, despite the atomic bomb, the USA had nothing to fear from the future ... technology could be relied upon to protect the American way of life.

One of the many plans for solving Japan's overcrowding problems is Marinopolis, a new city floating on the sea.

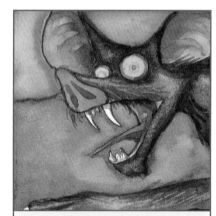

Over the next 50 million years the continents will break up. New isolated continents could develop their own unique animal life. Humans could become extinct – replaced by rabbits as big as kangaroos, sabre-toothed rats, and nightstalkers – man-sized flightless bats – which would hunt by echo-location.

Reading

World population to double by 2050

Current figures suggest the population of the world is going to double (to reach ten billion) by the year 2050. If estimates are correct, and over 90 per cent of that growth is urban, there will be a crisis in our cities. What will we do? How will we cope?

1 How would you react if you read this headline in a newspaper? How do you think the newspaper will answer its own questions: *What will we do? How will we cope?*

2 Read about one plan for coping with the problem. Did you think of this idea?

FUTUROPOLIS

One solution is to build cities underground

One solution is Japan's underground *Geotropolis*, on which work is due to start in the early part of the century. To expand Tokyo into a city 100 kilometres across, vast caverns will be excavated 50 metres below the ground and linked by high-speed railways. To reduce the negative effects of living underground, natural light will be reflected down shafts. Residents will be able to look out of 'virtual window' television screens and there will be various other gimmicks to imitate the sounds, smells, and breezes of above-ground conditions.

3 a What do you think daily life will be like in Geotropolis? Work in pairs and discuss normal routines such as eating, drinking, sleeping, travelling, working, relaxing.

b Would you like to live there? Why? Why not?

c What will the possible negative effects of living underground be?

Person to person

1 Predict some of the problems that might arise in the future in your country, or in the world.

2 Do you think it is possible to predict the future accurately? Why? Why not?

Grammar – Futures review, *will*, *going to*

1 The two most common ways of making predictions are with *will* and *going to*. How are these two kinds of predictions different?

a Over the next 50 million years the continents *will break up*.
If you don't like sad films, don't go. You*'ll cry* from beginning to end.

b Current figures suggest the population of the world *is going to double* (to reach ten billion) by the year 2050.
My nose is tickling. I*'m going to sneeze*.

2 *Will* has two other common uses. What are they?

a I*'ll be* 22 next Friday. Can you come to my party?

b **A** I'd love a coffee.
B Me too. I*'ll make* it.

3 *Going to* has one other main use. What is it?
I*'m going to stop* listening to weather forecasts. They're never right.
Are you *going to study* medicine when you leave school?

▶ **Language commentary p.126**

Check

4 Fill the gaps in these sentences with the correct form of *will* or *going to*.

a Can you drive? I'm really tired. I _____ fall asleep at any minute.

b I've had enough. I _____ look for another job.

c You leave for Japan tomorrow? Wonderful! You _____ love it.

d The sun goes down very quickly here. It _____ be dark in half an hour.

e Can't you eat any more? I _____ finish it for you.

Pronunciation

5 a How can *going to* be pronounced in formal speech (sentence 1) and informal speech (sentence 2)?

1 Polls suggest that the President is *going to* win the next election by a wide margin.

2 I don't know what I'm *going to* do, Fran, I really don't.

b **3.1** Listen and check your ideas.

c Listen again and repeat the sentences.

▶ Future continuous and Future perfect   p.26
▶ The language of contrast: *but*, *however*, *although*   p.29

Listening

1 David and Tanya are listening to a programme in which experts are discussing the short and long term future of the world and society.

What do you think the experts will say about these subjects? Note down some ideas.

- computers
- employment
- wealth and poverty
- natural threats

LOOKING FORWARD TO WHAT ...?

As you listen

2 **3.2** Do the experts mention any of the ideas that you predicted? What threat is mentioned?

Interpretation

What do you think the speakers mean in these extracts?

a *I definitely won't be worrying about comets in a hundred years' time.*
b *... by the year 2200 humans will ... have merged with computers ...*
c *... it'll be very embarrassing, because it means we won't be the most intelligent ...*
d *... the better your credit the higher up the citizen ladder you will be.*

Vocabulary

1 These words express the speakers' feelings about future events. Find the ideas or events in the tapescript on p.142 that these words describe.

incredible   scary   exciting   embarrassing   terrifying   horrendous   frightening

a Which four words have similar meanings? Rank these words in order of strength of feeling.
b Are there any aspects of modern life that you find *horrendous* or *terrifying*? What are they?
c What do you find *exciting* or *frightening* about the future?
d What ideas about the future do you find completely *incredible*?

2 *Like* has many different meanings and uses. Match the five examples of *like* in sentences **a–d** with meanings and uses **1–4**.

a *By about the year 2200 humans will have merged with computers, though I have to say I don't **like** the idea much.*
b *The idea of people merging with computers sounds **like** science fiction to me.*
c *He means we'll be spending more and more of our time working on computers – you know, we'll be, **like**, we'll be more dependent on them.*
d *You know, **like** nowadays people have pacemakers fitted to control their heartbeat – well, maybe in the future, people will be fitted with other kinds of devices, **like** those virtual reality helmets you wear on your head.*

1 *be keen on*
2 *for example / such as*
3 *similar to*
4 used as a pause in the conversation – to give the speaker time to think.

Speaking personally

1 Do you think Earth will ever be hit by an asteroid?
2 What do you think the advantages and disadvantages of mergers between computers and humans would be?
3 How would you feel about living in an *independent city* rather than a *country*?

— Grammar —

Future continuous and Future perfect

Exploring concepts

1 Underline the future verbs in these extracts. Which extracts contain Future continuous verbs and which contain Future perfect verbs?

a *I definitely won't be worrying about comets in a hundred years' time.*
b *... we'll be spending more and more of our time working on computers.*
c *... we'll all have been fitted with other kinds of devices, ...*
d *... we'll all be walking around with computer chips in our brains ...*
e *... fewer people will be paying tax.*
f *... by the year 2100, nations as we now know them will have broken up ...*

2 Compare these pairs of sentences. Explain the difference in meaning in each pair. Why or when would you choose to use a continuous or a perfect verb rather than a simple verb? (Think about the meanings of the continuous and perfect aspects – there are notes on these on p.7.)

  a In 2100 oil reserves *will be running out.*
   In 2100 oil reserves *will run out.*

  b By 2100 nations as we now know them *will have broken up.*
   In 2100 nations as we now know them *will break up.*

  c By 2100 nations as we now know them *will have broken up.*
   In 2100 nations as we now know them *will be breaking up.*

3 Which form refers to an action:

  a in progress at a particular point in time in the future?

  b which will be completed before a particular time in the future and which will have a direct effect on that time?

4 Here are some words and phrases we use to show how certain we are about what will happen in the future.

---

probably   definitely   almost certainly
maybe   It's possible that   perhaps
(un)likely   I'm sure   I've no doubt

Add each of the words and phrases in the list to these two sentences.
 • I'll be a millionaire.
 • He'll be running his own business.

▶ **Language commentary p.126**

Pronunciation

5 a How are the words in *italics* pronounced in natural speech?

  1 In the future, *we'll* all *be* working from home.

  2 By 2100 the world as we know it *will have* changed completely. War, however, *won't have* disappeared.

 b `3.3` Listen and check your ideas.

 c Practise saying the sentences with a partner.

Exploitation

Here are some headlines from newspapers of the future.

World oil supplies run out

City built on Mars

Smoking illegal in Japan

Computers take over 95% of world jobs

MOSCOW TO BE WORLD CAPITAL

Elephants now extinct

Worldwide ban on private cars

1 a When do you think the events in these headlines will come true? Choose one of these dates: 2010, 2050, 2100, 2200, 2500, 3000, or add your own.

  b Now make Future perfect sentences for the headlines with these dates: 2010, 2200, 3000. Say what will have happened and what won't have happened. Compare your ideas with a partner.

  Example
  By the year 2010 world oil supplies **will have run out.**
  They **won't have built** *a city on Mars by 2010.*

  c Choose three headlines and think about their implications. Make Future continuous sentences.

  Example

  World oil supplies run out

  Cars and planes **will probably be using** *electricity.*
  People **will be travelling** *to work on foot or by bike.*

2 One of the speakers on the radio programme said, *There'll be fewer people paying tax in the future.* Think about people in your country in the future and make sentences starting like this:
 a There'll be fewer people …   **b** There'll be more people …

3 a Think about personal and professional aspects of your future life in 20 years' time. What things will you be doing? What things will you have done? Write sentences using some of these expressions.

I hope … / I'm confident …
I (don't) think …
I expect … / I doubt if …
   I'll be … / I'll have …
   I won't be … / I won't have …

  Example
  In ten years' time, **I hope I'll be** *running my own business.*

 b Work in pairs. Make guesses or predict what your partner's life will be like in 20 years' time.
  Example
  I think you'll have visited Australia.

Free speech

4 If you could find out one thing about the future, what would it be? Is there anything you wouldn't want to know?

Reading

1 Work in pairs. Discuss these questions.

a Life is faster now than in the past. In what ways? How does this affect your life?

b You are going to read an article about attitudes to time and speed in which *Time-bandits* are mentioned. Who or what do you think they might be?

As you read

2 a Find out whether you were right about Time-bandits.

b What aspects of life are mentioned that are affected by speed and time?

c What is *Tempus* and what is its main aim?

Close up

1.14 + 1.21 What does *ever* mean in these sentences? How could the sentences be rephrased without the word *ever*?

1.24 What do you mean if you describe a discussion as *hot air*?

1.31 What is the opposite of *blind action*?

1.52 If someone *blurts* something *out*, do they say something thoughtfully or without thinking?

Time-bandits discover slowness

A curious 100m race takes place this week in the small town of Calw, near Stuttgart in Germany. The race is not for the world's best sprinters, because the challenge is
5 not to cover 100m in the shortest possible time, but to cover it in one hour.

Slowness rather than speed, patience rather than power, are the qualities needed to win the Calw
10 challenge, which is organized by *Tempus*, the society for the slowing down of time.

'The wheel of time is turning ever faster,' explains *Tempus*
15 founder, Peter Heintel, an Austrian philosophy professor. ' "Time is money" is the motto of the modern age, but what may be logical for industrial production has spread to all
20 areas of life,' Heintel explains. 'Leisure time is ever more packed. Politicians hurry through legislation because they need short-term success; discussion is regarded simply as hot air.'
25 *Tempus* started at Klagenfurt University in Austria and has spread to Germany and Switzerland. Since 1990 the organization has attracted more than 600 members, all Time-
30 bandits committed to slowing down any part of their lives where blind action has replaced thought-out deeds. *Tempus* is part of a larger movement that is beginning to question the modern glorification of
35 speed. What, for example, do we gain by jetting from one city to another when it takes hours to drive to and from the airports at both ends because of traffic?

More significantly, the time people spend working to maintain their living standards is on the increase. Jean Giono, the French novelist, observed: 'We have forgotten that our only goal is to live ... the days are fruits and our role is to eat them.' Ironically,
40 those who work the longest hours in Europe are often in the leisure and tourist industry. Management consultant Othmar Hill has bad news for hard workers: 'People who work 60–70 hours a week are employment parasites who steal other people's jobs.' Dr Rotraut Perner, a member of *Tempus* and a therapist who treats workaholics, even suggests that overwork is a
45 symptom of deeper personal problems. She reckons that politicians are among the worst offenders when it comes to living too fast.

Not all of us are obsessed with time in terms of increasing speed: in fact quite the opposite in the case of the German novelist Sten Nadolny, whose book *The Discovery of Slowness* has sold a million copies and become a cult
50 text among the Time-bandits. Nadolny explains the book's success like this: 'I am sure the title struck a chord with a lot of people longing to slow their lives down. Sadly, only speed is honoured in our society. I know from my days as a schoolteacher that quick pupils who blurt out the answers do better than slower, more thoughtful students.' He is keen to point out, however, that speed does have its place. 'Music would be very boring if there were only slow movements. Acceleration makes
55 music interesting. I am arguing for tolerance between the different speeds.' *The European Magazine*

Interpretation

1 Make a list of five key words or phrases from the text which will help you to remember the main points.

2 a Can you think of real-life examples which illustrate these statements from the article?

1 … *the time people spend working to maintain their living standards is on the increase.*

2 *People who work 60–70 hours a week are employment parasites who steal other people's jobs.*

3 … *overwork is a symptom of deeper personal problems.*

4 *Time is money.*

5 … *only speed is honoured in our society.*

b Do you agree or disagree with these generalizations?

Speaking personally

1 Read this advice from two members of *Tempus*. As you read the ten tips, tick ✓ the ones that are relevant to you.

Tips on how to slow your time

Othmar Hill, a management consultant, says:

1 ☐ Go home on time; the office won't collapse without you.

2 ☐ Throw away your mobile telephone.

3 ☐ Swap your office for a bar and a lap-top computer.

4 ☐ Take a holiday in Morocco and learn to walk as slowly as a Bedouin.

5 ☐ Change pace with a three-day retreat in a monastery.

Dr Rotraut Perner, a therapist who treats workaholics, says:

6 ☐ Learn to say 'no' and put up with the unpopularity this may cause.

7 ☐ Give up trying to be perfect.

8 ☐ Stop doing lots of things at once; instead, do one thing at a time and do it well.

9 ☐ Work out how many single tasks you can do in succession.

10 ☐ Delegate what you can to colleagues and machines.

2 a Do you want to slow down the pace of your life? Why? Why not?

b Which of the tips would you find difficult or impossible to follow? Why?

c Write two of your own tips for slowing life down.

— Grammar —

The language of contrast: *but, however, although*

Exploring concepts

1 Which words or phrases in these extracts from the text indicate contrast? What are the contrasts in each case?

Example

… *the challenge is **not** to cover 100m in the <u>shortest time</u>, **but** to cover it in <u>one hour</u>.*

a *Slowness rather than speed, patience rather than power, are the qualities needed to win the Calw challenge.*

b *Not all of us are obsessed with time in terms of increasing speed: in fact quite the opposite in the case of the German novelist Sten Nadolny.*

c *Nadolny believes that many people want to slow their lives down. He is keen to point out, however, that speed does have its place.*

d *Stop doing lots of things at once; instead, do one thing at a time and do it well.*

2 Which negative word could replace *rather than* in **1a**? Rephrase sentence **1d** using *instead of*. Where else could the word *however* be put in **1c**?

3 *But, however,* and *although* are common contrast words, but they are used in three different ways. Link these sentences using *but, however,* and *although* in turn. Think about word order. More than one answer may be possible in each case.

a *Nadolny believes in slowness.*　　b *He insists that speed has its place.*

▶ **Language commentary p.126**

Pronunciation

4 a In spoken English, contrast is indicated as much by stress and intonation as by the use of contrast words. Underline the words that you think would be particularly stressed in **1a–d** if they were read aloud.

b **3.4** Listen and check your ideas.

Exploitation

1 Finish these sentences in at least two different ways.

a I'd love a mobile phone but …　　d I'm not a workaholic; in fact, …

b Instead of criticizing me, …　　e Fast food may be convenient. However, …

c Although planes are quickest, …　　f My ambition is to be happy rather than …

Role play

2 Work in pairs. Take turns to be Student A.

Student A Your friend has been working far too hard and is looking tired and stressed. You are going to try to persuade them to change their pace of life by taking a three-day break. Think of some ideas for places where your friend could go and explain the benefits of your ideas.

Student B You appreciate your partner's concern and you sympathize with the ideas of *Tempus*. However, you are too busy to take a three-day break. Think of some immediate practical solutions to help you rather than going away.

Using a dictionary

The most common uses of a dictionary are to check the meaning or the spelling of a word. But most dictionaries contain a lot more information.

Investigation

1 a Work in pairs. Make a list of the different kinds of information you can find in a dictionary.

b Now look at this entry from the *Oxford Advanced Learner's Dictionary* to see what else you can find in dictionaries.

> **predict** /prɪˈdɪkt/ *v* to say in advance that sth will happen, [Vn] *accurately predict the outcome / result / possible consequences of sth* • *City analysts confidently predict a turnover of $300 million.* [V.that] *She predicted that the election result would be close.* [V.wh] *It is too early to predict who will win.* [V.n to inf] *Pre-tax profits are predicted to fall sharply.* ▶ **predictable** /-əbl/ *adj* (**a**) that can be predicted: *predictable behaviour / results / weather.* (**b**)(*often derog*) (of a person) behaving in a way that can be predicted: *I knew you'd say that – you're so predictable!* **predictability** /prɪˌdɪktəˈbɪləti/ *n* [U]. **predictably** *adv*: *Predictably enough the medical profession have condemned the proposals.*

c Compare your list with another pair of students.

2 a What do you think these abbreviations in the dictionary entry for *predict* stand for?

  1 *v*
  2 V.n
  3 *sth*
  4 inf
  5 *adj*
  6 *derog* (How would you feel if someone said you were predictable?)
  7 *n* [U] What is the opposite of (U)?
  8 *adv*

b Here are some more abbreviations commonly used in dictionaries. What do they stand for?

  1 *Brit* (What is the main alternative to *Brit* in an English dictionary?)
  2 *def art* (What other kind of *art* could you find in a dictionary?)
  3 *infml* (What is the opposite of *infml*?)
  4 *sl* (How is *infml* different from *sl*?)
  5 *sing* (What is the opposite or alternative to *sing*?)

Practice

Use your dictionary to answer these questions.

1 What are the main differences in meaning between these pairs of words?

  a predict / foresee
  b resident / citizen
  c extinct / dead

2 Which of these words rhyme with each other? There are three rhyming pairs.

tough	though	borough	through	enough	ought
thorough	bough	bought	cough		

3 Which word in these sets has a different stress pattern from the other three?

  a future   device   human   fiction
  b negative   natural   exciting   industry
  c technology   information   unemployment   independent

4 One meaning of *ring* is *phone*. What other meanings do you know for *ring*? Make a list (both verbs and nouns) and then look in your dictionary to check if there are other meanings.

Different dictionaries

Work in pairs or groups. Discuss these questions.

1 What are the advantages and disadvantages of monolingual and bilingual dictionaries?

2 What are the advantages and disadvantages of small, pocket dictionaries?

3 Why are electronic dictionaries becoming more popular? What can they do that traditional dictionaries can't do?

4 Why do some teachers prefer their students not to use dictionaries very often?

5 What kind of dictionary do you prefer?

Language in action

Reasons and explanations

Eavesdrop!

1 Look at the picture and guess the answers to these questions.
   - Who are the people and what is their relationship?
   - Where are they?
   - What could they be talking about?

2 Now imagine you are one of the people in the photograph. How do you feel about the other person? How do you think they feel about you?

Listening 1

1 **3.5** Listen, check your ideas and think about these questions.
   a How would you describe the attitude or the manner of the young man?
   b What would you do if you were the woman?

2 Work in groups of three. Listen to the conversation again.

   Student A Listen and note down expressions the woman uses to ask the man for reasons or explanations.

   Student B Listen and note down expressions the man uses to give reasons or explanations.

   Student C Listen and note down expressions the two speakers use when they want to change the subject of the conversation.

   Tell each other the expressions you heard. Make lists with the following headings:
   - asking for reasons or explanations
   - giving reasons or explanations
   - changing the subject.

Listening 2

1 **3.6** You are going to listen to another conversation in which people ask for and give reasons and explanations. As you listen, answer these questions.
   a What are the three people talking about?
   b What is the attitude of the two men to the woman and her ideas?

2 Listen again and read the conversation on the next page.
   a Mark any expressions used to:
      - ask for reasons or explanations
      - give reasons or explanations
      - change the subject of the conversation.
   b Add the marked expressions to the lists you have already made.

Conversation

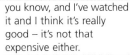

B Yeah, uh–huh …
T What on earth for?
B Well, I mean, the main reason is, I mean, on terrestrial television, you've just got five channels, erm, if you've got satellite, then you get about forty.
S But why d'you want more, more channels?
B Well, there's more choice, you know, you've got lots of films, you've got sport, lots of live sport.
T You'll never have, you'll never, never have the … all the time to watch all that TV.
B No, but, but you, I mean you've got more choice, so you can watch, you can choose what you want to see, I mean a lot, now a lot of the time there's nothing you want to see at a time you want to see it, there's

much more choice. You can see films when they're out much more quickly, erm …
T Do you really think you're going to have the time to sit down and go through all the choices and do all the recordings and watch the recordings afterwards? Come on, you'll never make it.
B No, I mean a friend of mine's, a friend of mine's got it and he's really pleased with it,

you know, and I've watched it and I think it's really good – it's not that expensive either.
T I don't understand why it's, you know, why it's so popular, why it's the thing to have. Four channels of terrestrial TV is fine.
B Well, five, Tony. Well, for the simple reason that it's, it just gives more choice, that's all.

And I mean, I think it's really good for the sports, you know, because you can't get live sports now on a lot of, erm terrestrial television.
S There must be another reason than sport, though, because there … there's quite a lot of sport on television already.
B Well, yes, certain sports …
T Too much sport …
S Too much, yeah …
B It depends, you know, there are certain sports you, you can only get if you've got satellite …

S By the way, did you see the tennis yesterday?
T Tennis?
S Yeah.
T Yeah. Who won?
S Erm … Can't remember who won …

Features of natural conversation

When we are speaking we often repeat words or phrases, sometimes making small changes. This repetition may occur because the speaker is thinking about what to say next, but it may add extra meaning.

Look at the highlighted parts of the extract and listen to the conversation again. What extra meaning, if any, does the repetition add?

Practice

1 a **3.7** Listen to people asking for reasons or explanations. How do the speakers sound – surprised, angry, frustrated, or sympathetic?

1 Why on earth are you here?
2 Why did you lie to me? There must be a reason.
3 Can you tell me exactly why you came?
4 What I don't understand is why you didn't phone.
5 Why didn't you tell me?

b Answer the questions above using one of the phrases in the list and one of the explanations below.

Mainly because …   For the simple reason that …
The main / real reason was …   … that's why!
that's the main / real reason …   Well, you see …

1 I thought you'd be angry.
2 I wanted to see you again.
3 I thought you'd be upset.
4 We had arranged to meet.
5 The phone was broken.

Example
Student A *Why on earth are you here?*
Student B *Mainly because we had arranged to meet.*

c **3.8** Listen to the speakers giving possible answers.

2 **3.9** Listen and repeat the expressions used for changing the subject.

Exploitation

Work in groups of three. Decide who is going to be Student A, then choose Situation **1** or **2**.

Situation 1

Student A You need to take time off work and you ask two colleagues to do a few things for you.
• Think of explanations for taking time off. (You don't want to give the real reason!)
• Explain and answer your colleagues' questions.
• When you think you have answered enough questions, change the subject.

Students B/C Student A needs to take time off work and wants you to do a few things for them. You are happy to help but you want to know why Student A needs time off.
• Tell your colleague you are willing to help.
• Try to find out your colleague's reasons.
• Try to find out the truth. (You don't believe them.)
• Don't let your colleague change the subject.

Situation 2

Student A You have decided to go abroad for a year.
• Decide where to go and what to do.
• Think of reasons why you want to go.
• You get increasingly annoyed by your friends' questions and you try to change the subject.

Students B/C Student A is your friend. You cannot understand why they want to go abroad.
• Ask for explanations.
• You are not satisfied with the first reasons your friend gives and you keep asking for the real explanation.

Writing

1 You are going to write a letter explaining a recent event.

  a First, think about the main differences between spoken and written explanations.

Spoken language

T I don't understand why it's, you know, why it's so popular, why it's the thing to have. Four channels of terrestrial TV is fine.

B Well, five, Tony. Well, for the simple reason that it's, it just gives more choice, that's all. And I mean, I think it's really good for the sports, you know, because you can't get live sports now on a lot of, erm terrestrial television.

S There must be another reason than sport, though, because there … there's quite a lot of sport on television already.

Writing (letter)

I am writing to explain why I was unable to attend the department meeting on Friday and to explain why I did not contact you beforehand to let you know that I would not be there. I was in fact on my way, but was involved in a minor accident on the motorway caused by thick fog. The reason I did not phone was that all drivers were told by police not to leave their cars.

  b In the conversation Tony asks for reasons and Barbara responds. What is the letter writer responding to?

  c Underline the language of explanation in the letter.

2 a Write an appropriate letter for this situation 1.

  ▶ **Writing guidelines p.155**

Situation 1

For various personal reasons you have to cancel an important business trip which has been arranged for months. Write a letter explaining why you cannot go.

Follow this paragraph plan.
1 Say you cannot go and apologise.
2 Give a brief but clear explanation.
3 Say you will be in touch again soon to make new arrangements.

  b Exchange your letter with a partner. Read each other's letters. How formal is the language? Do you believe the reasons and explanations given?

  c Discuss suggestions for improvements, then rewrite your letter including any improvements you discussed.

3 a Now read this explanatory note. How is it different from the letter in **1**?

Writing (note)

Sorry, couldn't make it to the meeting, had an accident on motorway and couldn't get to a phone.

  b Now write an explanatory note for this situation 2.

Situation 2

You arranged to meet a friend for lunch, but you find out rather late that you can't make it. You try to get your friend on the phone, but they are not available. Write a brief note which you could give to another friend to pass on.

  c Exchange and discuss notes with a partner. Can you make any suggestions for improvements?

Unit 3 Summary

In this unit you have worked on the following language points.
- ☐ *will*, *going to*
- ☐ Future continuous and Future perfect
- ☐ The language of contrast: *but*, *however*, *although*
- ☐ Using a dictionary
- ☐ Asking for and giving reasons
- ☐ Changing the subject of a conversation
- ☐ Writing letters and notes of explanation

Tick ✓ the points you are confident about and cross ✗ the ones you need to revise.

4 Children, parents, and ancestors

Preview

Your thoughts

Think back to your early childhood and compare your memories with a partner.

1 Do you have happy memories of your parents and of growing up?

2 Did you spend a lot of time with your parents? Were they strict? Did they spoil you? What did they do if you behaved badly?

Reading

1 Read these three situations involving parents and young children. If you were a parent, which situation would you find most difficult to deal with? Why? What would you do?

2 Compare your ideas with a partner.

1 When we get home from work in the evening, we're both worn out. Unfortunately, our two-year-old toddler is still wide awake. She's missed us during the day and she's delighted to see us. She just wants to play and flatly refuses to go to bed until she decides she's tired. Sometimes that's not until 10 o'clock. Of course, we want to play with her, but we're really tired – we need to rest.

2 I was on a crowded plane sitting next to a serious-looking businessman with my 18-month-old son William on my lap. William started saying 'Button! Button!' over and over. I looked down and saw that he'd pulled a button off the man's sleeve. I took the button and turned to the man and said, 'I'm sorry, but I believe this is your button.' Unfortunately, he didn't think it was funny.

3 I'm a nervous wreck. Ben, our three-year-old, is always taking risks. He climbs up everything and if there's a locked door he just has to get through it. Last Saturday he ran into the road without looking and this morning, while I was still half asleep, I heard Ben shouting, 'Mummy, look at me!' I looked out of the window. He was in his pyjamas riding up and down the pavement on his tricycle.

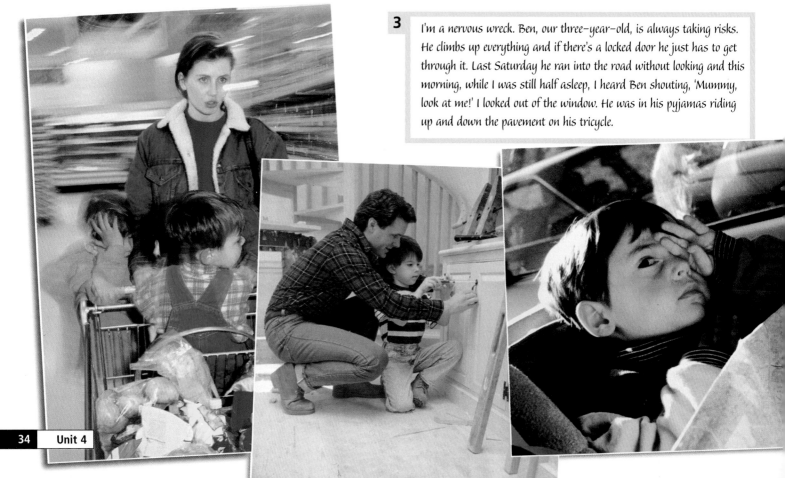

3 Now read these *Golden rules* of childcare.

a Do you think this kind of advice is useful? Why? Why not?

b Would any of the rules help the parents in the three situations?

c Think of two more rules of childcare.

Golden rules

1 Give your child self-confidence. Be on their side.

2 You shouldn't ask your child to make decisions – this will lead to confusion and insecurity.

3 Be consistent in your behaviour towards your child.

4 If you threaten your child, you must carry out the threat.

5 Don't say 'no' to your child without explaining why.

6 Encourage your child to experiment – how else will they learn?

7 Allow your child to develop their own personality.

8 Instead of using discipline, you should encourage self-discipline.

9 Remember that children learn from their parents, so you ought to set a good example.

10 Don't encourage your child to fight.

Person to person

Do you think children are more badly behaved today than in previous generations? Give examples.

Grammar – Rules, needs, duties, and advice review

1 What are the main differences in meaning between these pairs of verbs?

a need / want
1 *… we're really tired – we **need** to rest …*
2 *Of course, we **want** to play with her, …*
Which verb expresses:
• a physical necessity?
• a desire?

b have to / must
3 *Parents **have to** send their children to school.*
4 *If you threaten your child, you **must** carry out the threat.*
Which verb expresses:
• strong advice, or an order to be obeyed?
• an obligation resulting from an external situation or rule?

c should / ought to
5 *You **shouldn't** ask your child to make decisions.*
6 *… you **ought to** set a good example.*
Which verb is used:
• to give advice?
• to suggest a duty or obligation?

2 Change as many of the sentences **1–6** as you can so that they refer to the past.

▶ **Language commentary p.127**

Pronunciation

3 a How are the words in *italics* pronounced in natural speech?
1 You *must carry* on as usual.
2 You *must eat* less if you want to lose weight.
3 You *should go* and see the new Bond film.
4 You *should ask* for help if you don't understand.
5 You *ought to* do as you are told.

b ■ **4.1** Listen and check your ideas. When is the final letter of the modal verb not pronounced?

Check

4 Fill the gaps in the sentences with one of these verbs.

| have to | must | need to | ought to | should | want to |

a Generally, people only _____ sleep for about six hours a night.

b You _____ get up now, or you'll be late for work.

c My two-year-old son is no problem in the evening. Usually he _____ go to bed.

d You really _____ tell your parents. It's not fair to keep them in the dark all this time.

e You're working too hard. You _____ learn to relax a bit more.

f I _____ work late on Tuesdays. Unfortunately, it's in my contract.

▶ Modal verbs: prohibition / no obligation   p.37
▶ Modal verbs: speculating about past events   p.39

Listening

1 Work in pairs. Look at this family photograph. Try to work out the relationships between the individuals.

The generation game

2 Describe one of your older relatives to your partner. Talk about their personality. Say what you particularly like or liked about them. Ask each other questions.

3 You are going to listen to four people talking about their older relatives.

As you listen

a **4.2** Complete the chart with words or ticks ✓.

Speaker	1	2	3	4
1 Who is / are being described?				
2 Whose relative(s) is / are still fit and healthy?				
3 Whose relative(s) is / are over 70 years old?				
4 Whose relative(s) introduced them to a bad habit?				

b Do any of the descriptions remind you of any of your relatives? In what way? Discuss your ideas with a partner.

Interpretation

1 Why did the first speaker's Grandad not want him to tell anyone that he gave him cigarettes?

2 The second speaker says her mother is very independent. She says she *still lives on her own, cooks all her own meals, and that kind of thing*. What other things do you think she does for herself?

3 The third speaker says her Grandma never has any time for her grandchildren. How do you think she shows this?

4 a The fourth speaker's grandparents think *Mum and Dad are too easygoing*. How do *easygoing* parents treat their children?

b *Grandma thinks we have far too much freedom*. What do you think children with too much freedom are allowed to do?

Vocabulary

1 What are the differences in meaning between these pairs of words? Work out or guess the difference. Check your ideas in a dictionary.

a remember / remind
I **remember** my grandad really well.
I **remind** her of my grandad.

b favourite / special
I was his **favourite** grandchild.
I was his first and that made me sort of **special**.

c grow up / bring up
We **grew up** in the country.
Our parents **brought** us **up** quite strictly.

d patient / easygoing
She's the most **patient** person I've ever known.
They think Mum and Dad are too **easygoing**.

e angry / grumpy
My grandmother's nearly always **grumpy**.
He never got **angry** or shouted at me or anything.

2 Now discuss these questions in pairs or groups.

a Do you *remind* people of anyone in particular?

b What sort of a place did you *grow up* in?

c Are you a *patient* person? Give examples.

d What makes you *angry*?

Speaking personally

1 Think about people you know or have known well. Who is or was:
- the most patient?
- the kindest?
- the funniest?
- the most intelligent?

2 What are the opposites of these qualities? Think of people you know who have these qualities.

Modal verbs: prohibition / no obligation

Exploring concepts

1 a Read these sentences with *mustn't*, *don't have to*, and *needn't*. What is the difference in meaning between the three verbs?

1 You *mustn't* say anything to anyone ...

2 You *don't have to* say anything to anyone ...

3 You *needn't* say anything to anyone ...

b Match sentences **1–3** with the best continuations **4–6**.

4 you have the right to remain silent.

5 or we'll all be in terrible trouble.

6 I'll do the talking.

2 a These two sentences both express lack of necessity, but what is the important difference in meaning between them?

1 He *needn't have come* to meet me from school ...

2 He *didn't need to come* and meet me from school ...

b Match sentences **1** and **2** with these continuations.

3 but he did because he enjoyed the walk.

4 because he knew I was coming home with a friend.

▶ **Language commentary p.128**

Pronunciation

3 a How are *have / has* pronounced in these sentences?

1 I *have* two brothers.

2 I *have* to go.

3 He *has* a problem.

4 He *has* to work hard.

5 You don't *have* to come.

b **4.3** Listen and check your ideas. Then practise saying the sentences with a partner.

Exploitation

1 Complete these sentences about life in your country in two different ways, one with *mustn't* and the other with *don't have to* (or *needn't*).

Example
On underground trains ...
*You **mustn't** smoke. / You can sit down if you like, but you **don't have to**.*

a At the cinema you ...

b At colleges or universities you ...

c At school you ...

d At swimming pools ...

e On buses ...

f In hospitals ...

2 a Work in pairs. Take turns to be Student A.

Student A
Think of *have to* questions to ask your partner about their life at around the age of ten. Ask about things they *had to do* at home, at school.
Example
Did you have to do jobs at home for your parents?

Student B
Think of *have to* questions to ask your partner about their life. Ask about things they *have to do* at home, at work, as a student.
Example
What time do you have to get to work in the morning?

b Now talk about your life in the future. Exchange ideas about some of the things you think you'll have to do. Think about your professional and personal life.
Example
I'll probably have to move to another town if I want to get a good job.

Free speech

3 Work in groups. Tell each other about a club or organization you belong to. Talk about these aspects:

• why you joined and how long you've been a member

• what you do, how often you go, who the other members are

• what membership involves, e.g. rules, obligations, and privileges

• how much it costs.

Reading

1 You are going to read an article about Neanderthal Man.

   a Who was Neanderthal Man and what was important about him?

   b Why or how did Neanderthal Man disappear?

Exchange information with a partner. Make brief notes.

2 Read the introductory paragraph. Does it give you any new information?

As you read

3 One partner should read Part **1** of the article, and the other Part **2**.

   a Continue to look for the information for **1a** and **b**.

   b Underline or note any facts or ideas which you think suggest or help to explain why Neanderthal Man disappeared.

Close up

1.7 What is the opposite of *minimize*? Do you know any other words with the prefixes *mini-* and *maxi-*?

1.12 What is the opposite of a *meat-eater*?

1.12 A *mammoth* was a large elephant-like creature. What does the adjective *mammoth* mean? Example: *It's a mammoth job.*

1.16 The comparative form of *clever* can be *more clever* or *cleverer*. What other adjectives have two comparative forms?

Who were the Neanderthals?

The Neanderthals, who inhabited Europe about 230,000 years ago, were the descendants of *Homo erectus*, who walked fully upright about 1.6 million years ago. They were named after the German valley where their remains were first discovered in 1856.

5 **Part 1** At about 169 centimetres tall, the average male was not much shorter than his modern European descendant, but he had short limbs and must have been tremendously muscular – a compact body minimizes heat loss. He had a sloping forehead, a prominent brow, and a large, broad nose which must have evolved for warming and humidifying cold, dry air. Another feature of Neanderthal skulls

10 was their large front teeth: patterns of wear suggest that these might have been used to hold objects while they were being shaped with stone tools.

The Neanderthals were mostly meat-eaters. Occasionally they killed mammoths by driving them over cliffs, but they hunted mainly smaller animals like horses and reindeer. Hunting requires coordination and forward planning, but how

15 intelligent were the Neanderthals? If brain size was the only measure of intelligence, then the Neanderthals would have been about 6 per cent cleverer than humans. But brain size is not necessarily an indication of intelligence, and although they had mastered the technique of producing stone tools, the range was limited and did not develop much over 100,000 years. Despite the ability to control fire, they didn't

20 make permanent shelters or home bases. They could communicate, but the evidence indicates that their language can't have been very sophisticated.

Part 2 And the Neanderthals were facing a new challenge. That challenge came from us – or rather our ancestors, the Cro-Magnons, who appeared about 35,000 years ago. Physically, these newcomers were not as well adapted to the cold as the

25 Neanderthals. But technologically they were ahead with more varied and efficient weapons and tools, including spears that enabled them to kill their prey at a much greater distance with less risk to themselves. They may have used lunar calendars to calculate the seasonal movements of reindeer. They controlled their environment. At Kostenki in Russia, they survived by building villages from mammoth bones. For

30 about 500 years the Cro-Magnons shared their environment with the Neanderthals. But then all traces of Neanderthal culture vanished. Cro-Magnons may have killed them off or they may have interbred with them. Alternatively, the more resourceful Cro-Magnons might simply have displaced the Neanderthals to more marginal environments where they died of starvation.

35 There is evidence that, during their short coexistence, the Neanderthals tried and failed to imitate the Cro-Magnons. The most striking evidence of this comes from the explosion of cave art in Cro-Magnon times. All art is abstract, requiring an ability to replace real objects with symbols. The Neanderthals apparently couldn't make this association; the Cro-Magnons could.

Focus

Interpretation

Tell your partner the new facts or information you have learned about Neanderthal Man. Then discuss these questions together.

1 What was Neanderthal Man able to do?
2 What were Cro-Magnons good at?
3 Why did Neanderthal Man eventually disappear?

Speaking personally

How do you think human beings will develop in the future?

— Grammar —

Modal verbs: speculating about past events

Exploring concepts

1 There is a lot we don't know for certain about the past, but we can make intelligent guesses based on evidence.
How certain is the speaker in these two sentences? In one, the speaker knows what he is saying is true. In the other, he is almost certain.
  a The language of Neanderthal Man can't have been very sophisticated.
  b The language of Neanderthal Man was not very sophisticated.

2 Some modal verbs in their perfect form can be used to guess or speculate about the past. In which two of these statements does the speaker feel almost certain that what he says is true?
  a *Neanderthal Man had a large, broad nose which **must have evolved** for warming and humidifying cold, dry air.*
  b *Cro-Magnons **may have killed** them off ...*
  c *... the evidence indicates that their language **can't have been** very sophisticated.*

3 a Both of these statements show reasonable certainty. How are they different?
    1 Neanderthal Man *must have been* very artistic.
    2 Neanderthal Man *can't have been* very artistic.
  b Which of these sentences could follow **a1** and **a2**?
    3 The caves they lived in were covered in colourful drawings.
    4 The walls of the caves they lived in were bare. There was no sign of any drawings.

▶ **Language commentary p.128**

Pronunciation

4 a How are the modal verbs in **2** pronounced in natural speech?
  b **4.4** Listen and check your ideas.

Exploitation

1 a Read these comments made by people about the appearance or behaviour of their colleagues. Speculate about the possible reasons for their appearance or behaviour, using *could have* or *might have*. Use the explanations suggested, or your own ideas.
    1 *Ella's normally here by now. I wonder what's happened.*
      car accident, oversleep, late to bed last night
    2 *Marc's looking really happy today.*
      win a competition, letter from girlfriend, pay rise
    3 *Louis looks terrible this morning. He hasn't even had a shave.*
      lose razor, no sleep, get up late, think it's Sunday
    4 *Julia drove herself to work this morning.*
      her own car, pass driving test, too late for the train
    5 *There was a light on in Sam's room until the early hours of the morning.*
      work late, fall asleep with light on, come home late, read an exciting book

  b Work in pairs. Talk about comments **1–5**, giving what you think are the most likely explanations. Support your idea with a reason.
    Example
    Student A *Ella **might have** overslept. She's been working very hard recently.*
    If you agree with your partner, use *must have*, and add more supporting evidence.
    Student B *Yes, she **must have** overslept. She looked tired all day yesterday.*
    If you disagree with your partner, use *can't have* and support your idea with a reason.
    Student B *She **can't have** overslept. She rang me at eight o'clock this morning.*

Free speech

2 We often make assumptions about people from the expressions on their faces.

  a What would you assume about these people if you met them in a meeting or at a party? Compare ideas in pairs or groups.

  b Now speculate about the appearance or behaviour of someone both you and your partner know.

Word-building: suffixes

Suffixes and word class

Suffixes often show the class a word belongs to: verb, noun, adjective, adverb.

1 a Here are some words with suffixes from the texts in this unit. What class of word are they?

> competitive   decision   famous   humidify   independent
> intelligence   membership   visitor   technologically
> organization   personal   personality   personalize
> punishment   responsible   suggestion

b Mark the stress on the words, e.g. competitive.

c **4.5** Listen and check your ideas.

2 Make a list of the suffixes related to each class of words.
Examples

noun	verb	adjective	adverb
-ion	-ize	-ous	-ly

Noun suffixes

1 The suffix *-ion* can be used to form nouns from many verbs. What are the nouns formed from these verbs?

> associate   invent   explode   invade

How have these verbs been changed into nouns? What rules of pronunciation and spelling can you work out?

2 Now change these verbs into nouns.

> communicate   include   infect   react   regulate

3 a The suffix *-er* (or sometimes *-or*) is often added to a verb to form a noun referring to a person who does that action. Make your own lists under these headings.

	verb	**person**
Examples	*teach*	*teacher*
	visit	*visitor*

b How is the suffix *-er* or *-or* pronounced?

Verb suffixes

The suffix *-ize* (*-ise*) can be used to form verbs from some adjectives and nouns.

modern – modernize = to make modern.
What *-ize* verbs mean:

a to take or send someone to hospital?

b to change an agricultural country into a country based on industry?

c to turn a state-owned company into a privately-owned company?

d to bring something that is not particularly well known to people's attention and make it popular?

Adjective suffixes

1 The suffixes *-ous* and *-al* can be used to form adjectives from some nouns. How are the suffixes pronounced?
fame – famous   *person – personal*

2 a Make adjectives from these nouns.

> adventure   fame   humour   mystery   nature   nerve
> profession   religion   season   tradition

b Mark the stress on the nouns and their related adjectives.

c **4.6** Listen and check your ideas. What do you notice about the pronunciation?

d Which of the adjectives can be used to describe personalities? Think of people you know who have these qualities. Ask your partner questions.
Example
*Do you know anyone **famous**?*

Mini-discussions

Spend about two minutes discussing each of these questions.

a Should humans try to *communicate* with aliens?

b Does the press *invade* people's privacy?

c What is the most useful modern *invention*?

d How do people *personalize* their cars or their offices?

e How would you *modernize* your town or city?

Language in action

Remembering the past

Eavesdrop!

Look at the picture and guess the answers to these questions.

- Who are the people and what is their relationship?
- What do you think is happening?

Listening 1

1 a **4.7** Listen and check your ideas.
   b How would you deal with someone like Richard in this situation? Compare your ideas with a partner.

2 Work in pairs. Listen to the conversation again.

   Student A Listen and note down expressions Richard uses when he is remembering the past.
   Student B Listen and note down expressions the other people use to tell Richard to keep to the subject of the conversation.

   Tell each other the expressions you heard. Make lists with the following headings:

   - remembering the past
   - keeping someone to the subject of the conversation.

Listening 2

1 **4.8** You are going to listen to two more conversations in which people remember something in their past lives. As you listen, answer these questions.

   a What is the relationship between the speakers?
   b What situations are they talking about?
   c Are their memories happy or unhappy ones?

2 **4.9** Read and listen to the extracts from the conversations on the next page.

   a Mark any expressions used to remember the past.
   b Add the marked expressions to the lists you have already made.

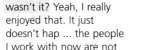

Extract 1

K Well, there was always so many things to do, weren't there, I mean you could always just sort of nip round the corner and go out for a drink or ...

R 'Cos it was so central.

K That's right.

R But it's a bit difficult now.

K Is it?

R Yeah, well ...

K I suppose if you ...

R It's only me.

K Yeah, that's true ...

R Nip out with myself round the corner, ... but, I'll never forget the time we all went to the restaurant together ... about ten of us, weren't there?

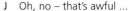
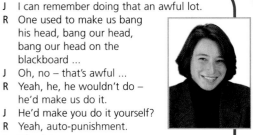

K Oh, that was wonderful, wasn't it? Yeah, I really enjoyed that. It just doesn't hap ... the people I work with now are not the same, I mean they're a lot older ...

R They don't like ...

K Well, they just have different interests, erm, and it's a lot harder to sort of get people together ...

Extract 2

J Well, I used to talk too much, I used to have to stand in the corner on my chair ...

H That's very Victorian ...

J I can remember doing that an awful lot.

R One used to make us bang his head, bang our head, bang our head on the blackboard ...

J Oh, no – that's awful ...

R Yeah, he, he wouldn't do – he'd make us do it.

J He'd make you do it yourself?

R Yeah, auto-punishment.

J Oh, dear.

H We used to get chalk flung at us.

R Oh yeah ...

J That's not very nice, is it, really? Oh dear ...

R And uniforms. Did you, did you have to wear uniforms?

J Yes, we did, we did, that's right.

Features of natural conversation

1 Look carefully at the extracts.

a Mark any examples you can find of unfinished statements. Why do people leave statements unfinished in informal speech or conversation?

b What do you think the speakers were going to say in these extracts?

  1 ... you could always just sort of nip round the corner and go out for a drink or ... (Extract 1)

  2 I suppose if you ... (Extract 1)

  3 They don't like ... (Extract 1)

  4 Yeah, he, he wouldn't do ... (Extract 2)

2 What is the effect of these question tags in the first extract? What do they tell the listener?

we all went to the restaurant together about ten of us, **weren't there**?
Oh, that was wonderful, **wasn't it**?

Practice

1 **4.10** Listen and repeat these expressions which people use to recall past events or situations.

a I can clearly remember (saying goodbye at the school gates).

b I can still see (my mother standing there crying).

c I can remember (walking into the classroom as if it were yesterday).

d I'll never forget the time (we played a trick on Mr Jones).

e I remember when (we had outside toilets).

f As far as I can remember, (we got homework most nights).

2 **4.11** Listen and repeat these expressions which we use to tell someone to keep to the subject. Which speaker sounds exasperated? Which speaker is giving the listener a gentle reminder?

a We're supposed to be talking about (school uniforms).

b We're not here to talk about (school rules in general).

c Can you stick to the point?

d Keep to the point.

Exploitation

Work in groups of three. Take turns to be Student A.

Spend two or three minutes thinking about what you want to say for each question before you start talking.

Discussion 1

What makes a good parent?

Student A Express your opinions, but include stories about your childhood from time to time.

Students B/C Express your opinions and try to keep Student A to the subject of the discussion.

Discussion 2

Should children have to wear school uniforms?

Student A Express your opinions and include stories of your own schooldays.

Students B/C Express your opinions and try to keep Student A to the subject of the discussion.

Discussion 3

What makes a good teacher?

Student A Express your opinions and include your views on why you would or wouldn't like to be a teacher.

Students B/C Express your opinions and try to keep Student A to the subject of the discussion.

Writing

1 You are going to write the beginning of a short story recalling an event from the past.

  a First, think about the differences between spoken and written memories.

Spoken language

R What about teachers – did you have any strange teachers?

J Oh, yes, – they were all Miss Somebody or another and they were very fierce …

R I can remember one – he was a French teacher – he used … if you did something wrong he'd put his hands all over your face and – but he was a heavy smoker and it used to choke you …

Writing

> I only have to close my eyes and I am back in the car behind the steering wheel heading towards Dublin. I can see the road quite clearly – it was a gentle downhill slope with occasional sharp bends. It had been raining and the fresh smell of damp leaves was in the air. The surface was still wet, so I was taking it easy. The crash came suddenly, without warning – all I remember now is the front of a black BMW, the sound of breaking glass, the screech of tyres, then silence.

  b Which words and phrases in the written memories show that the writer is describing a memory – something that happened to him?

  c How does the writer try to make the event 'come alive' for the reader?

  d What does the reader actually find out about the accident itself from the description?

▶ **Writing guidelines p.156**

2 Write the opening paragraph of a story, describing the background and the events leading up to a main incident. Choose one of these suggestions.

Suggestion 1

A memory of something that happened to you or someone you know – for example, an accident or a surprise.

Suggestion 2

An episode from a book, play, or film you have read or seen recently.

Think about how to make your story 'come alive'. Include details of the time of day, the surroundings, the smells, the sounds, and events before the episode took place.

3 Exchange your paragraph with a partner.

  a Read each other's stories, thinking about these points.
  • Does the story 'come alive' for you?
  • Does the description make you want to find out more?

  b Discuss each other's stories. Make any suggestions for improvements.

  c Rewrite your paragraph, including any improvements you discussed.

  d Finally, tell your partner how the story ends.

Unit 4 Summary

In this unit you have worked on the following language points.

- ☐ Rules, needs, duties, and advice
- ☐ Modal verbs: prohibition / no obligation
- ☐ Modal verbs: speculating about past events
- ☐ Word-building: suffixes

- ☐ Remembering the past
- ☐ Telling someone to keep to the subject of a conversation
- ☐ Writing the first paragraph of a story

Tick ✓ the points you are confident about and cross ✗ the ones you need to revise.

5 Judging by appearances

Preview

Your thoughts

1 When you meet someone new, how important are your first impressions? What sorts of things do you notice first?

2 What kind of person do you get on well with?

3 Do you generally get on better with people who are similar to or different from you?

Reading

1 Read the text and then match the couples.

Playing cupid is fun

We all like to introduce two people who we're convinced are perfect for each other. But how often do we get it right? Psychologists say that people choose partners with similar backgrounds, education, interests, and even physical features to themselves. But then there is that old saying 'Opposites attract'. Test your match-making skills: the six people photographed are three established couples. Can you guess who the couples are?

Name	Lucie Age 28	Ruth Age 33	Helen Age 30
Occupation	manager of an antique shop	jeweller	hair and make-up artist
Perfect weekend	at home doing nothing	in Paris	in the country with friends
Perfect holiday	skiing	a week on the beach, then a week sightseeing	trekking in Thailand
If I won the lottery, I'd buy …	a big country house	a new house	a Jaguar car
I worry about	death of myself and loved ones	things not being in my control	money and loss of innocence in children
Qualities I like	honesty, generosity	kindness, generosity	loyalty, sincerity
Qualities I dislike	deceitfulness	meanness, aggression	bitchiness, invasion of privacy
Children are	very important	not important	not important yet

2 Compare your ideas with a partner. Do you agree about which couples go together? Give reasons for matching particular women and men. Check your guesses by turning to p.159.

3 Do you think the three relationships are likely to be successful? Discuss your ideas.

Listening

1 5.1 Work in pairs. You are going to find out more information about the three couples. You are also going to listen to a psychologist's analysis of their relationships.

Student A As you listen, make a note of any new factual information you hear about the people.

Student B As you listen, make a note of any points the psychologist makes about what could affect the success or failure of the relationships.

2 From what you have heard, how successful do you now think each couple's relationship will be?

Person to person

1 Have your first impressions of someone ever been wrong? In what way? What happened?

2 Do you look for the same qualities in friends as you do in colleagues?

Nelson Age 30	Pip Age 26	Matthew Age 38
furniture designer	photographer	international banker
camping in the countryside	a country house with friends	watching football
visiting old cities	the US on my motorbike	skiing
a Scottish island	a new motorbike	an Aston Martin
burglary, family and friends being hurt	missed opportunities, a fatal motorbike crash	work
charity, compassion	loyalty, understanding	intelligence
ignorance	greed, selfishness, vanity	irrationality
not important	not important yet	very important

Grammar – Conditionals review

1 There are several common conditional patterns in English. What are the main differences in meaning between these pairs of sentences?

a 1 If I *get* money for my birthday, I *put* it straight in the bank. (Zero)
   2 If I *get* money for my birthday, I'*ll put* it straight in the bank. (First)

b 1 If I *win* the lottery, I'*ll spend* all the money on a luxury holiday. (First)
   2 If I *won* the lottery, I'*d spend* all the money on a luxury holiday. (Second)

c 1 If I *won* the lottery, I'*d buy* a new house. (Second)
   2 If I'*d won* the lottery, I'*d have bought* a new house. (Third)

2 Which of the sentences in **1** refer to:

a a possible but improbable future situation?
b a possible future situation?
c something which sometimes really happens?
d an imaginary past situation?

3 Compare these pairs of second conditional sentences.

a Which condition is possible?
   1 If I *were* a woman, I'*d have* children.
   2 If I *won* the lottery, I'*d give up* work.

b How certain is the speaker in these sentences?
   1 If I *won* a million pounds, I'*d buy* an island.
   2 If I *won* a million pounds, I *might buy* an island.

▶ **Language commentary p.128**

Pronunciation

4 a How are the words in *italics* pronounced in natural speech?
   1 If *he'd* won the lottery, *he'd have* bought a Ferrari.
   2 If *he hadn't* come, you *wouldn't have* known.

b 5.2 Listen and check your ideas.

Check

5 Choose the most appropriate form of these verbs.

a If I were five years younger, I'*ll go* / I'*d go* and live abroad for a year or two.
b If I *want* / *wanted* to make new friends, I go to a club or disco.
c I'll only tell you my secret if you *promise* / *you'd promise* not to tell anyone.
d I'd only change jobs if something much better *came up* / *had come up*.
e I'*d lose* / I'*d have lost* my temper if you'd been any later.

▶ The verb *wish*; mixed conditional sentences   p.47
▶ Past verbs with present or future meaning   p.49

Listening

1 Look at the logos. Discuss these questions in pairs or groups.

  a What consumer goods do you associate with the brands?

  b Which of these brands would you always or never choose? Why?

  c What other brand names do you know? Which are your personal favourite makes or brands at the moment? Think of cars, drinks, food, and clothes.

A brand new image

2 You are going to listen to four people talking about brand names. First, check the meaning of any of the following words and phrases you are uncertain of. Then think about how the people may use them in the conversation.

---

young people   create an identity   image   label
sort of uniform   status symbols   obsessed with brands

As you listen

3 **5.3** Listen and check your ideas.

4 Listen to the conversation again. Which brands are mentioned as examples of:

  a teenage fashion obsessions (jeans and shoes)?

  b trendy drinks?

  c cars which are status symbols?

  d ordinary department stores?

  e expensive designer clothes?

  f an exclusive place to go shopping?

  g a business which tries to protect the environment?

Interpretation

1 **5.4** Read the tapescript on p.144 and listen to the extract. What can you tell about the speakers' attitudes to the subject of brand names and to each other?

2 Underline the vague language in these extracts from the conversation, then decide what each vague term could mean.

  a *Did anyone see that article in the paper the other day about brand names?*

  b *It sounds pretty boring to me.*

  c *… clothes, drinks, food, cigarettes – things like that. It said that lots of young people need them to create an identity for themselves.*

  d *… when I was about 13, I wanted a pair of Levi jeans … they had to have that little orangey label.*

  e *I wish I'd gone to Marks and Spencer's instead – you know, somewhere more ordinary like that.*

  f *… I know loads of teenagers who buy soap and stuff there … (Body Shop)*

Speaking personally

1 Do you think young people need famous brand names to create an identity for themselves?

2 Do you agree that it isn't just kids that are obsessed with brands?

The verb *wish*; mixed conditional sentences

Exploring concepts

1 A wish is a desire for things to be different.
I wish I was taller means I'm short and I'd like to be taller but I know I can't be.

What do these speakers mean?

a *I wish you'd stop being so childish.*

b *I wish I had enough money to buy an Armani shirt.*

c *… to be honest, I wish I hadn't cut the label off now.*

2 Match the three wishes in **1** with one of these definitions.

1 a wish about one's own present situation

2 a wish about past behaviour

3 a wish about someone else's behaviour

3 Which sentence in **1** is:

1 a regret at having done something?

2 a complaint or criticism?

3 an expression of dissatisfaction or frustration with a present situation?

4 Like sentence **1c**, some conditional sentences refer to a past consequence of a past action or situation which cannot now be changed.

a *If I'd won the lottery, I'd have bought a new house.*

This third conditional sentence tells us that the speaker didn't win the lottery and didn't buy a new house.

Mixed conditional sentences also refer to the consequences of actions or situations in the past.

b *If they'd had more money, I'd probably be more worried about what I wear now.*

What are the main differences between the two conditional sentences **a** and **b** above? Think about the different meanings and the forms of the verbs.

▶ **Language commentary p.129**

Pronunciation

5 a **5.5** Listen and repeat these sentences.

1 I wish you wouldn't do that!

2 I wish you'd stop interrupting!

3 I wish I had hair like yours.

4 I wish I were twenty years younger.

5 I wish you'd listen when I'm talking to you.

6 I wish I could go.

b Which are complaints and which are regrets?

Exploitation

1 You are going to listen to extracts from six different conversations.

a **5.6** What is the situation in each conversation? What do you think was said just before each extract?

b Listen to the conversations again and convert what the speakers say into two wishes, one about the present situation and the other about past behaviour.

Example

I really hate being so tired.

I wish I wasn't so tired. (present situation)

I wish I hadn't gone to bed so late. (past behaviour)

2 Imagine you live with or are on holiday with someone who has a number of irritating habits.

a Write a list of things the person does that particularly irritate you.

Example

He / She always wakes me up early in the morning by being noisy.

He / She never stops talking.

b Work in pairs. Take turns to be Student A and make conversations with a partner.

Example

Student A *Why do you have to make so much noise in the morning? I wish you'd let me sleep a bit longer.*

Student B *But there are so many interesting things to do.*

Student A *That's not the point. And I wish you'd stop talking occasionally – it's really tiring listening to your voice.*

Free speech

3 a Think back over the last few years of your life. Is there anything which you did or didn't do which you now regret? Think about how your life might have been different. Here are some ideas.

• something you didn't do

• something you said to someone

• somewhere you didn't go

• someone you made friends with

b Compare your ideas with a partner.

c If you could change one thing in the past, what would it be?

Reading

1 You are going to read about a zoo where visitors can watch the typical behaviour of human beings in their natural environment.

a What kinds of typical behaviour do you think visitors will see?

b How would you react to seeing humans in a zoo?

c What do you think could be the purpose of watching typical human behaviour?

As you read

2 Check your predictions and note down anything you find surprising, interesting, or funny.

Close up

1.3 What other kinds of *primates* do you know?

1.4 Why does the writer add the word *literally* here? What is the non-literal meaning of *make an exhibition of yourself*?

1.34 What is the meaning of *get on with* here?
   • do something in a friendly way
   • continue

1.51 What are the main features of a *cage*? How is a *cage* different from a *cubicle* (1.4)?

BRAINY APES MAKE A SHOW OF THEMSELVES

Visitors to Copenhagen Zoo have been proving oddly reluctant to stare too long at the latest specimens in the monkey pavilion. For the latest primates are Malene Botoft, 27, and Henrik Lehmann, 35, who have been – literally – making an exhibition of themselves in a plastic cubicle in an attempt to place *Homo sapiens* in context in the animal kingdom.

An acrobat and a newspaper administrator in real life, they hope to raise environmental awareness by satisfying what they believe is one of the human being's most distinctive features: curiosity.

Their cubicle is supposed to look like a typical Danish home with a tiny kitchen, a hi-fi, lots of books, a little patch of grass with the Danish flag stuck in it. The couple are in their natural environment: reading books, drinking coffee, talking on the phone, fixing a computer which doesn't work and inviting guests, but all taking place in front of the zoo's daily visitors.

'Despite having little body hair, Man has spread through all climatic zones,' says the description of *Homo sapiens* in front of the cubicle. 'The numerous possessions and tools of Man are kept within the family's territory. Other representatives of the species respect that territory, usually without a fight.'

Botoft and Lehmann believe that western culture has created so many taboos regarding privacy that we do not question it, even when given the chance, although children have not yet learned to be so inhibited. Lehmann says: 'Kids are the only ones who dare cross the border and glue their noses to our cage.

'Visitors don't look at us so much as at what we have: the CDs, the kind of wine we drink, the books. What in fact they seek is to see

themselves,' continues Lehmann. 'Once we're inside the cubicle, we don't notice the people outside. Visitors tend to be too embarrassed to look us in the eye. We simply get on with our daily lives as if they didn't exist. If you talked to the other animals, you'd probably find they feel the same way.' Zoo spokesman Peter Haase says: 'They fit into our idea that the zoo should present animals in the most natural environment possible. What are people? Basically, primates with better means of grasping, binocular vision, and larger brains.' This is, however, the first time a zoological park has showcased the human being. In Copenhagen, no one denies that *Homo sapiens* has its place at the zoo, although it is unlikely the human corner by the monkey pavilion will be permanent.

It's about time people became more aware of their anthropological heritage. 'While we were building the cubicle,' recalls Lehmann, 'a sign had already been put up, saying *Homo sapiens*. Parents would say to their children: "Look, they're building a cage for *Homo sapiens*." Just one amused visitor realized that it was a cage for people.'

The European magazine

Interpretation

1 Why are adults *too embarrassed to look us in the eye*?

2 Why are visitors more interested in the couple's possessions than in the couple themselves?

3 Why is it *unlikely that the human corner will be permanent*?

Speaking personally

1 Do you agree with Peter Haase's definition of what people are (l.41–42)? Would you add any other characteristics?

2 Would you volunteer to be a human exhibit in the zoo? Why? Why not?

Past verbs with present or future meaning

Exploring concepts

1 The Past tense does not always refer to past time. Do the past verbs in these sentences refer to past, present, or future time?

a *If I **won** the lottery, I'd give up work and have children.*
b *I wish I **had** enough money to buy an Armani shirt.*
c *We simply get on with our daily lives as if they **didn't exist**.*
d *If you **talked** to the other animals, you'd probably find they feel the same way.*
e *It's about time people **became** more aware of their anthropological heritage.*
f *If only you **didn't have** to leave so early.*
g *I **thought** you might like to come round for the evening.*
h *Imagine/Suppose you **had** enough money to give up your job …*
i *I'd rather you **didn't stare** at me like that.*
j *Just one amused visitor **realized** that it was a cage for people.*

2 Why are past verbs used in sentences 1a–i? Choose one or more of these explanations.

1 Past verbs can express something unreal in the present, or something not true.
2 After some verbs and other expressions, past verbs can express a desire for things to be different.
3 In conditional sentences, past verbs show that actions or events are possible but improbable.
4 Past verbs can make questions or requests sound less direct, and so more polite.

▶ **Language commentary p.129**

Exploitation

1 a Rephrase these sentences using the past tense and the words in brackets to give a present or future meaning.

1 Can't we fly there? Sailing makes me feel sick. (rather)
2 He behaves like a single man. (as if)
3 Unfortunately people always seem to be in a hurry these days. (wish)
4 Hurry up! We're going to be late unless we leave immediately. (about time)
5 You shouldn't eat so quickly – it's probably why you always feel ill. (if)

b Compare your answers with a partner.

2 Imagine what the people in these scenes from old films are saying or thinking. Write down their thoughts or words using these expressions.

It's time …   I wish …   I'd rather …   Imagine we …   Suppose you …

Example
'**It's time** you bought a new hat.'
'**Imagine we** were twenty years younger.'

Role play

3 Work in pairs. Take the parts of the two people shown in one of the film scenes and make up a conversation between them. Remember the people would like things to be different.

Learning new vocabulary

Experiment

Here are some expressions or words with new meanings which have come into the language quite recently. Learn them now, using any method you know. You have five minutes.

couch potato an inactive person who watches a lot of television
graze eat small amounts of food often instead of having regular meals
gobsmacked almost speechless with surprise or shock
gutted very disappointed
infotainment the reporting on radio and TV of news in an entertaining way
naff unfashionable, unstylish, and therefore worthless

Couch potatoes don't have time for proper meals, so they graze.

Methods

1 a Answer these questions about how you learn vocabulary.

How do you do it?

1 How often do you try to learn new words in a deliberate way?
2 How many words on average do you try to learn at one time?
3 Do you have a special method?
4 When and where do you learn words? Do you have favourite times and places?
5 When you learn a new word what exactly do you learn? Just the spelling and the meaning in your language, or more than this?
6 How do you record vocabulary you want to learn?
7 Do you try to memorize long lists of words just before a test?
8 Do you think it is very important to try to learn a lot of new words? Why? Why not?

b Compare your answers with a partner.

2 Here are a few different methods for learning new words. Tick ✓ any of these you have tried.

☐ Group words in ways which mean something to you.
☐ Associate words with sounds, pictures, or objects.
☐ Associate words with words in your own language which sound similar.
☐ Remember words in useful phrases or sentences.
☐ Mark words in your dictionary with a highlighter pen.
☐ Write words and their meanings several times.
☐ Write words on pieces of paper then stick them in places where you will often see them.
☐ Repeat words aloud many times – in a normal voice or as a song.
☐ Make up a short story making use of all the new words.
☐ Write words and meanings in your language then cover the English words and try to remember them from the translation.

Test

1 Test each other to find out if you remember the six words you learnt in Experiment.

2 Here are some more words and expressions. Try learning them using a different method. Test yourself tomorrow.

gobbledygook language which seems meaningless because you can't understand it (the kind that is often used by bureaucrats)
miffed annoyed, often by how someone behaves towards you
plastic money general word used for credit or debit cards
wimp person who is not strong, brave, or confident
ginormous extremely large
freebie something you get for nothing (for no money)

Language in action

Checking understanding

Eavesdrop!

Look at the picture and guess the answers to these questions.

- Who are the people?
- Where are they?
- What is happening?

Listening 1

1 **5.7** Listen, check your ideas and think about these questions.
  a What is going to happen the following day?
  b Who do you think the person in the car is?

2 Work in pairs. Listen to the conversation again.

  Student A Listen and note down expressions the man uses to make sure the girl has understood his instructions.

  Student B Listen and note down expressions the girl uses to check she has understood the man's instructions.

  Tell each other the expressions you heard. Make lists with the following headings:
  - making instructions clear
  - checking instructions.

Listening 2

1 **5.8** You are going to listen to two more conversations in which one person gives another person instructions. As you listen, answer these questions.
  a How well do the speakers know each other?
  b What is their situation?
  c How does the person receiving the instructions react to what they are being told?

2 **5.9** Read and listen to the extracts from the conversations on the next page.
  a Mark any words or expressions used to:
    - make instructions clear
    - check instructions.
  b Add the marked expressions to the lists you have already made.

Extract 1

H Well, it depends on the time of day really, erm, I'll be here most of the time so you don't have to worry about that. Sometimes there will be questions which I can't answer, so we'll really have to find out the answers together, because you never know what people are going to ask you.

J So what you're saying is, I've got to learn as I go along.

H Yes, that's right. A lot of it is, is just learning, as you say, as you go along. You will also be asked by people for various documents – erm – now, you'll find in the file over in the corner that I have put a lot of specimen documents there – they are also on the computer, but the file will just give you the layout of the documents.

J Yes …

H Is that all right?

J Erm, yes, I think so. Erm, I think I'd like to …

Extract 2

K Right, OK.

B … and, erm, the ones in the kitchen – they need watering every other day really.

K Oh – right, OK.

B Is that clear?

K Yeah, I think so – that's fine. Yeah.

B I mean, it's not the end of the world, but … there are more important things. Erm … the washing machine …

K Right …

B … erm, just be careful that you close the door properly.

K Right – what, what, what do you mean?

B Well, er, I've had a few problems with it, so just make sure it's properly closed …

K Er, OK.

B … and, erm, try to avoid using that long programme.

K Do you mean I shouldn't use it?

B Well, it might be better if you didn't, yeah. Aha.

K Right. OK. Fine.

B OK, and erm, I've given you some keys,

K Yes.

B All right. Check when you leave that the back door's locked.

K Right, OK.

B And one of the keys is a bit dodgy …

K Right …

B … erm – you've got to sort of put it in quite, er, erm, hard and then turn it – so if you, if you don't get it the first time just try again.

K Right. OK.

B Are you all right with that?

K I'm fine, yeah. That's fine.

B Erm. Right. Do you just want, just to, just see if there's anything else?

K You mentioned something about the cleaner.

B Yeah.

K When does she come in?

B She comes in on Mondays – all right?

K Right.

B All right? She's got her own key so you don't need to worry about her.

K Right. So, do you mean – do I have to lock up after she's gone or will she … or do I have to stay while she's there?

Features of natural conversation

Read and listen to the extracts again.

1 How many different expressions do speakers use to give a positive reply to a question?

2 How are they pronounced?

Practice

1 a **5.10** You are going to listen to some speakers saying the words *right*, *all right*, and *OK*. Decide if the intonation in each group **1**, **2**, or **3** means: *Do you understand?*, *I understand*, or *I'm not sure*.

b **5.11** You are going to listen to someone giving instructions for looking after a pet. Repeat the dialogue.

2 a **5.12** Listen and repeat these phrases which check that someone has understood what you have said.
1 Do you see (what I mean)?
2 Does that make sense?
3 Is that all right?
4 Is that clear?

b **5.13** Listen and repeat the words and phrases which check that you have understood what someone has said.
1 What exactly do you mean?
2 Do you mean (I shouldn't use it)?
3 So, do you mean (I should be careful)?
4 So, what you're saying is (don't use it), right?
5 In other words, I mustn't use it, right?

Exploitation

Work in pairs. Take turns to be Student A.

Student A You have agreed to lend Student B something. Choose one of the items illustrated and explain how to use it. Check that Student B understands your instructions.

Student B Imagine you have never used the thing that Student A is going to lend you. Ask lots of questions to check you understand the instructions.

Writing

1 You are going to write some instructions.

a First, think about the main differences between spoken, and informal and formal written instructions.

Spoken language

B   … erm, just be careful that you close the door properly.
K   Right – what, what, what do you mean?
B   Well, er, I've had a few problems with it, so just, er make sure it's properly, er closed …
K   OK.
B   … and erm, try to avoid using that long programme.

Writing (informal)

> Turn the dial clockwise and wait – the water takes a minute to heat up.
> Check the temperature before you get in – it can get very hot.

Writing (formal)

> 1   Display the document in the active window.
> 2   Choose Page Setup and select the correct options.
> 3   From the menu box choose Print.
> 4   Choose OK or Print.

b What are the main language differences between informal and formal written instructions?

c How can you make sure the person reading your instructions understands exactly what they have to do? Remember, they can't ask you for clarification and you can't rephrase written instructions.

▶ **Writing guidelines p.157**

2 Choose one of these situations.

Situation 1

You are going away for the weekend and your best friend has kindly offered to help you out. You have already explained what needs to be done, but your friend has asked you to write a few clear instructions to remind them of the most important things. Here are some possible ideas.

- security: doors, windows, etc.
- plants / pets
- people: visitors / neighbours / deliveries

Situation 2

You are going to be away from work for two days next week and a colleague has offered to do two important tasks for you. You do the same kind of work, so you do not need to explain all the background. Write clear instructions saying exactly what your colleague should do. If time is important, say when each job should be done.

3 Exchange your piece of writing with a partner.

a Read each other's instructions. How clear are they? Ask your partner to explain anything you do not understand.

b Rewrite your set of instructions, taking account of any problems your partner had in understanding your first attempt.

Unit 5 Summary

In this unit you have worked on the following language points.

- ☐ Conditionals review
- ☐ The verb *wish*
- ☐ Mixed conditional sentences
- ☐ Past verbs with present or future meaning
- ☐ Learning new vocabulary

- ☐ Making instructions clear
- ☐ Checking instructions
- ☐ Writing instructions

Tick ✓ the points you are confident about and cross ✗ the ones you need to revise.

6 A certain age

Preview

Your thoughts

1 What are the advantages and disadvantages of being the age you are now?

2 What is the best age to be?

Reading

1 Read the six texts and match each one with a picture.

1 Laura sat up beside her father at the front of the cart and waved to the neighbours. 'Goodbye, Laura!' they called. As the cart moved on, more women came to their doors to see what the sound of wheels meant at that time in the morning. When they saw Laura and her trunk the women remained on their doorsteps to wave their farewells. Her going seemed to be causing quite a stir in the hamlet. Not because the sight of a young girl going out in the world to earn her own living was an uncommon one there, but they usually went on foot …

2 *It's been a really great day. Charlie has finally walked completely on his own, without holding on to a chair or anything. It was this morning – he just took off. He let go of the fridge and walked across the kitchen as if he'd never done anything else. I was really chuffed and he sensed that 'cos he kept looking at me. He went back and forth, a bit wobbly, so at times he grabbed the table legs, but mainly he was on his own.*

3 Until recently, Stephanie Ducker's life seemed perfectly ordinary. She was a psychiatric nurse, who was engaged to a scientist. All that has changed; she has left her job, broken off her engagement, and tomorrow she enters a closed order of nuns. From now on every day will be the same. She will get up at 5.30 a.m. for prayers and go to bed at 9.30 p.m. She will not be allowed to speak except in short periods of 'recreation'. She will have little free time or privacy.

4 It was a funny day, actually. Two of my friends and I were up till around five o'clock. And I spent all day preparing and then sitting around for about three hours just waiting for something to happen, and when it did happen I don't remember it happening. I can't forget the wedding cake. It was horrific what happened. It was sitting between Mick and myself and suddenly the columns gave way and fell into one.

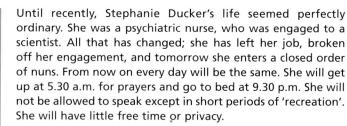

5 *In my twenties I worked non-stop, most of the time far from home, and enjoyed the incredible luxury of living to my own schedule. During that time there were decisions and discoveries that altered the course of my life, but then I made a conscious change: I wanted a child. Having Max is the most important thing that has happened to me. It has changed the way I look at everything.*

6 He called me into his office and said, 'I want to talk about reorganization. Unfortunately, it's bad news – there's no position for you. You're redundant.' It was a real blow because I've always been a company man, I've put in a long time, and I've always earned my keep. On the other hand, I was relieved to be out of that atmosphere. I went home and said to my wife, 'It's happened. He's given me the sack.'

2 Match these words and phrases from the texts with their meanings. (The text numbers are in brackets.)

a I was really *chuffed* (1)   unstable
b … *'cos* he kept looking at me (1)   not in bed
c … a bit *wobbly* … (1)   pleased
d … were *up* till around 5 o'clock (4)   disappointment
e It was a real *blow* … (6)   told me I've lost my job
f He's *given me the sack.* (6)   because

Person to person

1 At what age do the events described in texts **1, 2, 4,** and **5** usually happen to people in your country?

2 Do any of the events remind you of things in your life?

Grammar – Present perfect review

1 Underline the Present perfect verbs and circle the Past simple verbs in these extracts from the texts.

a *It's been a really great day.*
b *As the cart moved on, more women came to their doors …*
c *All that has changed; she has left her job, broken off her engagement, …*
d *It was a funny day … I spent all day preparing …*
e *Having Max is the most important thing that has happened to me.*
f *I went home and said to my wife, 'It's happened. He's given me the sack.'*

2 Look at **1b** and **c**. What different time periods do the two sentences refer to? What word could be added to **1c** to make the time period more obvious?

3 a What is the difference in meaning between these pairs of sentences?
    1 *It's been* a great day …   2 *She's left* her job …
       It was a great day …   *She left* her job …
   b Which is the continuation of each sentence?
    A … last December. Now she's self-employed.
    B … but it took me nearly a week to recover.
    C … but I'm really tired now.
    D … but she won't tell anyone why.

4 The Present perfect is used to link a past event with its present effect or result. What is the present effect or result of the events described in these sentences?

a *Charlie **has** finally **walked** completely on his own.*
b *Having a baby **has changed** the way I look at everything.*
c *I said to my wife, 'It**'s happened.** He**'s given** me the sack.'*

▶ **Language commentary p.130**

Pronunciation

5 a How are *have/has* pronounced in natural speech?
    1 What *have* you bought?
    2 *Have* you seen Lucy recently?
    3 No, I *haven't*, but Susan *has*.
    4 Michael *has* already told me.
    5 I *have* remembered.
   b **6.1** Listen and check your ideas. What rules of pronunciation can you work out?

Check

6 Choose the best form of the verbs in these sentences.

a I *went* /I*'ve been* to three birthday parties this week.
b My grandfather *travelled*/*has travelled* abroad for the first time last year.
c Maybe she*'s forgotten*/she *forgot* our meeting. She's over an hour late now.
d I *worked*/I*'ve worked* really hard all day. Now I need a rest.
e I *was*/I*'ve been* married in this church exactly ten years ago.

▶ Present perfect continuous (1)   p.57
▶ Present perfect continuous (2)   p.59

Reading

1. Look at the photograph of an old woman in traditional costume. From what you can see, what do you imagine her life is like? Think about work, food, and travel. Compare your ideas with a partner.

2. Look at the article title and the other photographs. What do you think the article is about? Note down your predictions.

As you read

3. Quickly look through the article to find out if your ideas about the old woman and your predictions were correct.

Close up

1.1 What does the word *it* refer to in *She does not realize it yet, but ... Cecilia has a good chance of living 100 years.*

1.21 *Taking care of the animals means a good hour's walk ... Does good* mean *pleasant* or *at least*?

1.39 What word could replace *Yet* in *Yet the village entered the world of technology four years ago ... ?*

1.41 The words *womb* and *tomb* are used figuratively to mean the beginning and the end of life. What are the normal equivalents? (Both end in *-th*)

Time has stopped in Campodimele

She does not realize it yet, but three-month-old Cecilia has a good chance of living 100 years. Her parents have not discovered the elixir of life – they just had the good fortune to be born in Campodimele, a small village on a rocky hilltop 120 km south of Rome, best known for the longevity of its 850 inhabitants.

'It is rare for anybody born in Campodimele to die before the age of 85,' says the mayor Paolo Zannella. His own grandfather died at 95, his grandmother at 97, and his aunt at 100. More than 90 people in the village are aged between 75 and 99 – such an astonishing proportion that the World Health Organization sent researchers to the village in 1985 to discover its secret. 'They did not believe their eyes when they saw the results of the tests,' recalled Zannella. 'The old people's cholesterol level was lower than in new-born babies.'

Since then, scientists from all over the world have been visiting this remote mountain village regularly. 'They all want to know my secret,' said Gerardo Pecchia, 99, the oldest villager. 'But what can I say? Maybe you live longer if you are not lazy. I've always worked hard. I only eat meat twice a year, at Christmas and on the feast of Saint Onofrio. There is no danger here and, when the weather is nice, I go to see the chickens.'

'Taking care of the animals means a good hour's walk at least twice a day,' said Zannella. 'But to list the ingredients of our recipe for a long, healthy life, I would mention first the Campodimelans' easygoing nature and sense of balance. Nobody suffers from depression and old people aren't lonely, as they live with their families.' Life is unhurried, stress is unknown, and traffic is banned in the centre.

To the outsider, it really looks as if time has stopped. Women wear scarves, just like their ancestors, who used to walk with pots of honey on their heads – Campodimele means 'field of honey' – and men gather in the paved square to gossip and play cards under a great oak. Even the tree is ancient. It has stood there for more than 400 years.

Yet the village entered the world of technology four years ago, when Pietro Cugini of Rome's Politecnico hospital began studying the old villagers for a project called *From the Womb to the Tomb*. Monitored 24 hours a day, the old people's blood pressure revealed rhythmic fluctuations significantly lower than the national average.

'A healthy blood pressure is the biological basis of longevity,' said Cugini. 'I have been studying the children and the grandchildren of the over-85s and I've found that they also have a substantially lower blood pressure.' However, genetic make-up is not enough to ensure long life. 'You need a well-structured lifestyle,' warned Cugini. In Campodimele, old people walk for at least two hours daily, eat at the same time each day, get up at dawn, and go to bed at sunset.

But for 93-year-old Erminia Spirito, baby Cecilia's great-grandmother, the secret is to eat lots of onions: raw, with oil, vinegar, and red pepper. 'Our diet is Mediterranean at its best. Lots of fresh vegetables, pulses, wild mushrooms, almost no butter, and not much salt.' The local speciality is the cicerchia, a pebble-like pea which is often served with home-made pasta. Then there are snails seasoned with pepper, and herbs. It will be the meal Gerardo Pecchia will probably eat on his 100th birthday.

The European magazine

4 Read the text again, underlining the parts that answer these questions.

  a What medical evidence is there that the people of Campodimele really are healthy?

  b What explanations are given for the fact that they live so long?

  c What gives outsiders the impression that time has stopped in Campodimele?

Interpretation

1 Why do you think scientists find Campodimele so interesting and need to visit the place regularly?

2 What lessons could 21st-century city dwellers learn from the people of Campodimele?

Speaking personally

1 From your point of view, what would be the greatest disadvantage of living in Campodimele?

2 Having read about Campodimele, are there any aspects of your lifestyle you would like to change? Would it be possible or practical to make these changes?

— Grammar —

Present perfect continuous (1)

Exploring concepts

1 Underline the Present perfect simple verbs and circle the Present perfect continuous verbs in these sentences.

  a *… scientists from all over the world have been visiting this remote mountain village regularly.*

  b *It has stood there for more than 400 years.*

  c *I have been studying the children and the grandchildren …*

  d *I've found that they also have a substantially lower blood pressure.*

2 a Which of the Present perfect forms, simple or continuous, refers to:

  A a continuous activity that takes place over a period of time up to and including the present?

  B a state (not action) which continues up to the present?

  C an action which is repeated during a period of time up to and including the present?

  D a completed past action or activity without specifying a time?

  b Match sentences **1a–d** with uses **A–D**.

3 Present perfect continuous verbs can refer to continuous or repeated actions. Are the actions in these sentences continuous or repeated?

  a *Scientists have been visiting this remote mountain village regularly.*

  b *I have been studying the children and the grandchildren of the over 85's.*

  c *He's been repairing his car all day.*

  d *I've been coming to Spain for holidays since I was fifteen.*

▶ **Language commentary p.130**

Pronunciation

4 a How are the Present perfect continuous verbs in sentences **3a–d** pronounced in natural speech? Read them aloud.

  b ■ **6.2** Listen and check your ideas.

Exploitation

1 a Think about your life in the last year. Write brief answers to these questions using the Present perfect simple and continuous.

  Example

  How have you kept fit? *I haven't done anything special. I've joined a gym. I've been going there twice a week.*

  1 How have you earned money?
  2 How have you spent your money?
  3 How have you spent your free time?
  4 Have you taken up any new sports or hobbies?
  5 Have you been anywhere interesting?
  6 What have you done to improve your education?
  7 What haven't you done that you would like to have done?

  b Now ask about your partner's life during the last year. Make a note of their answers, then talk about the similarities and differences between your lives.

Role play

2 Work in pairs. Take turns to be Student A.

Situation 1

Student A You arranged to meet your friend at 7 o'clock this evening. You arrive at 9.30. Make believable excuses.

Student B Your friend is two-and-a-half hours late. You are furious. Demand a full explanation.

Situation 2

Student A You bump into an old friend you haven't seen for years. Find out as much as you can about your friend's life since you last met.

Student B You meet someone you haven't seen for years. Since you last met you haven't done anything very interesting, so make up some facts to impress your friend.

Listening

1 a Here are some adjectives used to describe people. Which ages would you most commonly associate them with? Write the ages next to each adjective.

Example
adventurous = under 20,   relaxed = about 50

---
adventurous   ambitious   bad-tempered   bitter   depressed
easygoing   forgetful   independent   irritable   optimistic
patient   pessimistic   relaxed   sad   selfish   sentimental
stressed   stupid   wise

---

b Compare your ideas in pairs or groups. Try to agree about which adjectives are most appropriate to *old* people.

2 a You are going to listen to a radio interview with two British people who are over 100 years old. If you were the interviewer, what questions would you ask them? Make a note of your questions.

b Compare your ideas with a partner.

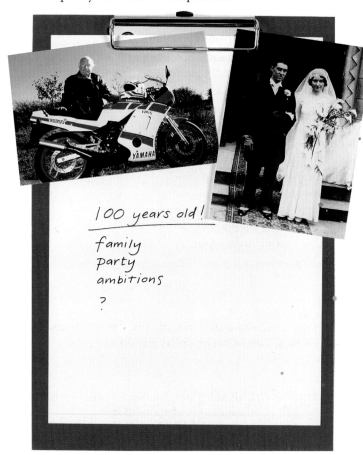

100 years old!

family
party
ambitions
?

As you listen

3 a **6.3** Does the interviewer ask any of the questions you would have asked?

b Do the old people seem generally happy or unhappy?

Interpretation

1 Which of the adjectives in **1a** would you use to describe Mary Craig and Edward Macintosh? Give reasons.

2 What is the attitude of Mary and Edward to:
  a education?
  b younger generations?
  c their own future?

3 What do you understand by the idiomatic expressions in **bold** in these extracts from the interview?

  a *As far as young people are concerned it's **easy come, easy go**. You see we had to **make do and mend** in our young days.*
  b *It was a much easier life when we were young. We were always **kept on the straight and narrow**.*
  c *I'm still trying to learn things, because I like **keeping my brain ticking over** but most of it **goes in one ear and out of the other** …*
  d *I can't remember names or names of places – **it drives me mad**.*

Vocabulary

The interviewer uses the phrase *senior citizens* as an alternative to *old people* to hide or soften the real meaning – in other words, to be polite. Words or expressions like these are called *euphemisms*.

1 Here are four more from the interview. What is their real meaning? (**a**, **b**, and **c** have the same meaning.)
  a *I've been travelling ever since my husband **passed away**.*
  b *I **lost** my wife in 1970 …*
  c *I still want to do a little more travelling before I **finish** …*
  d *People think I'm going **soft in the head**.*

2 Here are some more common euphemisms. What do you think they mean?
  a By comparison with her two beautiful sisters, she's rather *plain*.
  b You're *plumper* than when I last saw you, and you're *going thin on top*.
  c I had to explain it two or three times to him. He's *not very bright*.
  d You'll have to speak up – he's a bit *hard of hearing*.

Speaking personally

1 In your experience, are old people more selfish than other age groups? If your answer is yes, why do you think this is?

2 Why is it important for old people to keep their brains 'ticking over'? How do you think you might keep your brain ticking over when you are old?

Present perfect continuous (2)

Exploring concepts

The Present perfect continuous is often used to explain a present situation.
*If I sound slightly out of breath, it's because **I've been running** round the studio looking for my notes for today's programme.*
***He's been lying** on the beach all day. That's why he's so red.*

1 Here are five explanations. What is the present situation in each?

a She's been crying.
b They've been swimming in the sea.
c I've been eating less fat.
d He's been going to the gym three times a week.
e I've been decorating the apartment.

2 a The Present perfect continuous is also used in social situations to express politeness. In what situations might these statements have been made?

Example
***I've been hoping** you'd ring.*
The speaker has something important to tell the caller.

1 *I've been so looking forward to meeting you.*
2 *I've been longing to see you again. It seems so long since yesterday.*
3 *I've been meaning to write but I just haven't had the time.*

b How do you think the speakers of these statements feel? What impression do they want to make?

c In what situations might you choose not to use the Present perfect continuous? Compare these pairs of sentences.

1 a I've been so looking forward to meeting you.
  b I'm pleased to meet you.

2 a I've been meaning to ask you, do you find old people better company than young people?
  b Are old people better company than young people?

Pronunciation

3 a **6.4** Listen to the sentences in **2a**. In which sentences does the speaker sound polite and sincere?

b How does the speaker manage to sound like this?

▶ **Language commentary p.130**

Exploitation

1 a How might you respond to these comments? Think of explanations.

Example
'You're covered in oil.'
'I've been repairing my car.'

1 'You look exhausted.'
2 'You look terribly pale.'
3 'Your eyes look red.'
4 'You look really slim.'
5 'You're late again.'

b Compare your responses with other students, then together try to think of the most original (least likely!) explanations for the comments.

Example
'You're covered in oil.'   *'I've been swimming in olive oil!'*

2 Change these direct expressions into more polite language using the verbs in brackets.

a What shall I get you for your birthday? (wonder)
b Dinner was ready at 6 o'clock. You're late! (expect)
c How old are you? (want to ask)
d Why didn't you phone me earlier? (hope)
e Where did you buy that hat? (ask)
f I've forgotten your name. (try / remember)
g I know all about you. (hear)
h I'm glad we've met. (hope)

Role play

3 Work in groups of four. Make polite conversations in these situations. Prepare something to say to each person in the group before you start.

Situation 1

You have just arrived at a rather formal party.
Student A You are the host of the party. You know everyone.
Students B/C/D You know the host of the party, but only a little about each other.

Situation 2

You are at a college or work reunion.
Students A/B You are still at the college or workplace. Although you were not particularly good friends with the others you do remember a little about them.
Students C/D You don't remember the others at all.

Homonyms

There are three kinds of homonym:

- words that sound the same but look different and have different meanings. (Homophones)
  *He was the **sole** survivor of the accident.*
  *I love **soul** music.*

- words that look the same but sound different and have different meanings. (Homographs)
  *American scientists **lead** the world in computer technology.*
  *Petrol without **lead** is safer and less expensive.*

- words that look and sound the same but have different meanings.
  *I **saw** someone cut a tree down yesterday.*
  *He cut it down using a long **saw**.*

Homophones

1 What are the meanings of the words in **bold**, and what are the alternatives they sound like? There are clues to help.

   a *He went back and **forth**, a bit wobbly …*
      It's an ordinal number.

   b *… women came to their doors to **see** what the sound of wheels meant …*
      You might swim in it.

   c *… the World Health Organization **sent** researchers to the village in 1985 …*
      Perfume / small coin in the USA.

   d *I only eat **meat** twice a year …*
      Get together with someone.

   e *… traffic is **banned** in the centre.*
      A musical group.

   f *The women **wear** scarves …*
      In which place?

   g *… the secret is to eat lots of onions: **raw**, with oil, vinegar, and **red** pepper.*
      Animal noise; the past of an irregular verb.

   h *… they hadn't even asked us **whether** they could or not.*
      A topic of conversation if you're bored!

2 a **6.5** Listen and fill the gaps in these sentences with the correct words.

    1 I _____ the _____ forecast but I didn't _____ _____ to believe it or _____ .

    2 She didn't know _____ her glasses were _____ I had to _____ the letter to her.

    3 When I travel by _____ , I prefer to sit in an _____ seat.

    4 _____ _____ ago I was _____ for speeding.

   b Compare your answers with a partner. Decide what the alternative spellings and meanings are for each word.

Homographs

1 Read these sentences aloud with a partner. Decide how to pronounce the words in *italics*.

   a That's a terrible photo of me. Please *tear* it up immediately.

   b I prefer *live* recordings to albums made in a studio.

   c When I was younger, I liked sitting in the back *row* at the cinema.

   d When it's very hot, *bathing* in the sea is the quickest way to cool down.

   e My watch has a battery, so you don't need to *wind* it up.

   f In the end, the President had to *bow* to public opinion and change his mind.

2 **6.6** Listen and check your ideas.

3 Use a dictionary to check the other meanings and ways of pronouncing these words. Make up sentences illustrating these other meanings.

Words with different meanings

The words in **bold** in these sentences have several meanings. What is their meaning in these sentences and what other meanings do they have?

   a *When they saw Laura and her **trunk** …*

   b *… she has **left** her job …*

   c *… neighbours can be **pretty** awful.*

   d *… the people of Campodimele have an easygoing **nature**.*

   e *… it's making me so **cross**.*

   f *There's nobody there to ask what time you're coming home – you're **free**.*

Exploitation

Work in groups. Make up a story using one of these groups of words.

bathing	cross	left	live	pretty	sea	weather	wind
band	forth	free	meet	pretty	scent	see	tear
banned	cross	free	meat	raw	red	sent	trunk

Language in action

Expressing annoyance

Eavesdrop!

Look at the picture and guess the answers to these questions.

- Where do you think the people are?
- One of the people is annoyed about something that has just happened to him. What could this be?

Listening 1

1 **6.7** Listen, check your ideas and think about these questions.

   a What do they say about the ages of 13, 14, 16, 18?
   b How does this compare with your country?

2 Work in pairs. Listen to the conversation again.

   Student A Listen and note down expressions Daniel uses to say that he is annoyed.

   Student B Listen and note down expressions Daniel's friends use to calm him down.

   Tell each other the expressions you heard. Make lists with the following headings:

   - expressions of annoyance
   - expressions calming someone down.

Listening 2

1 **6.8** You are going to listen to two more conversations in which people express their annoyance about something. As you listen, answer these questions.

   a What is the relationship between the speakers?
   b Why are they annoyed?

2 **6.9** Read and listen to the extracts from the conversations on the next page.

   a Mark any words or expressions used to:
   - express annoyance
   - calm down the speakers who are annoyed.

   b Add the marked expressions to the lists you have already made.

Extract 1

Ju Well, we're going to have our coffee break reduced from twenty to ten minutes.

R You're joking!

J That makes me really angry. Why?

Ju Well, I wasn't told officially, but that's what I've heard and I think it's right.

R Oh, that's outrageous …

Ju I know, I, well …

J I can't believe it. Who said … ?

R That's not enough time to get your sugar in the cup. That's ridiculous.

Ju No, I know, no …

J Ten minutes, we don't even get back – just haven't got the time for that …

Ju Well, it's just a money-saving exercise, isn't it?

R Whose, whose brainwave was that?

J Yes.

Ju Well, I don't know. I don't know where it came from.

J Oh, that's so infuriating. Barbara?

B I mean, don't get so worked up about it. I mean you know, I mean, we've got to be a bit more flexible, perhaps. I mean …

R Flexible?

B Ten minutes is, ten minutes is …

J Barbara …

R Ten minutes is nothing.

Extract 2

J … and he's making me so cross …

B Have you spoken to him? Have you tried to reason with him?

J Well I've tried, yes. I've tried, and he says 'Oh, yes, hmm, hmm, hmm,' and then the next night it's the same thing.

B Well, I can understand your point of view, but I mean, I don't think, I mean, there are worse things.

J No, there aren't – it's making me lose nights and nights of sleep and I'm really, it's really getting me down. I don't know what to do any more, I really don't know what to do. I have tried talking to him.

S Well, neighbours can be pretty awful. I mean, we've, we got, the people next door to us, erm. We went … I went out one morning and they, they were in the process of building a wall between our house and theirs – they hadn't even asked us whether they could or not.

J Oh, you see, that's what's so irritating – people don't care.

S It's just so infuriating.

B Yeah, but I mean, you've got to, got to live with each other, you know, I mean …

J Well, not at night time …

Features of natural conversation

Why do the speakers use the phrase *I mean* so frequently? Find all the uses of this phrase in the extracts, then listen again. Compare your ideas with a partner.

Practice

1 a Underline all the syllables in these expressions which you think will be stressed. Which syllable do you think will carry the main stress?

1 That's ridiculous.
2 That really irritates me.
3 It's really getting me down.
4 That's really annoying.
5 That makes me really cross.
6 It really gets me.

b **6.10** Listen and repeat the expressions.

Role play

2 Work in pairs. Take turns to be Student A.

Student A Make up three statements that you think will annoy or shock your partner. Say each statement to your partner.

Example
Have you heard? They're doubling the price of cigarettes.

Student B Respond to your partner's statements using one of the expressions in **1**.

Exploitation

Work in groups. In each discussion one person should be annoyed and another should try to calm them down.

Discussion 1

You are either a group of teenagers discussing what annoys you about older people, or you are a group of older people discussing what annoys you about teenagers.

Discussion 2

You are either a group of cyclists and pedestrians discussing what annoys you about motorists and other road users, or a group of motorists discussing what annoys you about pedestrians and cyclists.

Writing

1 You are going to write a letter of complaint expressing annoyance.

a First, think about the main differences between spoken language and writing.

Spoken language

J   That makes me really angry. Why?
Ju Well, I wasn't told officially, but that's what I've heard and I think it's right.
R   Oh, that's outrageous …
Ju I know, I, well …
J   I can't believe it. Who said … ?

Writing

> Dear Sir,
> I find it quite appalling that, as an ordinary family, we should have to put up with this level of disturbance at all hours of the day and night. On numerous occasions over the last week, the noise of your road drills and other heavy machinery has woken my two young children. This is a completely unacceptable situation which I am not prepared to tolerate any longer. Unless I hear from you by the weekend, I shall consult my solicitor.

b Underline all the examples of formal language used in the letter. What impression does the writer want to make?

c The speakers use *really* to show how strongly they feel. What alternative words to *really* can you use when you write?

▶ **Writing guidelines p.155**

2 Write one of these letters.

Letter 1

Like one of the speakers in the conversations, you have a troublesome neighbour. You have asked them politely on several occasions to stop doing whatever it is that you find annoying, but nothing has made any difference. Write a letter to your neighbour. Follow this paragraph plan.

1 Say why you are writing. Describe what your neighbour is doing that annoys you and say how you feel about it.
2 Describe what you have already done to try to change your neighbour's behaviour. Say how you feel about this.
3 Say what you intend to do if the situation does not improve.

Letter 2

Your local council is planning to close a car park you use every day. You are not happy about this. Write a letter to the council expressing your annoyance. Follow this paragraph plan.

1 Say why you are writing. Describe briefly when and why you use this car park at the moment.
2 Say how annoyed you are at the council's plan and describe the inconvenience to you if the car park actually closes.
3 Suggest an alternative plan, then end your letter by saying what you will do if the council does not change its plan.

3 Exchange your letter with someone who has written the same letter as you.

a Read each other's letters. How formal is the language? How clear is it that the writer is annoyed? Make any suggestions for improvements.

b Rewrite your letter including any improvements you discussed.

Unit 6 Summary

In this unit you have worked on the following language points.

☐ Present perfect
☐ Present perfect continuous
☐ Homonyms
☐ Expressing annoyance
☐ Calming someone down
☐ Writing a letter of complaint

Tick ✓ the points you are confident about and cross ✗ the ones you need to revise.

7 Survival

Preview

Your thoughts

1 The Aborigines are a well-known minority group in Australia. Can you name any other indigenous populations and the countries they live in?

2 Is there a group like this in your country? Who are they? What problems do they face? Will their traditions and way of life survive?

Reading

1 What do you know about the situation of the Aborigines in Australia today? Compare your ideas with a partner.

2 Read these short texts to find out if any of your ideas are mentioned.

3 Read the texts again and make lists of facts under these headings.
- positive or improving features of Aborigine life
- negative features of Aborigine life

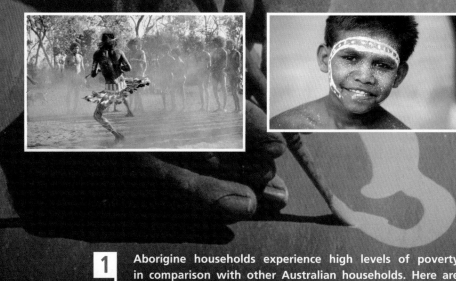

1 Aborigine households experience high levels of poverty in comparison with other Australian households. Here are a few facts and figures.
- They are larger – the average size of Aborigine households is four people compared with 2.9 people for other Australian households.
- They are more likely to be multi-generational and contain extended family members than other households.
- They are more likely to be multi-family households – 12.5 per cent of households include more than one family compared with 1.6 per cent of other Australian households.

  Although these disadvantages have mainly negative effects, there are some important plus points.
- Older people do not have to survive by themselves on low incomes, but can live with their extended families.
- In times of stress and financial hardship, family members in other households can look after young children.

2 Until relatively recently Aborigines could not vote. Now they can vote and receive state benefits. They have also been involved in political protest and this has helped improve their poor living conditions. Current issues of great importance are land rights, housing and health, and political representation at all levels. Many Aborigine communities have their own councils, engage in socio-economic ventures, and run many of their own affairs.

3 Many Aborigines live in urban communities which remain distinctively Aboriginal. For example, they can and do still speak their own language. In spite of appalling living conditions and widespread alcohol and drug problems, most urban Aborigines have retained much of their special bush knowledge, many traditional customs and ceremonies, and, most importantly, their dignity.

4 For Aborigines the landscape is a powerful spiritual force. It is a living environment of holy places and myths and is the basis of their culture and social life. Their history, which tells how rivers, animals, and plants were created, is passed from generation to generation through stories, song, and dance.

But, if you are an Aborigine, life in today's Australia is by no means easy. People are struggling with poverty, health problems, and unemployment dramatically worse than those of other Australians. Some communities are building themselves up and in places exciting projects, like tree-farming and eco-tourism, are showing signs of success.

For others, however, the struggle for economic independence is only just beginning. For these people, regaining their traditional lands is the fundamental first step. For many groups, it is important that their elders return from the cities to the country soon, to pass on the information, stories, and ceremonies that can only be communicated at home. Time is running out.

Person to person

1 Should groups like the Aborigines be persuaded to integrate with the rest of society or should they be encouraged to maintain their separate traditions and customs? Is there a position mid-way between these two extremes?

2 What could or should governments do to help groups like these?

Grammar – *can, could, be able to* review

1 In which of these sentences **a–e** do *can*, *could*, or *be able to* refer to:
- ability?   • possibility?   • permission?

a *… it is important that their elders return … to the country soon, to pass on the information, stories, and ceremonies that **can** only be communicated at home.*

b *… they **can** and do still speak their own language.*

c *It is only thanks to their resilience that they **have been able to** withstand the pressures on their traditions.*

d *Older people do not have to survive by themselves on low incomes, but **can** live with their extended families.*

e *Until relatively recently Aborigines **could** not vote. Now they **can** vote and receive state benefits.*

2 We can use *be able to* in most forms to express ability (we sometimes need to do this because *can*, and *could* only exist in a few forms). In sentences **a–f** which forms of *be able to* can be replaced with *can* or *could* without changing the meaning?

a He*'s able to* swim better than his brother.

b I*'ll be able to* walk better after the operation on my leg.

c At the age of eight he *was able to* run faster than any of his friends.

d She*'s never been able to* sing very well.

e I*'d love to be able to* speak another language.

f I *wouldn't be able to* play chess, if you hadn't taught me.

▶ **Language commentary p.130**

Pronunciation

3 a How is *can* pronounced in natural speech?
  1 *Can* you swim? Yes, I *can*. No, I *can't*.
  2 How far *can* you swim?
  3 I *can* play the piano, but I *can't* sing very well.

b **7.1** Listen and check your ideas. What rules of pronunciation can you work out?

Check

4 Complete these sentences with *can*, *can't*, *could*, *couldn't*, or the correct form of *be able to*. If more than one form is possible, write all the forms.

a My little brother _____ speak Spanish and English when he was four.

b You _____ check your spelling if you didn't have a dictionary.

c I've never _____ understand why people climb mountains.

d If I pass my driving test, I _____ drive to work.

e Would you like _____ play the guitar?

f Some people _____ do complicated mathematical calculations in their head.

▶ Ability and inability   p.67
▶ Articles   p.69

Listening

1 The newspaper headlines and photographs relate to stories of personal survival. Work in pairs. Discuss what the stories could be about.

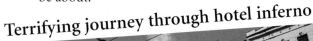

Terrifying journey through hotel inferno

Parachute fails at 1,000m.

2 You are going to listen to people talking about their involvement in the two incidents referred to in the headlines. Decide which story you think these words and phrases will be used in. Check any words you are uncertain of in a dictionary.

banging noises	blind panic
ejector seat	ladder
knotted sheets	roll the plane
soft landing	the floor below
torn parachute	two-seater
upside down	wall of flames

As you listen

3 **7.2** Listen and check your ideas. Look for mistakes in the photographs.

4 Work in pairs. Listen to the first speaker again. What is the significance of these things?

a bedroom curtains
b the toothbrush and straw hat
c the door at the bottom of the staircase
d the hotel car park and the fence
e a shoe and a hammer

Vocabulary

What are the differences in meaning between these sets of verbs from the first story? Work out or guess the differences, then check in a dictionary.

a bang   knock   hammer
   *I could hear **banging** noises and people shouting.*
   *Someone **knocked** on my door.*
   *The corridor was full of people **hammering** on doors.*

b grab   push   pull
   *A man **grabbed** my hand but I pushed him away.*
   *The man in front of me **pushed** and **pulled** at the door.*

c shout   scream   yell
   *I could hear people **shouting**.*
   *The corridor was full of people **screaming**. Someone **yelled** at me, 'Drop your things …'*

d smash   break
   *One girl escaped by **smashing** the window with her shoe, … another had her life saved by a man **breaking** her window with a hammer.*

Role play

Work in pairs. Read your roles, then listen to the second story again to check for any information you need. Take turns to be Student A.

Student A You are a reporter for a local newspaper and you are going to interview the man who survived the fall. Prepare four or five questions for your interview.

Student B You are the man who survived the fall. To prepare for the interview, think about the kinds of question you might be asked, then answer the reporter's questions about your experiences.

Speaking personally

Have you ever had a frightening experience? If not, do you know anyone who has? What happened?

Ability and inability

Exploring concepts

1 Underline the verbs and verb phrases in these extracts which express either ability or inability.

a *… all I could see was a wall of flames just a few centimetres from the window.*
b *We couldn't move there were so many people.*
c *Eventually we were able to make it round to the front of the hotel.*
d *… others managed to climb down on knotted sheets.*
e *The air was rushing in and for a moment I couldn't breathe.*
f *Amazingly he could still walk, and was already on his feet when the rescuers arrived.*

2 In the following sentences *could* is used to refer to an ability in the past. However, sentence **b** is not correct. Can you work out why? How is it different in meaning from **a** and **c**?

a By the age of six I *could* swim 500 metres.
b He tried once more and *could* open the door.
c When I was a child I *could* speak English and Spanish equally well.

3 a Here are some alternative ways of expressing ability. What meaning do these two expressions have in common?
  1 I tried very hard and in the end I *managed to …* + verb.
  2 After several attempts I eventually *succeeded in …+ -ing.*

b Rephrase sentence **2b** using these two alternatives.

4 *Can* and *could* are often used with verbs of perception.
I *could* see a wall of flames just a few centimetres from the window.
I *can* see someone waving from an upstairs window.
What other perception verbs do you know? Use them to make sentences like the two above.

▶ **Language commentary p.131**

Exploitation

1 a Read this story, then fill the gaps with the correct form of these words or phrases. You may need to change the verbs after the gaps.

| could/couldn't | be able | manage | succeed |

I turned off the main road on to a dirt track – it was narrow and bumpy with hedges on both sides. I drove quite slowly – then I noticed I was coming to a bridge over a stream. I .... **1** see that the road went steeply up to the bridge and dropped steeply again after the bridge. My car is very long and the bottom is close to the ground, which means that if you go over a bump it's easy to scrape the bottom. I knew by looking at the bridge that I .... **2** get over it without damaging the car. I'd have to go back. The problem was, because the road was so narrow I .... **3** turn the car round. The only option was to reverse the way I'd come. I remembered that about 500 metres back there was a farm entrance where I'd .... **4** to turn. I started reversing but by then there was another car behind me – of course he .... **5** overtake me so he had to reverse too. It was just as narrow and bumpy going backwards and there was an added problem: because of my bad neck I .... **6** reverse quickly. Eventually I .... **7** to reverse into the farm entrance and after a lot of to-ing and fro-ing, I .... **8** in turning the car round and driving forwards again. What a nightmare!

b **7.3** Listen and check your answers.

2 a Make lists of the following things.
- Things that you could do when you were younger but can't do now.
Example
I could swim two thousand metres.
- Things that you couldn't do when you were younger but can do now.
Examples
I couldn't play the piano until I was seventeen.
I didn't use to be able to play the clarinet.
- Things you'd like to be able to do.
Example
I'd love to be able to fly a plane.

b Compare your ideas with a partner.

3 Complete these sentences using *manage to* or *succeed in* together with ideas of your own.

a My car broke down on the motorway. I tried to get it started again, but couldn't. Eventually …
b She'd been trying to find a new job for over a year. In the end …
c My parents had always refused to let me have one. In the end …
d The pan caught fire while I was cooking. I poured water on it but that made it worse. Eventually …

4 Work in groups. Think back to any two of these occasions that you can remember, and describe what you could see, hear, and smell.
- your first day at a new job
- a visit to a farm or a zoo
- arriving at a party
- travelling on a crowded bus

Free speech

5 Work in pairs.
a Think of things you can do well.
b Compare abilities with a partner. Find out about one of your partner's abilities in more detail and make notes.
c Use your notes to write about or tell other students about your partner's ability.

Reading

1 Where do you think these photographs were taken? Which continents, countries, cities?

2 You are going to read about one of these cities. The article describes various aspects of life in the city. Work out from the words and phrases below what these aspects are.

better diet   bus lanes   vandalism
fruit and vegetables   fuel consumption
jams   rural exodus   recyclable waste

As you read

3 Answer these questions.

a Which aspects of life are described?
b Does life seem to be getting worse or getting better?
c Which of the photographs shows the city in the article?

Close up

1.2 What are the two possible meanings of *greenest* here?

1.11 Why is *mushrooming* a good word to use here? (How do mushrooms grow?)

1.17 What kind of noise does *purr* describe? Which animal purrs?

1.30 *Widen* means make wider, *sharpen* means make sharper. Do you know any other similar verbs?

Paradise? No, but one of the world's greenest cities

Jaime Lerner, the architect who has transformed Curitiba in southern Brazil into one of the world's greenest cities, says the secret is simplicity. 'People try to sell you complexity, they see the destiny of the city as tragedy, but if you're pessimistic about cities you are pessimistic about
5   people.' Lerner has been twice re-elected to run the city and is now the state governor. He thinks Curitiba, population 1.5 million, is not a paradise. 'We have the same problems as any other Brazilian city, we have shanty towns, crime, and poverty. The difference is in the respect for people, the quality of service provided.' Lerner's creed is revolutionary: 'The poorer you
10   are, the more important it is for you to have good services.' ⚙

When he first became mayor, Curitiba was mushrooming as the rural exodus of the seventies sent people into the cities, and the transport system was heading for chaos: 50 bus companies competed in the city centre, the jams worsening every day. Something had to be done. An
15   underground system would have cost too much, and taken too long to build. So planners identified the factors that made underground systems fast and applied them to the bus service. Huge red buses purr speedily along special lanes, stopping at stations where passengers buy tickets before boarding. Bus jams never happen, vandalism is unknown. 'People
20   don't vandalize it because they like it. They feel respected, they show respect,' says the president of Urbs, the company which regulates ten private companies. Now, 80 per cent of people go to work by bus; 28 per cent of car owners take the bus instead, which
25   has led to a 20 per cent drop in fuel consumption. Lerner says, 'The less importance you give to cars the better it is for
30   people. When you widen streets for cars you destroy identity and memory.' ⚙

Curitiba has also revolutionized the concept
35   of waste: it can mean food, books, or even Shakespeare. Last month 700 schoolchildren each paid four kilos of recyclable rubbish to watch King Lear, performed by one of Brazil's best theatre companies. They came from the poorest area of the city and it was the first time they had been to a theatre. ⚙

40   And 35,000 low-income families exchange recyclable waste for food once a fortnight. At the Parque Mane Garrincha, I saw people pushing wheelbarrows and carrying bags with tins, old toys, paper, plastic, and bottles. A young woman brought a broken window, another an old gas cooker. Council workers weighed the waste and loaded it onto a lorry. The
45   women then both received free food. Each four kilos meant a kilo of fruit and vegetables from another lorry. That day it was potatoes, bananas, and cake. In one month, the 54 exchange points collected 282 tonnes of waste at a cost of $110,000 – lower than before; the fruit and vegetables are bought at market prices from small farmers. This scheme has resulted
50   in major benefits, including a better diet for citizens and less risk of flooding from rubbish in streams and canals. ⚙

Lerner dismisses the critics who say that these schemes will not work in bigger cities: 'Every city could do the same. Curitiba is only different because it has made itself different. We have gone against the flow and
55   humanized the city.' ⚙

The Guardian

Comprehension

1 Why was transport in Curitiba so bad in the 1970s?

2 Why did the authorities decide not to build an underground railway?

3 Why is there no vandalism on the buses in Curitiba?

4 Why didn't the authorities widen the streets of the city?

Speaking personally

1 What are the pros and cons of using a car in large modern cities? How do you prefer to travel around cities?

2 What do you think of Jaime Lerner's scheme to reduce the amount of traffic in Curitiba? Would it work in any of the busy cities in your country?

— Grammar —

Articles

Exploring concepts

1 a Look at l.37 to l.46 in the text. (*They came … another lorry.*) Circle all the definite articles.

b Which reason, **1**, **2**, or **3**, explains the use of the definite articles in that part of the text? Sometimes more than one explanation is possible.

  1 Common knowledge – we know or can tell from the context who or what is being referred to.

  2 Repetition – this is not the first mention of the person or thing.

  3 Uniqueness – the only one(s) – things or people – in the world, or in this context (this includes superlative forms).

2 a Now underline all the indefinite articles in l.37 to l.46.

 b Which reason, **4**, **5**, or **6**, explains the use of the indefinite articles? Sometimes more than one explanation is possible.

  4 Non-specific – one, but it doesn't matter which one

  5 First mention of something specific

  6 Single – one, not two, three, or four

3 What two groups of nouns are used without articles? Mark ✗ in front of them in l.37 to l.46.

4 Read these *the … the …* constructions from the text.

 a *The poorer you are, the more important it is for you to have good services.*

 b *The less importance you give to cars, the better it is for people.*

 1 In constructions like these *the* is always followed by a comparative word or phrase. What kind of word or phrase follows *the* in sentences **a** and **b** above (e.g. noun, adverb)?

 2 Think of different endings to this sentence: The poorer you are, the …

 ▶ **Language commentary p.131**

Pronunciation

5 a How are these articles pronounced?
  1 *the* end   3 *an* umbrella   5 *a* university
  2 *the* film   4 *an* hour   6 *a* holiday

 b **7.4** Listen and check your ideas. What rules of grammar and pronunciation can you work out?

Exploitation

1 Fill the gaps in this article with *a*, *an*, or *the*. If no article is needed, write ✗.

All the rage!

There is .... **1** large crowd of .... **2** people standing by .... **3** side of .... **4** busy London road. In .... **5** middle of .... **6** road .... **7** bus driver is shouting and hitting .... **8** front window of .... **9** black London taxi. .... **10** driver of .... **11** taxi has decided to lock his doors and wait for .... **12** bus driver to calm down and return to his bus and .... **13** passengers waiting there. .... **14** scenes like this are becoming more and more common and increasingly they are ending in .... **15** violence and .... **16** criminal charges. In .... **17** United Kingdom, as in .... **18** other countries, there seems to be .... **19** epidemic of .... **20** incidents like this.

2 Work in groups. Each person should speak for a maximum of one minute on one of these topics. Talk generally and give any examples you can think of.

| poverty | pollution | traffic | city life | rubbish | road rage |

Writing

3 Write about one of these topics in relation to your town or city.
 • Public transport   • Waste disposal   • Poor areas

Exchange your description with a partner. Quickly read and talk about what your partner has written. Then read the description again, more carefully, and decide whether articles are used correctly.

Connotations

Positive or negative?

The *connotations* of a word are the particular ideas or feelings associated with that word in addition to its basic meaning.
- If you say to someone 'You look **slim**,' the person will be happy.
- If you say 'You look **thin**,' they may or may not be pleased.
- If you say 'You look **skinny**,' they will probably feel offended.

Slim, *thin*, and *skinny* have similar meanings but different connotations. Sometimes dictionaries tell you whether words have positive or negative connotations. Look at these entries for *skinny*, *slim*, and *thin*.

> **skinny** (*infml usually derog*) very thin
> **slim** (*approv*) not fat or thick, thin
> **thin** (*sometimes derog*) not having much fat on the body
> (*approv* = approving, positive / *derog* = derogatory, negative)

1 Think about the pairs of adjectives in *italics* in each of these sentences. Decide if the words have positive, negative, or neutral connotations. Check your ideas in a dictionary.

  a He has a very unusual lifestyle. Everyone thinks he's *eccentric / mad*.

  b My baby sister has got *chubby / fat* arms and legs.

  c My brother has always been a *serious / stuffy* person.

  d If you're in business people expect you to be *ambitious / pushy*.

  e He's made a success of his life by being *stubborn / determined*.

  f He's always been *keen on / obsessed with* football.

  g Most people would agree that Stalin was a *famous / notorious* man.

  h You have to be *confident / big-headed* to be a good actor.

  i Our hotel room was full of *cheap / inexpensive* furniture.

  j Children who do well at school usually have *proud / arrogant* parents.

2 Here are some pairs of similar-sounding adjectives. Which have a positive connotation and which have a negative connotation? Write sentences which show the meaning of the negative words. Check your ideas in a dictionary.

  a childish / childlike

  b effeminate / feminine

  c macho / masculine

Other associations

1 In English, the word *conservative* has political associations and *green* has environmental associations. Look at the words in **A**. Which subjects in **B** do you associate each one with?

A	belief campaign class climber confession creation defence harmony march minister score service power freedom
B	artistic military social political religious musical legal sporting

Check your ideas in a dictionary.

2 a Word associations are often personal. What ideas do you associate with these colour words?

  For example, the colour red has political associations for some people, whereas to others it expresses danger or prohibition.

red   blue   green   white   black yellow   pink

  b Work in pairs. Compare and explain your associations.

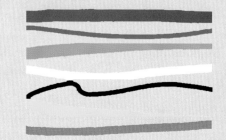

Language in action

Persuading someone not to do something

Eavesdrop!

Look at the picture and guess the answers to these questions.

* Who do you think the three people are?
* Where are they?
* What is the young man doing?
* What could the two older people be thinking? (Look at their expressions.)

Listening 1

1 a **7.5** Listen and check your ideas.

  b What do you think the young man is going to do when he reaches his destination?

2 Work in pairs. Listen to the conversation again.

Student A Listen and note down expressions Martin's parents use to persuade or advise him not to go.

Student B Listen and note down the expressions they use to make generalizations.

Tell each other the expressions you heard. Make lists with the following headings:

* persuading someone not to do something
* making generalizations.

Listening 2

1 **7.6** You are going to listen to two more conversations in which people try to persuade someone not to do something. As you listen, answer these questions.

  a What is the relationship between the speakers?
  b What is the subject of the conversation?
  c What are they persuading or advising someone to do?
  d What do they suggest as alternatives?

2 **7.7** Read and listen to the extracts from the conversations on the next page.

  a Mark any expressions used to:
    • persuade or advise someone not to do something
    • make generalizations.

  b Add the marked expressions to the lists you have already made.

Extract 1

S Oh, come, just think about it. Bananas for one, a whole day of bananas. Are you going to be able to stand that?

B Yeah, I can put up with that for …

K Shouldn't you be thinking about doing, things like exercise, not just about diet?

J That's a good idea.

B Well, you know, I mean, I haven't really got much time for that, you know. I'm just too busy. What time have I got to exercise?

K Oh, I don't know, it just seems much more sensible to just, be … just eating …

J That's all the good advice you always do read about, isn't it? You know, exercise as well as diet.

S Yeah. Most peo … most people who are thin, or reasonably slim, are like that because they take exercise, I think, as a rule, anyway.

K Or I think what you were saying about balance, I think that's generally right. You've got to have a balance of everything.

Extract 2

J Oh, I wouldn't if I were you, you know – I'd really think again and perhaps buy a new car, I mean …

R No, that's the whole point of a classic car is that it's not new, that, it's, it's, something, something they … you can't get any more …

J Well, you know …

R It's like buying a piece of history …

J Yeah, but I think you're making a big mistake, because if you're going to use it for travelling to and from work, I mean, is it really suitable for that sort of thing?

R Well, I'm not going to use it to and from work every, every day perhaps, maybe during the summer, but erm, I'm not going to sort of …

J I wouldn't if I were you, you know, it could be very difficult on the roads in traffic jams and all that sort of thing.

R Yeah, but it's a car, it goes, that's what it was made for.

J Mmm, mmm, I mean, what can I say to persuade you? I mean, what, what, have you really thought it through? Have you thought where you're going to park it, for inst … You can't park it on a street.

Features of natural conversation

1 Find all the examples of *you know* in the extracts, then listen to the two extracts again.

a How is *you know* used?

b Do you know any other words or phrases of the same kind?

c Where might *you know* be added to this extract of conversation?

> R Well, I've really made up my mind. I'm gonna buy that car.
> J Oh, I really don't think you should because, have you thought about the costs involved, Roger? It's an awful lot of money.
> R Of course I have, yeah.
> J Mmm. Well, I'm not so sure. What about insurance, for example, for a car like that – it's a very specialist car. Isn't it going to cost a lot?

2 What do you think the two speakers were going to go on to say?

a Yeah, I can put up with that for …

b … maybe during the summer, but erm, I'm not going to sort of …

Practice

1 **7.8** Listen and repeat these expressions for persuading or advising.

a I wouldn't do that if I were you.

b I think you're making a big mistake.

c Have you really thought it through?

d Surely it would be more sensible to (wait a bit longer).

e What can I say to persuade you not to?

2 Work in pairs. Take turns to say these sentences. Try to persuade your partner not to do things by using the expressions above and your own ideas.

a I'm fed up with this job. I'm going to resign at the end of this week.

b I'm going to sell my guitar – I don't play it any more.

c I think I'm going to start smoking again.

d University life doesn't really suit me. I'm leaving at the end of the year to get a job.

e Sorry. I've made up my mind. I'm definitely going to do the parachute jump at the weekend.

Exploitation

Role play

Work in groups. Take turns to be Student A. In each situation Student A should add details and then tell the rest of the group what they intend to do. The others should try to persuade Student A not to do whatever it is and generalize about what normally happens in situations like these.

Situation 1

Student A You intend to give up your steady job to join a travelling group of some kind. For example, a rock band, a theatre group, or a circus.

Situation 2

Student A You intend to change your appearance dramatically – maybe by having all your hair cut off or by having plastic surgery.

Situation 3

Student A You intend to cancel a holiday with your friends or family. You've got too much work to do.

Writing

1 You are going to write a radio script to give advice and persuade the public not to do something.

   a First, think about the similarities and differences between normal conversational language and a carefully written script.

Spoken language

J I wouldn't if I were you, you know, it could be very difficult on the roads in traffic jams and all that sort of thing.

R Yeah, but it's a car, it goes, that's what it was made for.

J Mmm, mmm, I mean, what can I say to persuade you? I mean, what, what, have you really thought it through? Have you thought where you're going to park it, for inst … You can't park it on a street.

Writing

Can you honestly say you've thought of the long-term consequences of what you're doing? Have you really considered the effects on your family, your children? You can't pretend you don't know – the scientific evidence is now overwhelming: everyone knows it's a dangerous, life-threatening habit.

So, how can we persuade you to give up? We've tried putting prices up; we've tried banning it in public places; we've tried showing you people suffering …

   b How does the writer of the radio script try to get listeners to think about what they are doing?

   ▶ **Writing guidelines p.157**

2 Write one of these radio scripts. The script should take no more than 30 seconds to read aloud.

Script 1

Write a script to persuade people not to drive too fast in residential areas.

Script 2

Write a script to persuade people not to spend too long in the sun when it is at its hottest.

3 a Work in pairs. Read your scripts aloud to each other.

   b Discuss how effective the script would be in persuading people not to drive fast or spend too long in the sun.

   c Rewrite your script incorporating any improvements you discussed.

Unit 7 Summary

In this unit you have worked on the following language points.

- [ ] *can, could, be able to*
- [ ] Ability and inability
- [ ] Articles

- [ ] Connotations
- [ ] Persuading / advising someone not to do something
- [ ] Making generalizations
- [ ] Writing radio scripts

Tick ✓ the points you are confident about and cross ✗ the ones you need to revise.

8 In the family

Preview

Your thoughts

1 Why do you think children often work in the same jobs or professions as their parents? Can you think of some famous examples?

2 Would you like to do the same job as either of your parents? Why? Why not?

Reading

1 Work in pairs. Look at the pictures to see who you recognize and then try to answer these questions.

a Why is the Fonda family famous? What different careers has Jane Fonda had?

b What do you know about the Kennedy family? Which members of the Kennedy family were or are active in politics? What happened to them?

2 Now read the texts to check your answers.

The Fonda family – father Henry, daughter

Jane, and son Peter – is one of the few family acting dynasties in the American film industry. Henry Fonda, who died in 1982, had a long and distinguished acting career, making over 100 screen appearances. In 1981, he won an Academy Award for best actor for his performance in *On Golden Pond*.

His daughter Jane, was once as well-known for her outspoken views on socio-political issues as for her films. She has received two Academy Awards for best actress, one in 1971 for *Klute*, and the second in 1978 for *Coming Home*. In 1981, she published her own books and videos on exercising, which have proved very successful.

Her brother, Peter Fonda, is still best-known for his performance in the cult sixties film *Easy Rider*, which he also produced. His daughter, Bridget, appeared in her first film in 1989.

The Kennedy family achieved a

prominence which was unique in American politics. Joseph Kennedy, whose grandparents were poor Irish immigrants, was head of the Kennedy clan. Although he never ran for election himself, he and his wife Rose had great political ambitions for their sons.

In 1960, their second son, John Fitzgerald Kennedy, was elected President of the USA, becoming the first Catholic and the youngest person to hold that office. However, his achievement was short-lived – on 22 November 1963, he was assassinated in Dallas, Texas. The man who is alleged to have shot him, Lee Harvey Oswald, was himself shot and killed two days later. Five years later, while campaigning for the Democratic nomination for the presidency, his brother Robert was also assassinated. In 1962, Edward Kennedy was elected to the Senate. In 1979, he was forced to withdraw as a presidential candidate, following a car accident in which his personal secretary was drowned. Although he was still influential, his involvement in this scandal was the reason why his political ambitions were never fulfilled.

3 Do you know anything that has happened to members of these families recently?

Person to person

1 What kind of ambitions do parents have for their children?

2 Did your parents have ambitions for you? Have you achieved them? Has this affected your relationship with them?

Grammar – Relative clauses review

1 Relative clauses give additional information about people, things, possessions, places, times, and reasons. In these sentences, which words join the relative clauses to the rest of the sentence?

   a *Dallas, **where John F. Kennedy was assassinated in 1963**, is the capital of Texas.*
   b *The man **who is alleged to have shot him**, Lee Harvey Oswald, was himself shot and killed two days later.*
   c *Joseph Kennedy, **whose grandparents were poor Irish immigrants**, was head of the Kennedy clan.*
   d *The Kennedy family achieved a prominence **which was unique** in American politics.*
   e *Many older people will never forget the day **when John F. Kennedy was killed**.*
   f *Edward Kennedy's involvement in this scandal was the reason **why his political ambitions were never fulfilled**.*

2 There are two kinds of relative clause. *Defining relative clauses* tell us which person or thing is being referred to. *Non-defining relative clauses* simply give us additional information about the person or thing that has already been identified. Say whether the clauses in sentences **1a–f** are defining or non-defining.

▶ **Language commentary p.132**

Pronunciation

3 a ▐ **8.1** ▌ Listen to two sentences with relative clauses. Write them down. Pay attention to punctuation.
   b Which sentence has a defining and which has a non-defining relative clause?

Check

4 Fill the gaps in these sentences with one of the relative words below, adding commas where necessary.

who   which   whose   where   when   why

   a Bridget Fonda _____ aunt is Jane Fonda was born in 1964.
   b She spent four years at the 'Lee Strasburg Theatre Institute' _____ she studied method acting.
   c *Scandal* was the film _____ brought her to the attention of the public in 1989.
   d 1992 was an important year in Bridget's career. It was the year _____ *Single White Female* and *Singles* were released.
   e Bridget grew up with actors. That's the reason _____ she chose a film career.
   f Henry Fonda _____ was Bridget's grandfather won an Oscar for his part in *On Golden Pond*.

▶ Relative clauses (2)   p.77
▶ Emphasizing words and structures   p.79

Reading

1 a What do you know about or associate with the name Benetton? Compare your ideas in pairs.

b Write two or three questions you would like to ask about the Benetton company or family.

As you read

2 Read the text quickly to see if your questions are answered. What was the most interesting piece of information you read?

UNITED COLORS OF BENETTON.

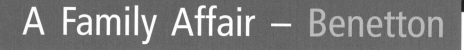

A Family Affair – Benetton

In the mid-1950s, Giuliana Benetton made her elder brother Luciano a multi-coloured pullover. 'It was the pullover which started the whole thing,' Luciano tells me as we sit in his villa near Treviso in north-eastern Italy, where he was born. 'The colours
5 were more exciting than the ones normally used in men's sweaters at that time. I saw that my friends liked it and I thought that it had market potential.' And so Benetton was born. The bright, vibrant colours in which the original sweater was knitted became its trade mark. Today the gigantic multinational
10 clothing empire is one of the world's biggest suppliers of casual clothes.

In the 1960s the two younger brothers, Carlo and Gilberto, joined Giuliana and Luciano to build what is probably the most remarkable family venture of the late 20th century, a corporation which has now diversified into banking, supermarkets, sporting equipment, restaurants, and Formula One racing cars.

15 Of the four founders, Carlo, the youngest, is the production director of Benetton Group worldwide. He also supervises the sheep ranches in Patagonia, where ten per cent of Benetton wool is produced. Gilberto, vice-president, is the financial expert. Giuliana is the design director, the creative genius behind Benetton clothes. The eldest, Luciano, is
20 president of Benetton Group and responsible for the company's long-term and global strategies.

The firm's success depends on a family structure which is now rare in Italy and the rest of Europe. Luciano is convinced that Benetton could never have taken off without the family partnership. 'The
25 crucial pillars of the operation were my sister and two brothers,' he says. 'Undoubtedly, the success of this relationship depended on a division of work and on our total trust in what each of us is doing.'

Six of their eleven children also work in the company. However, Luciano has also come to include friends and colleagues in the
30 business once they have demonstrated a solid commitment to the firm, which is why he is unconcerned about the group's future and the role of his immediate family in it. 'The future of the firm does not depend on the presence of our children within it eternally,' he says. 'If they prove themselves and want to enter the firm, then they are
35 welcome to make their career on their own merits. If they want to do something else, there is absolutely no pressure on them to enter Benetton.'

But despite his wealth, Luciano Benetton does not live a five-star lifestyle. One of the things which he most likes doing is eating out with friends, chatting into the night in the many family-run restaurants in and around Treviso.
40 For Luciano, maintaining friendships is one of the explanations for the success of his company.

The European magazine

UNITED COLORS OF BENETTON.

Close up

1.1 The *mid-1950s* is the period from 1954–1956. What could you call the periods 1950–1953 and 1957–1959?

1.17 What does the prefix *vice* mean in *vice-president*?

1.30 What word and phrase means the same as *once*?

1.37 What does the word *five-star* refer to normally? What do you think a *five-star lifestyle* would be like?

1.39 What does *chatting into the night* mean?

Interpretation

1 Why do large companies like Benetton get involved in other businesses?

2 Why do you think there are so few large family businesses like Benetton nowadays?

3 What characteristics do you think Luciano Benetton looks for in the people he employs? Do family members have an advantage over friends and colleagues?

Speaking personally

1 What star lifestyle do you have? Would you like to live a five-star lifestyle? What would you do?

2 If you owned a company, would you employ members of your own family? Why? Why not?

Relative clauses (2)

Exploring concepts

1 Underline the word or words that *which* refers to in these extracts.

 a *It was the pullover* **which** *started the whole thing.*

 b *… and the bright, vibrant colours in* **which** *the original sweater was knitted became its trade mark.*

 c *Luciano has also come to include friends and colleagues in the business once they have demonstrated a solid commitment to the firm,* **which** *is why he is unconcerned about the group's future …*

 d *One of the things* **which** *he most likes doing is eating out with friends …*

2 Answer these questions about sentences **a–d**.

 a *That* can replace *which* in sentences **a** and **d**, but not in **b** or **c**. Why?

 b The relative pronoun can be left out in sentence **d**. Why? Why can't it be left out in sentence **a**?

3 a Compare these ways of expressing the same information. Which are the most formal and the least formal?

   1 The bright, vibrant colours which the original sweater was knitted in became its trade mark.

   2 The bright, vibrant colours the original sweater was knitted in became its trade mark.

   3 The bright, vibrant colours in which the original sweater was knitted became its trade mark.

 b What do you notice about the position of the prepositions in relative clauses in formal and informal English?

4 Which words or phrases in these sentences means *the thing(s) that* or *anything that*?

 a Our success depends on our total trust in what each of us is doing.

 b Whatever they choose is all right by me.

 c You can do whatever you like on holiday.

 d What you need is a break from work.

▶ **Language commentary p.133**

Exploitation

1 Complete the sentences by adding appropriate prepositions and relative pronouns from this list.

| in | for | with | by | whom | which |

 a First, complete them in a formal style.
 Example
 The name **by which** *Robert Zimmerman is better known is Bob Dylan.*

   1 The song _____ Bob Dylan is most well known is 'Blowin' in the wind'.

   2 Woodie Guthrie is the musician _____ Dylan was most influenced.

   3 The guitar and the harmonica are the musical instruments _____ he is most closely associated.

   4 The style _____ his son sings is very reminiscent of his father's.

 b Now, rewrite the sentences in an informal style.
 Example
 *The name (**which**) Robert Zimmerman is better known* **by** *is Bob Dylan.*

Free speech

2 Work in pairs.

 a Interview your partner. Ask questions to find out things about them that you do not already know. Ask follow-up questions to get more information and make notes.
 Example
 Where were you born?   Where's that?   What's it like?

 b Write a brief profile of your partner using your notes. Use relative clauses to add information.
 Example
 Pilar was born in Bilbao, which is …

Listening

1 Think about your family.

  a What is your position in the family? Are you the eldest, the youngest, a middle, or an only child?

  b Do you think your personality has been influenced more by your relationship with your parents, or by your position in your family?

2 Now read this extract about children in families and see if any of the information is true for you.

THE GOOD, THE BAD, AND THE SPOILED: HOW CHILDREN REACT

Psychiatrists have acknowledged that environmental influences and relationships with parents are important factors in the development of personality. But, they say, it is birth order and relationships with siblings that is the most reliable predictor of human behaviour.

 First-borns – lots of attention but high parental expectations. Must then cope with the arrival of subsequent children. Try to win back parents' attention by meeting parents' expectations. Conservative, responsible, and insecure, but high achievers because they try hard.

 Second children – probably rebel against parental authority and goody-goody elder sibling. Attention-seeking, more relaxed attitude to life. May try to outdo elder child.

 Middle children – enjoy no clear status, often searching constantly for a role in the family. Attention-seeking.

 Youngest – plenty of attention from parents and siblings. If spoiled, can lack ambition.

 Only children risk being parent-bound or may find parental relationship claustrophobic and leave home early. Probably precocious and self-sufficient.

3 Now work with a partner who is in the same place in their family as you and compare your ideas and experiences. Do you agree or disagree with the information? Would you add anything to the descriptions?

Listening 1

You are going to listen to Jo, Emma, and Clare talking about themselves.

As you listen

1 **8.2** Answer these questions about the speakers.

  a Where are the three speakers placed in their families?

  b How have their personalities been affected?

  c Are the speakers and their sisters similar to or different from the stereotypes described in the text?

Listening 2

2 You are now going to listen to part of an interview with a successful athlete, Jenny Marshall, and her younger brother, Ben. Before you listen, discuss these questions.

  a How might Jenny's sporting success have affected Ben's personality?

  b Jenny's father was also her trainer. What effect do you think this had on the rest of the family?

As you listen

3 **8.3** Listen and check your ideas.

Interpretation

1 What kinds of behaviour do you think Jenny is referring to when she says, 'I think a lot of athletes are very selfish.'?

2 Jenny says her mother and father didn't worry about *normal family things*. What kinds of things is she referring to?

3 Jenny says her father wasn't there to do *any of the things fathers do with their sons*. What activities is she thinking about?

Speaking personally

Is there anyone in your family, or in another family you know, whose job, hobbies, or interests affect everyone else in the family? In what way are people affected?

Emphasizing words and structures

Exploring concepts

1 The auxiliary verbs *do* and *did* can be used to emphasize information. In which of the sentences **a–d** does the auxiliary verb:

- show that the speaker feels strongly about what they are saying?
- introduce contrasting information?

a I think being an only child *does* make you very spoiled and intolerant.

b James isn't very good at keeping in touch – he *did* phone last week, though.

c I get home late, but I *do* always spend time with my children at the weekends.

d I know you don't believe me, but I *did* try to contact you. Honestly.

2 a Underline the emphasizing words and phrases in these sentences.

1 Why on earth do you want to do that?
2 We get on really well.
3 I think myself that when you're the elder child …
4 Whatever does Karen see in him?
5 We're all very different indeed.

b Now answer these questions about the sentences above.

1 Which words are used in front of an adjective or adverb for emphasis?
2 Which word follows an adjective or adverb for emphasis?
3 In which two sentences do the emphasizing words show that the speaker has no idea of the answer?
4 In which two sentences are the emphasizing words or phrases interchangeable?
5 Which word is used to emphasize a personal pronoun?

► **Language commentary p.133**

Pronunciation

3 a **8.4** Work in pairs. Listen to sentences **1a–d**. Which words are stressed?

b **8.5** Decide which words are stressed in sentences **2a**. Listen and check your ideas.

Exploitation

1 This short text about Jackie is written in normal, unemphasized language.

a Rewrite the text using the emphasizing words and structures so that the information in *italics* is emphasized.

Example
Why didn't you tell me Adam was your brother? I *think* you could have told me.
Why on earth didn't you tell me Adam was your brother? *I* **do think** *you could have told me.*

> Jackie was *young* when she got married – just seventeen. Now, *she* admits it was a mistake. 'I *thought* it would work. My parents *warned* me that I was too young but I didn't listen.' So, *what* went wrong? 'I *love* Dave,' said Jackie, 'but we've changed. We both want *different* things from life now.'

b Prepare to read the paragraph aloud. Which words should be stressed? Work in pairs and read the paragraph.

c **8.6** Listen and check your ideas.

Role play

2 Work in pairs. Take turns to be Student A.

Situation 1

Student A
You are showing your partner round your new house or flat. You have just finished decorating it and have bought a lot of new furniture. You are very pleased with the results. Start the conversation and answer any of your partner's questions.
Example
This is the living room …

Student B
Your partner is showing you round their new house or flat. Be as complimentary as you can about the house itself, the furniture and fittings, and ask questions.
Example
It's lovely. I do like the colour. It's very nice.

Situation 2

Student A
Your partner has completely changed their appearance (hairstyle, clothes, jewellery). Compliment them on the changes and ask questions.
Example
You look great! Your hair does suit you short like that! Where did you get it cut?

Student B
You have completely changed your appearance (hairstyle, clothes, jewellery). You are not sure if you have done the right thing. You need reassurance from your partner.

Informal words

The adjective *nice* and the verb *get* are very commonly used in spoken English and in informal written English (e.g. letters to friends). In more formal English, alternative words with more specific meanings are used.

nice

1 The word *nice* can have several different meanings. Match the examples of *nice* to the words with a similar meaning.

complimentary enjoyable kind likeable smart

  a It was very *nice* of you to offer.
  b I've heard a lot of *nice* things about you.
  c You're looking *nice* today.
  d We had a really *nice* holiday.
  e John's a *nice* person.

2 Now make up sentences of your own to show the different meanings of *nice*.

3 We can also use *nice* in front of adjectives describing something we think is pleasant, attractive, or necessary.
*When I got home I had a **nice cool** shower.*
When the adjectives come after the word they describe, the word *and* must be added.
*The service wasn't very good but the food was **nice and hot**.*

Match the adjectives from list **A** with the nouns from list **B**, then make up sentences like these examples.
*I went for a **nice long** walk yesterday.*
*The weather was **nice and hot** when we were in Athens.*

A	cold comfortable easy large long sunny

B	bed (glass of) orange juice exam legs room weather

get

1 The verb *get* is common in informal English and has many different meanings.

annoy arrive at become buy earn obtain receive take understand fetch

Match these examples of *get* with their meanings.

  a I *get* tired quite easily nowadays.
  b Can you *get* my purse for me? I think it's on the table.
  c I *got* a nice long letter from Joe last week.
  d What time did you *get* to the airport?
  e James *got* a new car yesterday.
  f Sonia *gets* £30,000 a year for doing nothing.
  g I'm trying to *get* a bank loan.
  h Amy never *gets* my jokes. I always have to explain them to her.
  i We can *get* the bus to the airport.
  j It really *gets* me when he does that! It breaks my concentration.

2 Make up some sentences of your own with these meanings of *get*.

Language in action

Requests

Eavesdrop!

Look at the picture and guess the answers to these questions.
- Who are the people?
- Where are they?
- What is happening?
- How does the man feel?

Listening 1

1 **8.7** Listen and check your ideas.

2 Work in pairs. Listen to the conversation again.

Student A Listen and note down expressions the man uses to make a request.

Student B Listen and note down expressions the woman uses to respond to the man's requests.

Tell each other the expressions you heard. Make lists with the following headings:
- making requests
- responding to requests.

Listening 2

1 **8.8** You are going to listen to four more conversations in which one person makes a request and the other person responds. As you listen, answer these questions.

a What is the subject of the conversation?
b What is the relationship between the speakers?
c Does the other person agree to the request?
d If not, what excuse do they make?

2 **8.9** Read and listen to the extracts from **three** of the conversations on the next page.

a Mark any expressions used to:
- make a request
- respond to a request.

b Add the marked expressions to the lists you have already made.

Extract 1

H Might be possible, Tony. It depends how long you would want me to work for, though.

T Well, is there any chance of working, er, a couple of evenings and maybe Saturday, or sometime at the weekend, perhaps?

H I'm not sure if I can do that.

T Er … Are you sure? 'Cos really we need to get it now. We need to get it finished by Monday and it's going to be very difficult to get it done, you know, just in the normal working hours.

H I would if I could, Tony, but it very much depends on when you would want me to work.

T Well, how about, erm … How about tomorrow evening? Say till about six or six-thirty, something like that, and maybe Saturday morning? Is that any good?

H I'm afraid I can't do the weekend. No. I can do tomorrow evening, but not the weekend.

Extract 2

K Erm … Heather, I know this is really short notice … erm … Would it be possible … em … to borrow your car this evening?

H Oh, Karen, I'm sorry. I'd lend it to you if I could, but I've really got to go to a meeting tonight.

K Oh, right. Erm … Oh, OK. Well, thanks anyway.

H All right …

Extract 3

K Em. Em … Simon? Is it …? em, I really, I've got a bit of a problem. I need to, em, I need to get hold of a car this evening. Em … I need to give a friend of mine a lift and I was wondering, would it be possible to borrow your car at all?

S To, to borrow mine?

K Yeah …

S Em … I'm not sure, really. When do you want it?

K Well … about seven, really, this evening.

S This evening? That's about in an hour and a half's time.

K Well, yeah, I know it's short notice. Em …

S I've got to … the thing is, I've got to go and pick up …

K Right.

S … my daughter from the station …

K Right. What, what? Would, would, would, er …

S I know, I mean it's, it's possible, em …

K Yeah? I mean, I could, I could come round. I mean it, it, maybe I could make it a bit later. Seven-thirty?

S … That might be OK, actually, seven-thirty …

Features of natural conversation

1 When we request something which might be difficult for the listener, we do not simply make the request – we prepare the person first. We do this by saying a short preparatory phrase, or by saying several sentences.

  a Underline the phrases and sentences in Extracts **2** and **3** which prepare the listener for the request. What is the purpose of each of these?

  b Why do you think Karen spends so long preparing the listener before she makes the request in Extract **3**?

2 ▮8.10▮ Listen to these extracts from the conversation again. What does the word *OK* mean in each instance?

  a H I've really got to go to a meeting tonight.
      K Oh, right, Em … Oh OK. Well, thanks anyway.
      H All right …

  b K Thanks. Speak to you soon.
      H Yes, OK …
      K OK, bye.

  c K Maybe I could make it a bit later. Seven-thirty? …
      S … That might be OK, actually …

3 What does the phrase *the thing is* in Extract **3** mean?
  … the thing is, I've got to go and pick up …

Practice

1 ▮8.11▮ Listen and repeat these requests. Make sure you sound polite.

  a Do you think I could (use your phone)?

  b Could you possibly (give me a lift)?

  c Would it be possible to (bring a friend)?

  d Is there any chance of (lending me that video)?

2 ▮8.12▮ Listen and repeat these expressions for agreeing to and refusing requests.

  a Certainly.

  b No problem.

  c Yes, OK.

  d I'm afraid that's not possible.

  e It's quite out of the question.

  f I would if I could.

  g I'm afraid not.

  h I'm sorry.

  i I can't.

3 ▮8.13▮ Listen to the expressions of refusal. Which speaker refuses politely or diplomatically? How does the other speaker sound?

4 Work in pairs.
Student A Make up four requests to ask your partner.
Student B Respond to your partner's requests using expressions from **2a–i**.

Exploitation

Role play

Work in pairs. Take turns to be Student A. In each situation Student B can agree to the request or refuse and give excuses.

| Situation 1

Student A You want to buy a car but you can't afford it. Ask someone in your family to lend you the money.

Situation 2

Student A Your flight is going to arrive at 3 a.m. on a Sunday morning. There are no buses or trains until 9 a.m. Ask a friend to pick you up.

Situation 3

Student A You have just bought a new computer. You don't know how to set it up. Ask a colleague to do it for you.

Writing

1 You are going to write a letter requesting information or help.

   a First, think about the differences between spoken and written requests.

Spoken language

T Would it be possible to do a couple of evenings, then? Say, tomorrow evening and Thursday evening?
H I'm afraid not. One evening would be all right.
T Erm … Hmm. Any chance of working through till, say, about seven, then?

Writing

Jenny Bright gave me your name and address. She said you had studied French at London University. I was wondering if you could possibly give me some information about the course. I've got all the brochures that they send to all interested students, but I was hoping you might be able to let me know what living and studying in London is really like. Would it be all right for me to phone you some time for a chat? Perhaps this weekend if you can spare the time.

   b Underline all the request phrases in the letter extract.
   c How does the writer make the requests sound polite?

▶ **Writing guidelines p.155**

2 Write one of these letters.

Letter 1

You want to study English at a language school in an English-speaking country. You have received some details about a school which you think would be suitable but you need more information. Write a letter to the school asking for further details. Follow this paragraph plan.

1 Say why you are writing.
2 Make particular requests about paying fees, lessons, and accommodation.
3 Finish your letter concisely and politely.

Letter 2

You are planning to go on a world tour. You haven't got much money so you are hoping that acquaintances in the countries you will be visiting will be able to help you. Write a letter to one of them asking them to help with accommodation and to show you round. Follow this paragraph plan.

1 Remind them of the last time you met and tell them about your plans.
2 Make your requests.
3 Ask them politely to reply as soon as possible.

3 Exchange letters with someone who has written the same letter as you.

   a Read each other's letters. Is the language appropriately polite or formal? Is it clear what the writer's requests are? Make any suggestions for improvements.
   b Rewrite your letter including any improvements you discussed.

Unit 8 Summary

In this unit you have worked on the following language points.

☐ Relative clauses
☐ Emphasizing words and structures
☐ Informal words – *nice* and *get*

☐ Making and responding to requests
☐ Writing a letter of request

Tick ✓ the points you are confident about and cross ✗ the ones you need to revise.

9 On the move

Preview

Your thoughts

Look at these photographs of three groups of people who live a nomadic life.

1 Who are the three groups? Match the pictures with these names: Gypsies, Bedouins, New-Age Travellers.

2 What do you know about each group?

3 What are the advantages and disadvantages of travelling as opposed to living permanently in one place?

Reading

1 Which groups in the photographs are mentioned?

2 Does the text mention any of the disadvantages of travelling you discussed?

Travelling through life

Travellers

It is estimated that the total number of travellers in England is about 90,000. 'New-Age Travellers' account for around 50,000. The remainder are gypsies.

Where do they live?

Whereas Gypsies traditionally travelled around the country in brightly-coloured wagons, nowadays they are more likely to live in modern caravans and stay in one place, usually a municipal caravan site. New-Age Travellers follow a more itinerant lifestyle, travelling around the country in convoys of trucks following seasonal work and music festivals.

Who are the New-Age Travellers?

Some New-Age Travellers are well-educated, literate people, mainly in their 20s and 30s, who are anti-consumerist and have 'green' beliefs. In many cases it is their strongly-held opinions that make them take to the road. Others opt for the

travelling life for different reasons. Some have had their homes repossessed or have otherwise fallen on hard times.

New-Age Travellers try to live as close to nature as the modern world will allow. They also try to stop new development schemes such as road-building and airport extensions.

A case study

Fiona Earle is a typical New-Age Traveller. She lives in a truck with her three children but, as she needs to supplement her income, Fiona occasionally puts on smart clothes and teaches in secondary schools. 'I use teaching to get the money I need to fund my alternative lifestyle,' she says. 'Initially schools I work in don't know that I'm a New-Age Traveller. When I eventually mention it, teaching colleagues say, "Oh, you don't look like one of those".'

Education

Whereas Gypsy parents generally insist on primary education for their children, and withdraw them as soon as they reach secondary age to join in the working life of the family, New-Age Travellers do things differently. One-third educate young children at home. The problem comes at secondary age. Because they want their children to get a proper education, many parents decide to come off the road and move into houses so that their children can attend school regularly. But when parents are dependent on nomadism for their livelihood, settling down can be difficult.

The Times Educational Supplement

Person to person

1 What sort of travellers are there in your country? How do people feel about these groups? What problems do they have?

2 Should people have complete freedom of movement? For example, should they have the right to live where they want?

Grammar – Time and reason clauses review

1 a Which words connect the two clauses in these sentences?
   1 Fiona teaches in a school when she needs extra money.
   2 Some people become New-Age Travellers because they have strong 'green' beliefs.

   b Which of the two words introduces a time clause and which introduces a reason clause (it answers the question why)?

2 Now underline the time words and phrases and circle the reason words or phrases in these extracts from the text.

   a *… as she needs to supplement her income, Fiona occasionally … teaches in secondary schools.*

   b *When I eventually mention it, teaching colleagues say, 'Oh, you don't look like one of those.'*

   c *Because they want their children to get a proper education, many parents decide to come off the road and move into houses …*

   d *Gypsy parents … withdraw them (their children) as soon as they reach secondary age …*

3 a Look at the tenses of the verbs in *italics* in these sentences.
   1 After Ricardo *finished / had finished* university, he did his military service.
   2 Emma takes the dog for a walk before she *goes* to school.
   3 After Giuseppe *leaves* school, he'll go to work for his father.

   b What verb tenses can be used with *before* and *after* when we are referring to:
   1 a present situation?
   2 a past situation?
   3 a future situation?

   c What other time words or phrases could you use instead of *before* and *after* in the sentences in 3a?

4 What is the difference in meaning, if any, between these pairs of sentences?
   a 1 He decided to stay on at school when he was seventeen.
     2 He decided to stay on at school until he was seventeen.
   b 1 As I have time, I'll take you out for a driving lesson.
     2 When I have time, I'll take you out for a driving lesson.
   c 1 When he left university, he became a New-Age Traveller.
     2 As soon as he left university, he became a New-Age Traveller.
   d 1 While I was still at school, my twin brother was already working.
     2 When I was still at school, my twin brother was already working.

   ▶ **Language commentary p.134**

Check

5 Choose an ending 1–6 for each beginning a–f, then link the two parts with a word or phrase from the list. Use each word or phrase at least once.

after   as   as soon as   because   when

Beginning	Ending
a People are suspicious of gypsies	1 … there was a violent thunderstorm.
b The farmer phoned the police	2 … it was light.
c The travellers moved off the land	3 … it got dark.
d They set up camp by the roadside	4 … they have a strange lifestyle.
e They didn't sleep well	5 … the police arrived.
f The convoy set off again	6 … the travellers started to cross his field.

   ▶ Participle clauses   p.87
   ▶ Cause and effect   p.89

Reading

1 Look at these photographs from a magazine article and read the headline. Predict in as much detail as possible what the article is about.

As you read

2 Read the text quickly to check your ideas and for general comprehension.

Close up

1.8 What does *break up* mean here? What else can *break up*?

1.16 What does *shine* mean in this context? What other, more usual meanings do you know?

1.17 Students who fail an exam often *cram* for *re-takes*. What do these words mean?

1.25 + 1.37 The words *via* and *en route* are not English words. What do they mean?

1.30 How would you feel if you were *under the eagle-eye* of someone? What kind of eyesight has an *eagle* got?

Tourists move in as city locals flee the big heat

Deserted streets, shuttered shops, and an eerie silence: summertime in the suburbs of any one of a number of European capitals.

The Parisians take to the countryside and the Madrileños escape to the coast. Romans visit family or head for the sea. The summer exodus from these three
5 cities is legendary.

'You never hear French spoken during August,' said Aline Carasso, head of promotions at France's National Federation of Tourism Bureaux.

In Paris, holiday-makers depart early, as soon as schools break up in July. Major roads out of the city become clogged with
10 motorists heading for the countryside. City suburbs are left virtually deserted.

Parisians, not surprisingly, avoid city locations for their holidays, heading instead to mountain retreats and country cottages. Children are often sent to holiday camps, where the
15 lucky ones can enjoy outdoor pursuits while those who failed to shine in end-of-year examinations open up their schoolbooks again to cram for re-takes.

Although tourist shops remain open, businesses shut down throughout the capital, and even some food shops close their
20 doors. For those who remain in the city, this makes day-to-day life a little more complicated.

However, all is not lost for the tourist. Paris is a welcome sight with calmer streets, and a much appreciated absence of car horns, and the city authorities strive to ensure that there is still plenty for
25 tourists to see and do via a programme of street theatre, concerts, puppet shows, and other events.

The oppressive heat of Madrid in August forces most inhabitants to seek respite by the coast. Again, the streets are quieter during the day, but night-time is more hectic than ever. Spaniards tend to live at home
30 under the eagle-eyes of their parents until a later age than many other Europeans. But as mother and father head for their holiday home in August, many youngsters make the most of the opportunity to party until sunrise.

Many open-air terraza bars and night-clubs do not get going before midnight, and locals and holiday-makers revel in the relative cool of the early
35 hours of the morning.

Madrid tends to attract short-term visitors during the summer. Most stay just two or three days to see the sights while en route to somewhere else.

In contrast, the centre of Rome is a major tourist attraction in the summer. The locals also head for the sea and the difference in traffic levels in the capital is
40 more noticeable than in Paris or Madrid. Ironically, travel is still difficult for those without a car because so many bus drivers are also on holiday.

Again, open-air activities, including a film festival, are organized by the city council as tourists replace locals.

Romans are now beginning to stagger their summer break, but the outskirts
45 of the city still resemble a ghost town in August. Even bars and restaurants tend to shut down in all but the most popular tourist areas. As in Madrid, many of the businesses and offices that do remain open adopt summer working hours, closing early in the afternoon to allow staff to enjoy themselves.

The European

Interpretation

1 Why do you think Parisians leave their city as soon as they can?

2 In what ways do you think life is more complicated for the Parisians who do not leave the city in the summer?

Speaking personally

1 Have you ever spent the summer or part of the summer in a city, either where you live or in another country? What was it like?

2 Do many tourists visit your city or country? Why do they come? What effects can tourists have on the people who live there?

— Grammar —

Participle clauses

Exploring concepts

1 In written English, participle clauses can be used to link two parts of a sentence. How are the present and perfect participles formed?

  a *In July Parisians go on holiday,* **leaving the city to foreign tourists.** (present participle)

  b **Being impatient to get away,** *they often drive all night long to reach their destination.* (present participle)

  c **Having spent two or three days in Madrid,** *foreign tourists go on to other places.* (perfect participle)

2 Participle clauses like these can be used as alternatives to:

  • relative clauses
  • time clauses
  • main clauses joined by *and* or *but*
  • reason clauses
  • result clauses.

Look at sentences **a–f**. Which type of clause does the participle replace?

  a *Major roads out of the city become clogged with motorists* **heading for the countryside.**

  b *Parisians … avoid city locations for their holidays,* **heading instead to mountain retreats …**

  c *Some food shops close,* **making day-to-day life more complicated.**

  d **Travelling around Paris in August,** *I couldn't help noticing how quiet it was.*

  e **Not needing to explain their every move to their parents,** *young Madrileños stay out till all hours.*

  f **Having done well in end-of-year exams,** *lucky children are sent to holiday camps.*

3 In which other position can the participle clause come in sentences **e** and **f**?

4 What do you notice about the time relation between the two clauses in **d** and **f**?

  ▶ **Language commentary p.134**

Exploitation

1 Fill the gaps with an appropriate participle clause. You will need to use the negative form in some sentences.

  a _____ to speak Greek, I couldn't make myself understood.

  b _____ octopus before, I didn't know if I would like it.

  c The shop was full of tourists _____ souvenirs to take home.

  d After lunch everyone has a siesta, _____ the streets deserted.

  e _____ the Acropolis on my last trip, I decided not to bother this time.

  f _____ most of my money by the end of the first week, I couldn't afford to eat out for the rest of the holiday.

2 Fill the gaps in the story with the present participle of one of these verbs.

| believe | carry | cause | hear | help | hit | knock over | ride | stare | trap |

Driving through a small town south of Rome, my eye was caught by a large billboard which began with the word *Automobilista!* (motorist). ....1 that the advertisement was meant to attract my attention, I momentarily took my eyes off the road and the cyclist ....2 in front of me to read it. Unfortunately, at this precise moment a policeman, ...3 a blind man, and a man with a ladder to cross the road, instructed the cyclist to stop.

............4 at the advertisement, I ran into the cyclist, ...5 him to be thrown forward off his bicycle and to trap his head in the ladder.

The force of the cyclist ....6 the ladder caused the man ....7 it to spin, fall over, and trap his fingers in the spinning wheel of the bicycle. Meanwhile, the ladder hit the policeman on the back of the head and knocked him unconscious.

Not ....8 all the noise, the blind man walked in front of a bus, which was carrying school children. In an attempt to avoid him, the driver was forced to go onto the pavement, ...9 a telephone box and ....10 the person inside.

I am pleased to report that no one was seriously hurt. The advertisement, which was the cause of it all, read, 'Motorist! Why are you looking at this? You should be watching the road!'

Listening

1 Decide whether you agree or disagree with the following statements. Then discuss each statement in groups.

a People shouldn't be allowed to drive until they are 26.

b Young drivers take more risks than their parents do.

As you listen

2 You are going to listen to part of a radio broadcast about young people and driving.

a **9.1** Listen to Part 1 and make a note of any arguments that support statements 1a and b. Compare your ideas with a partner.

b Listen to Part 2 where three young people give their views on driving. As you listen, make a note of any information which contradicts statement 1b. Compare your ideas with a partner.

Interpretation

1 What questions might the researchers have asked to test young people's attitude to driving?

2 One of the young drivers says she picked up her bad habits from being a passenger. Can you think of any bad driving habits?

Vocabulary

1 What do you understand by the words and expressions in **bold** in these extracts from the radio programme?

a *How good a driver you are has less **to do with** your age than your attitude.*

b *… it's attitude that makes some people drive like maniacs and overtake every car **in sight**.*

c *There isn't really much **in the way of** public transport.*

d *Me and most of my friends **stick to** soft drinks if we're driving.*

e *I've had **the odd** accident.*

2 What do you think the same words and expressions mean in these contexts?

a I'm thirsty. I *could do with* a drink.

b It seemed that an end to his problems was *in sight*.

c Would you mind standing over there? You're *in the way*.

d Athletes who don't *stick to* the rules risk disqualification.

e I left the house in *odd* socks. Green and blue look the same in the dark.

Speaking personally

Are you a driver? If you are, work in a group with other drivers. Discuss these questions.

1 Do you consider yourself a safe driver? Have you been involved in any accidents? Were you at fault?

2 What do you think makes a good driver?

If you are not a driver, work in a group with other non-drivers. Discuss these questions.

3 How do you feel about being a passenger in a car and having to rely on a driver?

4 What do you think makes a good driver?

Cause and effect

Exploring concepts

1 The verbs or verb constructions in **bold** all express the idea of cause and effect. Underline the causes and circle the effects in these sentences.

  a It's attitude that **makes** some people drive like maniacs ...

  b They drive up really close and flash their lights. It **makes** me furious.

  c The desire to impress friends **causes** some young drivers to take unnecessary risks.

  d Driving slowly **causes** just as many accidents as driving fast.

  e They often end up taking unnecessary risks, which can **lead to** accidents.

  f Advertising campaigns have **brought about** a change in public opinion towards drinking and driving.

  g High accident rates for young drivers have **resulted in** higher insurance charges for this age group.

2 Which of the verb constructions in **1a–g** are followed by:

  • object + infinitive (with or without *to*)?

  • object + adjective?

  • object (noun or noun phrase)?

  ▶ **Language commentary p.135**

Exploitation

1 Complete the sentence beginnings **a–h**, using the appropriate form of one of the cause and effect structures from **1a–g** and one of the endings **1–8** below.

Beginnings

  a Being able to drive ...
  b Cars ...
  c Poor air quality ...
  d Sitting in traffic jams ...
  e Talking on a mobile phone while driving can ...
  f Selfish driving can ...
  g The wet road surface ...
  h New tougher driving laws ...

Endings

  1 an increase in diseases like asthma and bronchitis.
  2 a heavy fine.
  3 the car to skid.
  4 you more independent.
  5 people irritable.
  6 a decrease in serious accidents.
  7 a lot of pollution.
  8 me lose my temper.

2 Use your imagination to complete sentences **a–c** and write your own sentences for **d** and **e**.

  a Waiting for buses makes ...
  b If we build more roads, it will only lead to ...
  c Increased fines for motorists who break the law should bring about ...
  d (*result in*) ...
  e (*cause*) ...

Free speech

3 Imagine that the government of your country has raised the price of petrol dramatically (for example, to five times its current price), and allowed each family to have only one car. What effect do you think this would this have on:

  • people's lives?
  • the economy?
  • the environment?
  • you and your family?

Synonyms

1 Synonyms are words or phrases with similar meanings.
*The film was rather **dull/boring**.*

  a The words on the left are all from texts in this unit. Match each word with a synonym on the right.

    1 ☐ *head*   a choose
    2 ☐ *deserted*   b dawn
    3 ☐ *eerie*   c decent
    4 ☐ *depart*   d director
    5 ☐ *lucky*   e empty
    6 ☐ *open-air*   f fortunate
    7 ☐ *opt for*   g ghostly
    8 ☐ *proper*   h leave
    9 ☐ *smart*   i outdoor
   10 ☐ *sunrise*   j stylish

  b Write synonyms for the words in *italics* in these sentences.

    1 In some countries you have to *do* an entrance *exam* to get into university.

    2 The government *plans* to *do* a survey on the number of people who use public transport.

    3 *Once* all the information has been *gathered*, the results will be published.

    4 Zoe's manners are *awful*. She always speaks with her mouth full.

    5 It was a long, *hard* climb, but the view from the *summit* was *spectacular*.

2 Sometimes certain words can be synonyms in some contexts, but not in others. Look at these sentences.
*In August, the Parisians **take to/head for** the countryside.*
*As soon as Paul got in, he **headed for** the fridge.*
Head for and *take to* are synonyms in the first sentence, but *take to* cannot replace *head for* in the second sentence.

  a Decide which of the words or phrases in brackets is the appropriate synonym for the word in *italics*. Check your ideas in a dictionary.
    Example
    He's a very *smart* (stylish/<u>clever</u>) boy. He always gets high grades.

    1 A lot of shops close in August, which makes *daily* (normal/usual) life *difficult* (uncooperative/complicated).

    2 The lucky children can *enjoy* outdoor pursuits. (take part in/appreciate)

    3 I *learned* something interesting about David yesterday. He's been married three times before. (picked up/discovered)

    4 It's *clear* we're having no success. Let's try something different. (obvious/definite)

  b Now think of a context where the other synonym given would be correct.
    Example
    *He always wears **stylish** clothes.*

3 Sometimes words are synonyms, but one word is more appropriate in a particular context than another because of its register (formal/informal). Replace the formal words and phrases in *italics* with more appropriate synonyms, making any necessary changes.
Example
I'll work out *an approximate* (a rough) estimate.

  a Don't let it *depress* you. It isn't the end of the world.
  b I'll *distribute* the books if you like.
  c I *apologize* for being rude. I shouldn't have said that.
  d Anthea's parents must be *wealthy*. They bought her a Mercedes for her birthday.
  e What do you do in your *leisure time*?

4 Work in pairs. Ask and answer these questions. Use synonyms for the words in *italics* in your answers.
Example
Student A When was the last time you *apologized* to someone and why?
Student B The last time I *said sorry* was about a month ago. I was late for work.

  a What do you like doing in your *leisure time*?
  b If you were *wealthy*, how would your life be different?
  c What sort of things *depress* you?

Language in action

Suggestions

Eavesdrop!

Look at the picture and guess the answers to these questions.

- Who are the people?
- Where are they?
- What are they doing?

Listening 1

1 a **9.2** Listen and check your ideas.

  b In the conversation, Nick expresses his ideas cautiously. Why do you think he does this?

2 Work in groups of four. Listen to the conversation again.

Student A Listen and note down expressions the speakers use to make suggestions.

Student B Listen and note down expressions the speakers use to accept suggestions.

Student C Listen and note down expressions the speakers use to reject suggestions.

Student D Listen and note down expressions one of the speakers uses to end the conversation.

Tell each other the expressions you heard. Make lists with the following headings:

- making suggestions
- accepting suggestions
- rejecting suggestions
- ending conversations.

Listening 2

1 **9.3** You are going to listen to two more conversations in which people make suggestions. As you listen, answer these questions.

  a What is the conversation about?

  b What suggestions are made?

2 **9.4** Read and listen to the extracts from the conversations on the next page.

  a Mark any expressions used to:

- make suggestions
- accept suggestions
- reject suggestions
- end the conversation.

  b Add these expressions to the lists you have already made.

Extract 1

R Well, look, I've, em, … you know, got to go, so, er … well, what do you think?
J Oh, right, erm …
R What do you think?
K Well, what about we try and combine both? I mean …
J Yeah, I think that's a good idea.
K Is it a nice idea to try and do a bit of both?
R Yes … mmm …
J Mmm, mmm, mmm …
K Some place in London and a bit of, sort of natural …

J And some countryside or something, er … yes, the Welsh hills. Would that suit you?
R Well, yeah, I'd go along with that, yes.
J Yeah, all right then.
R So, I mean, we could …
J Just a few days in each, sort of thing. Would

that be a good idea?
K Might be a good idea …
R Yes. So, I mean, we can continue this maybe …
K Well, it'd be nice to make a …
J Yeah …
K … you know, a sort of decision today really …
J Yeah, I think it would be a good idea to do that …
K What would you … what do you want to do? Where would you take them?
R Well, I think outside of London. I think they see enough of London, anyway …
J Mmm, I'd agree with that.
K So where? Where would you go?
R York, as I said, Edinburgh, somewhere like that. Anyway, look … erm … you know … can we carry on with this maybe …?

Extract 2

J Wouldn't it be a good idea to try and get that little door open? Has anybody anything we could …?

S Mmm … we could try. Have you got something?
B Oh, I wouldn't do that!
K No. Don't fiddle with it.
B I wouldn't, I wouldn't do that …
S Why?
B Well, you don't know, I mean …
R Just, just, play, play with the buttons …
S Well, wouldn't that be a way of letting anybody know …?
K Yeah, they'll know … Why don't we just, just wait? I mean it's only just … you know …
B We could, em, bang on the door? Sing and shout?
J Actually, this has happened before so, hmm, it's nothing new.
S Is it?
J So perhaps if we just wait …

Features of natural conversation

Just is commonly used to fill a gap in the conversation or when we are hesitating. But it also has other meanings.

1 **9.5** Listen and match sentences a–e with the most appropriate meaning of *just* 1–5.

a *Just, just*, play, play with the buttons.
b Why don't we *just, just* wait …?
c A Hurry up! We're going to be late!
  B I'm *just* coming. I'm *just* finishing this letter.
d Can I *just* borrow your pen a minute?
e I've *just* finished my course.

1 To be polite when making a request, interrupting, changing the subject.
2 To show that something happened a short time ago.
3 To emphasize that something is easy or simple to do.
4 For emphasis when you are telling someone to do something.
5 To show that you are doing something or will soon finish doing something.

2 **9.6** What are the different uses of *actually*? Listen and match sentences a–e with meanings 1–5. Sometimes more than one meaning is possible.

a *Actually*, this has happened before …
b A I imagine the weather was pretty awful.
  B *Actually*, it was quite good. It only rained once.
c We don't *actually* allow non-members into the club, I'm afraid.
d *Actually*, it might be better if we stop for a break now.
e A Did you know that Joe was thinking of leaving?
  B I'm not surprised, *actually*. He never really settled in, did he?

1 To contradict something another person has said.
2 To make something sound less direct or more polite.
3 To introduce a personal opinion.
4 To mean *in fact* or *this is true*.
5 To introduce new information.

Practice

1 a **9.7** Listen and repeat these suggestions.
  1 Would it be an idea to (go by train)?
  2 Don't you think it'd be a better idea to (fly)?
  3 We could always (hire a car).
 b Which speaker sounds enthusiastic?

2 **9.8** Listen and repeat these expressions for accepting and rejecting suggestions. Make sure you sound appropriately enthusiastic or unenthusiastic.

a That's a good idea.   e I'm not keen on that idea.
b I'd agree with that.   f I'm not sure we should do that.
c Great idea!   g I wouldn't do that.
d Definitely!

3 **9.9** You and a group of colleagues are planning how to celebrate a small win on the lottery. Listen and respond to the five suggestions, using appropriate expressions from **2**.

Exploitation

Work in groups. In each situation you should take turns to make suggestions, and agree or disagree with each other's suggestions. Try to decide on the best plan of action.

Situation 1

You all arrive at the main rail terminal of a foreign capital city. You have planned to spend a week with a friend, who lives in that city. Your friend was supposed to meet you there but has not turned up. You have been waiting for several hours. Unfortunately, you can't phone or go round to their house as you have lost their address. You are not sure what you should do.

Situation 2

You are on holiday in an exotic foreign country. Your hire car has broken down. You appear to be in the middle of nowhere, it will be dark in two hours, you don't have a mobile phone, and you don't speak the language.

Writing

1 You are going to write a letter containing some suggestions.

a First, think about some of the similarities and differences between spoken and written suggestions.

Spoken language

J Wouldn't it be a good idea to try and get that little door open? Has anybody anything we could …?

S Mmm. We could try. Have you got something?

B Oh, I wouldn't do that!

Writing

I'm sorry to hear about your problems at work. We had a similar situation last year, but luckily we managed to resolve our difficulties quite amicably in the end. I have one or two ideas which might help. Have you considered discussing the problem directly with your colleague? As a first move, you could try inviting him for a drink after work one evening. If that doesn't work, I suggest you make a formal complaint to your manager.

b What suggestion expressions does the letter writer use? Underline or highlight them in the extract.

► **Writing guidelines p.156**

2 Write one of these letters. Follow this paragraph plan.

1 Refer to the letter you are replying to. Describe the problem briefly.

2 Make two or three different suggestions.

Letter 1

You have had a letter from an old friend who moved away from your town several years ago to live in the countryside. They would like to return to the town, but are worried that they may not fit in any longer. Reply to your friend's letter, suggesting how this problem could be resolved.

Letter 2

Somebody you work with has written to you from a holiday resort in another country. They are enjoying their holiday so much that they are thinking about staying there. Reply to your friend's letter, suggesting alternatives to this rather drastic course of action.

3 Exchange your letter with someone who has written a different letter from you.

a Read each other's letters. What do you think of the suggestions? Make any suggestions for improvements.

b Rewrite your letter including any improvements you discussed.

Unit 9 Summary

In this unit you have worked on the following language points.

☐ Time and reason clauses
☐ Participle clauses
☐ Cause and effect

☐ Synonyms
☐ Making, accepting, and rejecting suggestions
☐ Ending conversations
☐ Writing a letter making suggestions

Tick ✓ the points you are confident about and cross ✗ the ones you need to revise.

10 Playing with reality

Preview

Your thoughts

Under what circumstances might you:

- lie about your age or your experience?
- pretend to be another person?

Compare your ideas with a partner.

Listening

1 Look at the photograph of three students in their final year at a secondary school. One of these students deceived the school, a university, and the general public by lying about their identity.

   a Which of the three students do you think it was?

   b Why do you think they lied?

   c Compare your ideas with a partner. (If you know this true story, note down anything you remember about it.)

As you listen

2 **10.1** You are now going to listen to part of the story about the student who lied.

   a Check whether any of your ideas or 'facts' are correct.

   b Who is Brandon Lee?

3 Listen to the story again. Put the events in the order in which they happened. The first one has been done for you.

This person:

☐ followed a degree course in experimental pathology
☐ enrolled at the school
☐ went back to the university as a librarian
1 went to Glasgow University to study medicine
☐ went to Canada
☐ had an important conversation with their father
☐ left university because they failed their exams
☐ returned to Britain
☐ got an unknown illness
☐ began a pre-medical course of study

Reading

1 a How do you think the story ended?
  b Compare your ideas with a partner, then read this text.

Brandon Lee stayed at the school for a year, passed his exams, and was accepted by Dundee University medical school. Because of money problems, he had to leave during his first year, but was told he could return later. In the meantime, the headmaster of his school was informed that Brandon Lee and Brian McKinnon were the same person. The headmaster got in touch with Brandon Lee and asked him to produce his birth certificate. When he failed to do this, the head contacted Dundee University and told them of his suspicions. By then the information had been passed to the press and the story of Brandon Lee filled newspapers and radio and TV news bulletins.

2 What do you think of what Brian McKinnon did? Could you imagine doing this yourself?

Person to person

1 How far would you be prepared to go to get a job you really wanted?

2 Who would you choose to become if you could change your identity?

Grammar – Passives review

1 Underline the passive verbs in these sentences.
  a *… he failed his exams and was asked to leave …*
  b *… that route too was blocked when he realized that his immigrant status would prevent him from completing his studies.*
  c *… he had been educated by private tutors, not in normal schools.*
  d *He thought he might be asked for his birth certificate.*
  e *… the headmaster was informed that Brandon Lee and Brian McKinnon were the same person.*
  f *… the information had been passed to the press …*

2 Why do we sometimes choose to use passive verbs in English? Compare these two pairs of sentences.
  a 1 Brandon Lee *had been educated* by private tutors.
    2 Private tutors *had educated* Brandon Lee.
  b 1 The headmaster *was informed* that Brandon Lee and Brian McKinnon were the same person.
    2 Someone *informed* the headmaster that Brandon Lee and Brian McKinnon were the same person.

3 a What is the *agent* of a passive verb?
  b In which sentences **1a–f** are agents mentioned?
  c Why is no agent mentioned in the other sentences? Choose one or more of the reasons **1–4**.
    1 The agent is not important – the focus is on the action.
    2 The agent is obvious – we already know or can guess.
    3 The identity of the agent is unknown or a secret.
    4 The agent is nobody in particular, or people in general.

4 Say or write sentences **1a** and **c–f** without using passive verbs.

  ▶ **Language commentary p.135**

Pronunciation

5 a How are passive verbs pronounced in natural speech? Read sentences **1a–f** aloud.
  b **10.2** Listen and check your ideas. What are the weak forms of *be* in all the tenses?

Check

6 Make these sentences more formal. Rewrite them using passive verbs. The beginnings of the answers are given.
  a The university have accepted me on a course starting next week.
    I _____ .
  b Nobody recognized the President in his old jeans.
    The President _____ .
  c Amateur photographers sent their photos to national newspapers.
    Photos _____ .
  d The police took two years to discover the fraud.
    The fraud _____ .
  e They might send one of the directors to prison.
    One of the directors _____ .
  f Someone has just told me I've got an interview.
    I _____ .

  ▶ Passive constructions   p.97
  ▶ The pronoun *it*   p.99

Reading

1 Do a quick class survey to find the answers to these questions.
   a Which students in the class own pets?
   b What are the most common and the most unusual pets?
   c Are any of the pets dangerous or difficult to look after?

2 Look at the article title and the photograph.
   a What does *virtual* mean?
   b Do you know any other expressions with the word *virtual*?

As you read

3 What do you think is special about the pet in this article? In what ways does it 'live life to the full'?

4 Make a list of the advantages and disadvantages of the norns mentioned in the article.

Close up

1.6 to 1.9 Why are speech marks used like this in this paragraph? If you were reading the extracts aloud, how would you say them?

1.10 What is the difference in meaning between *slap* and *tickle*? What effects do slapping and tickling have on 'victims'?

1.16 What is the difference in meaning between a *groan* and a *cry*?

Virtual pets live virtual lives to the full

Artificial life will soon reach new heights when computer owners will not only be able to play with 'virtual pets', but will be able to breed them as well.

Since breeding works as in real life, but with digital DNA, nobody knows what might ultimately result. Stephen Grand, the senior programmer responsible for
5 developing norns, admits, 'We've no idea what we've started.'

The 'pets', furry cartoon-like 'virtual creatures' called norns, are said to be no harder to care for than hamsters, but cost nothing to feed and don't make a mess or smell. They will be distributed on floppy disk as 'virtual eggs' for users to hatch and feed.
10   It is claimed that norns respond to being slapped or tickled and can even learn simple words. After six to ten hours of computer time, they reach adolescence and become interested in the opposite sex. But there's nothing indecent about their breeding. 'They just kiss for a bit longer,' says Mr Grand.
15 The norns can also, apparently, get drunk or sick. They exhibit a range of groans and cries, shake or sneeze, and sometimes die. Toby Simpson, one of Mr Grand's colleagues at the firm developing the program, says, 'If they're really ill, there's no reason why you
20 shouldn't send them back to us to look at – perhaps for a small fee!'

According to Mr Simpson, people who use the program will be able to exchange eggs or send creatures to one another over the
25 Internet. 'If you're going away, you'll be able to send them on holiday,' he says. 'The drawback is that other people almost always teach them to swear.'

Although 'virtual pets' have a long history, these new creatures are far
30 more complex than anything attempted before. They have a complete but simplified bio-chemistry, and you can even examine their brains to see neural patterns developing. Scientists trying to develop thinking machines are believed to be interested in this feature.
The Guardian

Interpretation

1 Stephen Grand says: 'We've no idea what we've started.' (l.5) What could they have started?

2 How interested do you think these people would be in owning a norn?
   a someone who loves animals
   b someone who is interested in computer technology
   c someone with a busy, stressful life
   d someone who is lonely or bored

3 Why do you think scientists are interested in virtual pets?

Speaking personally

1 Why do people own pets?

2 Do you think certain kinds of people prefer certain kinds of animals as pets?

3 Would you like a norn as a pet? Why? Why not?

Passive constructions

Exploring concepts

1 Compare these pairs of sentences. What difference does the passive make in each pair?

a 1 The 'pets', furry cartoon-like 'virtual creatures' called norns, *are said to be* no harder to care for than hamsters.

2 The 'pets', furry cartoon-like 'virtual creatures' called norns, are no harder to care for than hamsters.

b 1 Scientists trying to develop thinking machines *are believed to be* interested in this feature.

2 Scientists trying to develop thinking machines are interested in this feature.

c 1 *It is claimed that* norns respond to being slapped or tickled.

2 Norns respond to being slapped or tickled.

2 Which of these uses of the passive apply to sentences **a1**, **b1**, and **c1**?

A To focus on the person or thing affected by the action.

B When you don't know or don't want to say who did the action.

C To make the writing sound less personal and more formal.

3 What other verbs could be used instead of *said*, *believed*, and *claimed* in sentences **a1**, **b1**, and **c1**?

4 a Compare sentence **c1** with sentences **a1** and **b1**. Rewrite **a1** and **b1** starting with *It is …*

b Rewrite **c1** starting with *Norns are …*

5 a In sentences **1a–c** the writer uses passive constructions to show that he is not sure if what he is saying is true. How is the same idea expressed in these sentences?

1 *The norns can also, apparently, get drunk or sick.*

2 *According to Mr Simpson, people … will be able to exchange eggs …*

3 *They say that more and more people are buying computer pets.*

b Rephrase these sentences using passive constructions.

▶ **Language commentary p.135**

Exploitation

1 Read this advertisement for a different computer pet program.

a What is the main purpose of the program?

KyttyKyts the screen saver you'll just love.

KyttyKyts protects your computer screen and give you hours of fun.

• Watch KyttyKyts eat and drink what you offer them
• Watch KyttyKyts dreaming of mice and birds
• Watch KyttyKyts chase mice across your screen
• Listen to KyttyKyts purr when you stroke them

Ten different KyttyKyts to choose from, each with a different personality.
In just a day or two you'll wonder how you lived without KyttyKyts

b Write about the program from the point of view of someone who has not used it and who has doubts about the truthfulness of the advertisement. Show doubt by using passive constructions.

Example

It is said / claimed that these computer pets (can) eat and drink.

2 Work in pairs. You are going to report a number of 'facts' to each other using passive constructions. **Student A / B** both turn to p.159.

Finally, discuss any of the statements that interest, amuse, or surprise you. Say which you think is or isn't true.

Free speech

3 a Read these newspaper headlines. What do you think each story could be about? Discuss your ideas in groups.

GOVERNMENT HIT BY SCANDAL – TOP POLITICIAN RESIGNS!

ROCK STAR DENIES ALLEGATIONS

Food company cheating public

b Talk about a similar story of public interest at the moment in your country.

Writing

4 Write the story behind one of the three newspaper headlines.

• Write the main details of the story in one paragraph (60–70 words).
• Use formal language.
• Use passive constructions to protect your sources of information and / or to express your own doubts about the accuracy of the information.

Listening

1 Look at the optical illusions on this page.
   a Do you find them intriguing or irritating? Why?
   b Have you any ideas or theories about how the *Kennel of Confusion* in this photograph was made? (Turn to p.159 to see the answer.)

Don't believe your eyes!

As you listen

2 **10.3** Listen to the first part of a popular science radio programme called *Don't believe your eyes!* Which four of the impossible objects below are described? What is the name of the object described but not shown?

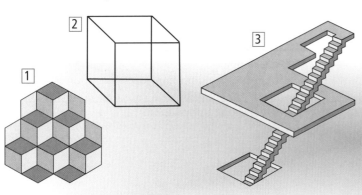
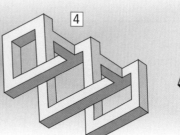
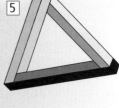

3 a Why do you think our brains are tricked by these impossible shapes? Compare your ideas with a partner. You might find these words and phrases useful.

---
illusion   light and shade   perspective   shadow   signal
three-dimensional   visual data   perception   trick
---

   b Listen to the second part of the programme and check your ideas.

Interpretation

1 What situations can you think of when people *need to convey a sense of three dimensions on a piece of paper*?

2 What kind of judgements are being referred to here? *They (our brains) evolved to make* **life-saving judgements** *in a world where it was vital to interpret visual information very fast.*

Vocabulary

1 Think of synonyms for *look at* and *see* in these sentences from the radio programme.
   a *… we're going to* **look at** *ways in which the human brain processes visual information.*
   b *… let's* **look at** *some of the impossible objects artists have created …*
   c *If you can't* **see** *two different images, try turning the page 45 degrees.*

2 Here are some more uses of *look* and *see*. What are their meanings here?
   a I've been *looking for* you. Where have you been?
   b *Look at* me when I'm talking to you.
   c He *looks like* his mother.
   d It *looks like* rain.
   e I *see* what you mean.
   f I'll *see* you tomorrow.
   g I'll *see* if I can help you to find your keys.

Speaking personally

Have you ever had the feeling that you have already experienced in the past exactly the same sequence of events as is happening at the present moment? (This feeling is sometimes called *déjà vu*.) What was the experience? When and where did it happen? Why do you think this happens?

The pronoun *it*

Exploring concepts

1 The pronoun *it* (like *he* or *she*) is often used instead of a noun to avoid repetition. What nouns does *it* refer to in this extract?

*When we look at any picture, the brain instantly processes the visual data and allows us to see the three-dimensional object on a flat surface, although we know **it** cannot actually be there. That illusion is commonplace – and is very useful to us. The art of painting depends on **it** for a start, …*

2 *It* can also be used as the subject of a sentence or clause when it does not refer to a specific noun. Match the examples **a–f** with some common uses **1–5**.

a *It* is our brains, however, that sort out the information, not our eyes.

b They evolved to make life-saving judgements in a world where *it* was vital to interpret visual information very fast.

c … *it* seems that interpreting the patterns is much harder.

d Programmers have found *it* extremely difficult to 'teach' even super-computers to recognize quite simple images.

e … *it*'s not surprising that the human brain can be fooled.

f … *it* wasn't until halfway through the present century that artists thought …

1 For emphasis – to show that the word or phrase that follows is important.

2 To introduce a subject (an infinitive expression or another clause) that comes up later in the sentence.

3 To introduce an object (an infinitive expression or another clause) that comes up later in the sentence.

4 In expressions referring to certain conditions: the weather, times, and distances.

5 As the subject of verbs relating to what appears to be true (e.g. *appear*).

▶ **Language commentary p.136**

Exploitation

1 Make sentences using a beginning, one of the *it* clauses, and your own ending.

Beginnings	*it* clauses
a When you're on holiday,	it's important / sensible …
b If you're travelling abroad,	it's (not) a good idea …
c When you go for an interview,	it would be a pity / shame …
d If you want to stay healthy,	it makes sense …
e After all your efforts,	it would be silly / pointless …

2 Finish these sentences about yourself. Compare your ideas with a partner.

a I find it easy to …

b I find it very difficult to …

c I find it impossible to …

d I like it when …

e I hate it when …

3 Write five true sentences about other students in the class.

Example

Pablo is going out with Suzy.

Change the names of the people to make the sentences incorrect. Then read your sentences to a partner who has to respond with a true statement.

Example

Student A *Phil is going out with Suzy.*

Student B *No, he isn't. It's Pablo that's / who's going out with Suzy.*

4 Work in groups. Have short conversations on these subjects.

• today's weather compared with yesterday's

• distances between places of interest in your country

Free speech

5 Look carefully at this picture. Describe what you can see and then discuss what you think is happening.

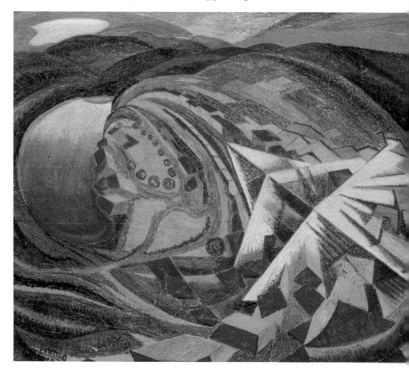

Metaphorical language

1 Many English words have *literal* and *metaphorical* meanings. The *literal* meaning is the word's most basic (often physical) meaning; the *metaphorical* meaning often involves a more abstract use of the same word in a different context. Here are three pairs of sentences in which are words used *literally* and then *metaphorically*. Work out or guess the meanings.

Literal use	Metaphorical use
a We couldn't leave the city – all the main *routes* were *blocked* by army tanks.	Brian McKinnon went to Canada and started a pre-medical course. However that *route* too was *blocked* when he realized that his …
b After the accident I had to *bend* my bicycle wheel back into shape.	… let's look at some of the impossible objects artists have created by *bending* the rules.
c When the minister arrived, I took a *step* forward and shook his hand.	It is a small *step* from the Necker cube to the truly impossible tribar.

2 Newspaper headlines frequently use metaphorical language. Why is this?

  a Read these headlines and identify the word or phrase being used metaphorically. Can you explain its meaning? (You may need to refer to a dictionary.)

> **1** Prices tumble after government tax announcement
>
> **2** New company takes off after slow start
>
> **3** Government closes the door on new pay talks
>
> **4** Economic plan shot down in flames
>
> **5** Mars robot unlocks the secrets of the Red Planet
>
> **6** Frosty reception for President at New York summit meeting

  b Now use the words and phrases from **2a** (with their literal meanings) in the correct form to fill the gaps in these sentences.

    1 I can't _____ my suitcase – I've left the key at home.

    2 'It's a cold, _____ morning – you ought to wear a hat.'

    3 The pilot had a lucky escape when his helicopter was _____ over the sea.

    4 Even though it was foggy, our plane _____ on time.

    5 I tripped over the cat and _____ down the stairs.

    6 We argued for ten minutes outside his office, then he just _____ in my face.

3 Here are some nouns being used metaphorically as verbs.

  a What are the literal meanings of the words as nouns?

  b What are their metaphorical meaning as verbs?

    1 It was three days since he'd eaten, so when the food was put in front of him, he *wolfed it down* in a few seconds.

    2 I know he's your brother, but you shouldn't let your personal feelings *cloud* your judgement.

    3 I know you're busy, but you should have a break – you've been *beavering away* all day on the computer.

    4 We argued for an hour, then he just turned round and *stormed out*.

    5 She didn't really love him – he knew she was only *toying with* him.

    6 We're the same age, but John absolutely *towers over* me.

  c Work in pairs or groups. Discuss these questions.

    1 What can be the effects of *wolfing down* your food?

    2 Are you the kind of person who *beavers away* at things for long periods of time?

    3 Have you ever been so angry that you *stormed out* of a room?

Language in action

Announcing decisions

Eavesdrop!

Look at the picture and guess the answers to these questions.

- Who are the two people?
- What is the relationship between them?
- What is in the letter the woman is carrying?

Listening 1

1 a **10.4** Listen and check your ideas.

b Which of these words best describes the tone of the conversation you have just heard? Compare your ideas with a partner.

warm	casual	informal	formal	cold

2 Work in pairs. Listen to the conversation again.

Student A Listen and note down expressions the woman uses to announce or confirm decisions.

Student B Listen and note down expressions the man uses to question the woman's decisions.

Tell each other the expressions you heard. Make lists under the following headings:

- announcing or confirming decisions
- questioning decisions.

Listening 2

1 **10.5** You are going to listen to two more conversations in which people question the decisions of others. As you listen, answer these questions.

a What is the relationship between the speakers?
b What decisions are being discussed?
c What is the main reason for the decisions?
d What arguments are made against the decisions?

2 **10.6** Read and listen to the extracts from the two conversations on the next page.

a Mark any expressions used to:
- announce or confirm decisions
- question decisions.

b Add the marked expressions to the lists you have already made.

Extract 1

T You don't speak Czech.
J No – awful, I shall …
B It's quite a difficult language.
J Yeah, I think so, mmm, I'll have to get some lessons sorted out, won't I?
T Sounds a bit …
J Aren't you excited? Don't you think it's great?
B Well, I mean …
T Well …
Ju I just wish I had your confidence.
J Oh, but it's nothing. I mean, if you want to have change in life, why not do it?
B Well, I mean, it just seems a big risk to me to take – I mean you've got a … I mean,

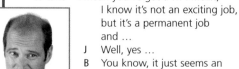

  I know it's not an exciting job, but it's a permanent job and …
J Well, yes …
B You know, it just seems an awful big risk, I mean, what, just what happens if it doesn't work out?
T And what do you do about friends? You're leaving all your friends here. Think about that.
J Well, I shall make new friends and, I mean,

I'm outgoing and sociable and I shall meet an awful lot of new people in the school I'm going to.
T I'm not so sure. • Sounds a bit risky to me.
J No, no they're a very nice lot. I've, I've talked to them quite a lot and I've, I've talked to some other people who've been there and they're very enthusiastic about it so, you know, I've got to make a move, really I've, well, I've made my mind up – I have to have a change in life, I think.
B Well, I think you should really, you know, think twice before you take it – it's a big decision.
J Well, it is a big decision and I have been thinking about it for, well, to be honest …

Extract 2

R Yes it is, it's, it's, it's exciting, there are things to do, I mean, the country • slow death.
Ju Yeah, but then you can choose, you can choose to go into the city to do the pastimes you want and then you just escape to the peace and quiet of the country.
S Yeah, what happens if it's, like, the weekend

and you think – what can I do at the weekend? There's nothing to do, is there? What do you do?
Ju Oh, you read and you go for walks and

you listen to music and just listen to the, the countryside and it's all quiet.
R I mean, what would you do if you … suddenly had an emergency, you, you got ill or …
Ju Oh, well, it's not, it's not out in the outback, there are … we still get sort of … the emergency services …
R • Sounds like it.
S You hear terrible stories of people getting stuck when they're …
R Yeah, I mean in winter.
S Yeah, • cut off …
Ju Well, yes, you can get cut off, yes, yes. I have heard stories of that, but that, that's just a small price to pay for, for just a life.

Features of natural conversation

In informal speech people often leave out words or phrases which would be necessary in more formal speech or in writing.

1 a Look at places marked • in the extracts and work out what is missing.

Example
• Sounds a bit risky to me.
sounds has no subject – *it* or *that* is missing.

b Here are some more everyday conversations. Work out what is missing.
1 A Got the time?
   B Yes, just gone six.
2 A Nice day, isn't it?
   B Not bad.
3 A Been here long?
   B About ten minutes.
4 A Sorry. Must dash.
   B OK. See you later.

2 a What does the speaker imply by asking negative questions?
Aren't you excited?
Don't you think it's great?

b How are these questions different?
Are you excited?
Do you think it's great?

Practice

1 a Before you listen to these expressions, decide which syllables you think will be stressed.
1 I've made up my mind – (I'm leaving).
2 (I'm leaving, and) I'm not going to change my mind.
3 My mind's made up – (I'm going).
4 I've decided to (go) – you won't change my mind.
5 I'm definitely (leaving).

b **10.7** Listen and check your ideas. Which syllables carry the main stress?

c Listen again and repeat the expressions.

Exploitation

Role play

Work in small groups. Take turns to be Student A and announce a decision to the rest of the group. In each situation the rest of the group should raise doubts about the decision, ask questions, and make suggestions to get the decision-maker to change their mind.

Situation 1

Student A You have decided to give up your present job and train to be one of these: a teacher, a police officer, an actor, a pilot, a circus performer. Announce your decision to a group of close friends. Make it clear you are not going to change your mind.

Situation 2

Student A You have decided to become a vegetarian. Announce your decision to the people you live (and eat!) with. Make it clear you are not going to change your mind.

Situation 3

Student A You have decided to ban smoking in the place where you work. Announce your decision to the people you work with and employ – you are the boss! Make it clear you are not going to change your mind.

Writing

1 You are going to announce decisions in writing.

  a First, think about the differences between spoken and written decisions.

Spoken language

T I'm not so sure. Sounds a bit risky to me.

J No, no they're a very nice lot. I've, I've talked to them quite a lot and I've, I've talked to some other people who've been there and they're very enthusiastic about it so, you know, I've got to make a move, really I've, well, I've made my mind up – I have to have a change in life, I think.

B Well, I think you should really, you know, think twice before you take it – it's a big decision.

J Well, it is a big decision and I have been thinking about it for, well, to be honest …

Writing

> After careful thought I have finally decided to leave the company and return to full-time education. I have been thinking about this move for a number of years now, but friends and colleagues have always persuaded me to think about my career, my salary, and other practical considerations. This time my mind is made up and I have accepted a place at Oxford University to study biochemistry.

  b What words and expressions does the writer use to express the firmness of their decision?

  c How does the writer deal with possible doubts or questions in the mind of the reader?

▶ **Writing guidelines p.155**

2 Choose one of these situations.

Situation 1

Write a letter saying you are withdrawing from a committee, or any position of responsibility, in a real or imaginary organization or club that you belong to. Follow this paragraph plan.

1 Say why you are writing and state your main decision.

2 Explain briefly the reasons for your decision. Think about the objections the club may raise and make sure you answer/cover them. Say that you will not change your mind again.

3 Finish on a friendly note – for example by saying that you will continue to show an interest in the work of the club/organization.

Situation 2

You have decided to move to another city or country to live and work, and you're going to announce this decision to colleagues at a party at your workplace. To make sure you can remember everything you want to say, you decide to read out a prepared statement. You want to keep your announcement brief and to the point, but include the following information in your statement.

- Say where and when you are moving.
- Give a reason for your move, making it clear that you have thought about some of the possible problems you will face.
- Say how much you have enjoyed working with your colleagues and wish everyone well for the future.

3 Exchange your piece of writing with a partner.

  a Read each other's work. How firmly are the decisions expressed? Has your partner included enough explanation and predicted the most likely doubts in the minds of readers or listeners? Make any suggestions for improvements.

  b Rewrite your letter or prepared statement, including any improvements you discussed.

Unit 10 Summary

In this unit you have worked on the following language points.

☐ Passives
☐ Passive constructions
☐ The pronoun *it*
☐ Metaphorical language

☐ Announcing / confirming decisions
☐ Questioning decisions
☐ Announcing decisions in writing

Tick ✓ the points you are confident about and cross ✗ the ones you need to revise.

11 Followers

Preview

Your thoughts

Which newspapers and magazines in your country contain the latest gossip about famous people? Who reads these publications? Why do you think they are popular?

Reading

1 Work in pairs and discuss these questions.

a Do famous people need to have a relationship with the press? Why? Why not?

b Why do *paparazzi* photographers go to extremes to get interesting photographs?

2 Read the text to find out whether any of your ideas are mentioned.

In the public eye

2169364

1:3.5~4.5

35~105mm

We love to look at photographs of celebrities and celebrities love to be looked at. Until, that is, they get too famous. When they first start out, they spend all their time trying their hardest to get into the newspapers. Then, once they are household names, everything changes. All celebrities desperately desire Press attention when they want it, and then cry 'invasion of privacy' when they don't. You can even sympathize with them at times. What photographers will do to get a shot is sometimes outrageous, but we all love to see the results. And as long as we do, the financial rewards for these pictures are so huge that any risk is worth taking. The irony is that when a celebrity blows his top, makes obscene gestures, and / or attacks a photographer, the sky really is the limit when it comes to the price of the pictures. One photographer commented, 'I just love it when they make a stupid gesture. It's a mystery to me why they don't just walk to their car.'

Options Magazine

Zoom

Listening

1 You are going to listen to two *paparazzi* talking about their jobs. Before you listen, predict their answers to these questions.

a Why do you do this job?

b How do you get your photographs developed?

c What kinds of things are you prepared to do to get a photograph?

d Do you think that the general public supports what you do?

2 **11.1** Listen and check your ideas.

Person to person

1 Do you think the activities of the *paparazzi* should be restricted? Why? Why not?

2 Does the general public have the right to know everything about a famous person?

Grammar – Causatives review

1 What are the differences in meaning between the sentences in the two groups **a** and **b**?

a 1 I have the photos developed.
  2 I have developed the photos.
  3 I develop the photos.

b 1 I had my room decorated before going on holiday.
  2 I had decorated my room the previous week.

2 In which two sentences in **1** does the speaker arrange for something to be done? These two sentences contain causative verbs. How are these formed?

3 The causative verb structures, *get something done* and *have something done*, are sometimes completely interchangeable. *He **has / gets** his teeth checked every six months.*

a Which of the two forms *have* or *get* is more formal than the other?

b In some contexts only one of the forms is possible, and in others, one form is more usual than the other. Match these three sentences 1–3 with a use a–c, and a rule A–C.
  1 'Get your hair cut!', the officer shouted at the soldier.
  2 I had to get my car brakes fixed. They were dangerous!
  3 Have you had your windows cleaned recently?

  a in the Present perfect tense
  b to show an action is, or was urgent
  c for imperatives (e.g. orders)

  A *have* is possible but *get* is more usual
  B *get* is used
  C only *have* is possible

▶ **Language commentary p.136**

Check

4 The words in these sentences are jumbled up. Rewrite them in the correct order.

a your better cooker you'd get checked. (It smells of gas in here.)

b you had tested your eyes have recently?

c having some new made bookshelves am I.

d cut down that get tree. (It could fall on the house.)

e we had resprayed after our car the accident.

5 Fill the gaps with a causative structure using *get* or *have* and the words in brackets. Add any other necessary words.

a We must _____ before winter comes or we'll freeze. (windows / repair)

b _____ you _____? It looks different. (hair / cut)

c We _____ next year. (house / paint)

d _____! It might have a virus. (computer / checked)

e Susan's handbag's been stolen from her flat. If I were her I _____. (locks / change)

▶ Causative verbs and the passive; non-causative use of *have something done* p.107
▶ Question tags p.109

Reading

1 What do you know about tornadoes? Are these statements true or false?

a Most tornadoes occur in the USA.

b Scientists can now predict exactly when and where tornadoes will occur.

c Tornadoes generally move forward quite slowly.

As you read

2 Check your ideas in the article.

Many of the residents of Pampa (Texas) had their homes destroyed when a tornado hit the town. Roofs were torn off; trees were ripped out of the ground.

Close up

1.3 What does a *mecca* mean? Where is Mecca? Why is it important?

1.6 What is the meaning of *hard* here?
• difficult to understand
• factual or definite

1.7 What is a *flock* of sheep? What do you think the verb *flock* means?

1.25 *Twisting* describes the internal movement of the tornado. Which other two words in this paragraph have the same meaning?

Twister-chasers

'Tornado Alley', a belt of the American Midwest, is a mecca for research scientists and amateur tornado-chasers alike
5 during the months of May and June, the tornado season. Seeking either hard data or a pure rush of adrenalin, they flock to the vast open spaces of Oklahoma, Texas, and Kansas, armed with satellite scanners,
10 video cameras, and a case full of maps.

Eric Rasmussen, a world authority on tornadoes, does most of his work here, where a staggering 75 per cent of the world's tornadoes occur. But not all the tornadoes happen within convenient reach of the
15 scientists whose mission it is to understand them. 'We can predict where a tornado could form,' he said 'but we can't be sure that it will.' So quite often a team of 120 experts may travel hundreds of kilometres in a day and have a
20 wasted journey.

Although it is known that most tornadoes develop in *thunderheads* – giant unstable clouds which reach high into the atmosphere – it is still not known how tornadoes get to the ground. Discoloured by dirt
25 from a field, a tornado may appear as a twisting umbilical rope, a grey spinning funnel, or a hissing column of rotating debris.

At first, to the untrained eye, it may appear stationary. A tornado's typical forward progress is
30 only around 32 kilometres per hour. The damage they cause is done by the velocity of the internal, rotating winds which can reach 400 or possibly 480 kilometres per hour. Nobody is quite sure, because most wind speed measuring equipment is
35 destroyed when a tornado passes over it.

What can be measured, however, is the damage they cause. In the United States this century they have claimed between 15,000 and 20,000 lives. On a single March day in 1925, nearly 700
40 people lost their lives as seven tornadoes surged over 320 kilometres of the American Midwest. *The Tristate Tornado*, as it became known, was the most destructive ever recorded, reaching speeds of 120 kilometres
45 an hour and travelling for most of its journey in an unbroken straight line across Missouri, Illinois, and Indiana.

Events like that, and the Wichita tragedy of 1991, continue to fuel a search for the
50 causes of this dangerous but curiously exhilarating phenomenon. But the answers may be many years away and tornado-chasers, professional or amateur, may be bound together, not just by
55 obsession, but by frustration for some time to come.

Savage Skies

Interpretation

1 Explain the purpose of the things the scientists carry around with them.

2 Why does the writer describe the tornado as *a curiously exhilarating phenomenon*? What other phenomena or events could be described in the same way?

3 Find evidence in the text which tells you what problems scientists and tornado-chasers face when researching tornadoes.

Speaking personally

1 Would you like to chase tornadoes as a hobby? Give reasons.

2 Have you ever experienced a tornado, a hurricane, a violent thunderstorm, or something similar at close range?

— Grammar —

Causative verbs and the passive; non-causative use of *have something done*

Exploring concepts

1 The passive and the causative are similar in meaning, but have a different focus. Look at the two sentences below. Which form is used to tell you who was responsible for arranging, but not doing the action? Which form is used to focus on the action?

  a Alex's flat *was redecorated* last month.

  b Alex *had his flat redecorated* last month.

2 In these sentences, *have something done* has a different (non-causative) meaning. What does it mean here?

  a He *had his telephone disconnected* because he didn't pay his bill.

  b We *had our roof torn off* in the storm.

  c Hugh *had his car stolen* at the weekend.

3 We can express the sentences above in the passive.

  a His phone *was disconnected* because he didn't pay his bill.

  b Our roof *was torn off* in the storm.

  c Hugh's car *was stolen* at the weekend.

Which form, the causative or the passive, emphasizes the dramatic nature of the action?

  ► **Language commentary p.137**

Exploitation

1 Look at the photograph. What effect do you think the flood has had on the farmers who live in the area?

  a Match the nouns from list **A** with the verbs from list **B**. Sometimes more than one answer is possible.

    Example
    crops ruin

| **A** | crops | livelihoods | trees | walls |
| | fences | furniture | | |

| **B** | destroy | uproot | ruin | knock down |
| | wash away | damage | | |

  b Now write two sentences for each idea above. Use a passive verb in one sentence and a *have something done* structure in the other.

    Example
    Their crops have been destroyed.
    They have had their crops destroyed.

Role play

2 Work in pairs. Student A interviews Student B.

Student A You are a journalist interviewing people who have been affected by the flood. Prepare your questions.

Student B You live in the area which has been flooded. Prepare what you are going to say. Use the ideas in **1** to help you.

Example

Student A *Have you been badly affected by the flood?*

Student B *Yes, we have. The farmhouse has been flooded, as you can see. We've had a lot of furniture and carpets damaged by the water – in fact almost everything downstairs has been ruined.*

3 Now use your ideas to prepare a short written bulletin on the floods for a local radio news programme. Use passive verbs and *have something done* in your report. Begin like this.

Farmers in Aylesforth woke up this morning to terrible scenes of devastation. During the night the River Ayle rose and flooded …

Listening

1 What is a *fan*? Why do you think some fans become obsessed? What extremes do some obsessed fans go to?

2 You are going to listen to part of an interview with Chuck McDonald, who claims to be Elvis Presley's number one fan. What do you think he does?

As you listen

3 **11.2** Listen and check your ideas.

Interpretation

1 Answer these questions about the interview.
  a Why do you think Chuck McDonald's wife left him?
  b Why do you think Chuck McDonald's son became a fan of Elvis?
  c Why do you think Elvis Presley 'hated sunlight'?
  d Chuck McDonald says that he never actually met Elvis because *there was always too many folks between us*. Who were these people?

2 Notice how Chuck McDonald leaves out certain words when he speaks. Write in the missing words from these extracts.
  Example
  Called him after the King … = I called him after the King.
  a *Hell, just one of those things …*
  b *It's signed to me. See?*
  c *Course, I keep the drapes closed all the time …*
  d *Matter of fact, I was at 'Graceland' day before he died.*
  e *Who'd have thought?*
  f *Greatest sorrow of my life is that I never actually met the King.*

Vocabulary

1 Many words in American English are the same as in British English, but some are different. What are the British English equivalents of these words?

drapes folks howdy kid movies

2 Work out the British English for these American English words. Use the context to help you.
  a The *elevator* was out of order so we had to climb the stairs.
  b The *truck*, which was carrying logs, almost hit a pedestrian on the *sidewalk*.
  c We put our *baggage* in the *trunk*, jumped in the car, and set off on a two-week *vacation* to Florida.
  d The customer asked the waiter if he could have the *check*.
  e He loves sweet things but he knows that *candy* is bad for his teeth and *cookies* are bad for his waistline.

Speaking personally

1 Are you, or have you ever been, a fan of a sports team, sports person, movie star, or musician?

2 Can you think of anyone alive today who will have as many followers as Elvis Presley 20 or 30 years after their death?

Question tags

Exploring concepts

Question tags are small questions that can come at the end of sentences in spoken and informal written English. They are used to check whether something is true – like a real question – or to ask for agreement.

Pronunciation

1 a **11.3** Listen to the sentences. Are the question tags asking real questions or are they asking for agreement? Does the intonation rise or fall on the question tag?

1 Now, you know more about Elvis than anyone else in the world, don't you?
2 That's what you're here for, isn't it?
3 It's come out really well, hasn't it?
4 We still can't believe he's gone, can we?
5 He doesn't exactly sing it, though, does he?

b What rules of pronunciation can you work out?

2 Read these rules on forming question tags and then match them with sentences **a–j**. In some sentences more than one rule may apply.

If the main clause contains …	the question tag contains …
1 an auxiliary verb	an auxiliary verb
2 the verb *be*	the verb *be*
3 a negative verb, auxiliary, or modal or a negative word	an affirmative verb, auxiliary, or modal
4 an affirmative verb, auxiliary, or modal	a negative verb, auxiliary, or modal
5 non-auxiliary verb *have*	an auxiliary verb
6 *let's*	*shall*
7 no auxiliary	*do*
8 an affirmative imperative	*will* or *would*
9 a negative imperative	*will*
10 *nobody*, *somebody*, etc.	*they*
11 *nothing*	*it*
12 a modal verb	a modal verb

a He never apologizes, does he?
b Patrick left early, didn't he?
c Don't forget to send me a postcard, will you?
d Let's take a break, shall we?
e She's got three sisters, hasn't she?
f Stefan has a shower every morning, doesn't he?
g Nobody phoned for a taxi, did they?
h Nothing's wrong, is it?
i You can't speak Swahili, can you?
j Close the window, would you?

3 **11.4** Read and listen to these requests. Which sentence in each pair is less formal?

a Can you lend me ten pounds?
b You can't lend me ten pounds, can you?
c Could you give me a hand?
d You couldn't give me a hand, could you?
e Do you mind if I smoke?
f You don't mind if I smoke, do you?

▶ **Language commentary p.137**

Exploitation

1 You are going to listen to ten incomplete sentences.

a **11.5** Listen and write down the missing question tags.
b **11.6** Listen and check your answers.
c Listen again and repeat the sentences, using the appropriate intonation, depending on whether the speaker is checking information or asking for agreement.

2 a Make these requests less formal by using a negative sentence and a question tag.

1 Can you come back tomorrow?
2 Could you help me with my homework?
3 Would you be able to come a bit later?
4 Would it be possible for you to work late tomorrow?
5 Do you mind if I invite Tom?

b **11.7** Listen and check your ideas.

3 Work in pairs. Each think of five statements you think your partner will agree with and have a short conversation.

Phrasal verbs are difficult to pick up, aren't they?

Yes, I keep having to look them up!

4 Work in pairs. Take turns to make requests to each other. Don't agree to the request immediately. You can begin with the questions in **2** above.

Word-building: prefixes

Prefixes and opposite meanings

1 The prefixes *un–*, *in–*, *im–*, *ir–*, *il–*, and *dis–* can be added to the beginning of some words to give them a negative meaning. Add the appropriate prefix to these words to give a negative meaning.

Example
trained – **un**trained

~~trained~~   literate   mature   efficiency   approve   legally
dress   responsible   agree   relevant   practical   experienced

---

2 Think of definitions for five of the negative words and test your partner.

Example
Someone who can't read is …

3 Complete the rules of use for these three prefixes.

a *il–* is used before words which begin with the letter _____ .

b *ir–* is used before words which begin with the letter _____ .

c *im–* is generally used before words which begin with the letter _____ .

4 **11.8** Mark the stress on the words. Does the stress change when the prefix is added? Listen and check your ideas.

5 Fill the gaps in these sentences with the correct form of the words in brackets. You will need to add a prefix.

Example
*Caroline's such a **disagreeable** person. She's always so unpleasant.* (agree)

a The decision was totally _____ . We were really surprised by it. (expect)

b She was _____ dressed for the cold weather and had to borrow a sweater. (appropriate)

c The boy's mother reported his _____ to the police. (appear)

d The _____ of winning the lottery does not stop people buying a ticket. (probable)

e He writes so _____ that even he can't read what he's written. (legible)

Prefixes and other meanings

1 Match the prefixes in italics with their meanings **a–g**. Use the example sentences 1–7 to help you.

1 ☐ *over*   a many
2 ☐ *anti*   b of, or by oneself
3 ☐ *multi*   c again or back
4 ☐ *auto*   d against
5 ☐ *re*   e not enough
6 ☐ *mis*   f too much
7 ☐ *under*   g badly or wrongly

1 I left the vegetables cooking for an hour. So I'm afraid they were *over*cooked.

2 If you want your car to start in the winter you need to use *anti*freeze.

3 America is a *multi*racial society. There are people there from all over the world.

4 His *auto*biography, which took him three years to write, will be published soon.

5 I'll *re*wind the tape so that you can listen another time.

6 I thought the meeting was tomorrow, not today. I obviously *mis*understood.

7 The strikers demanded more money, saying that they were grossly *under*paid.

2 Fill the gaps in these sentences with one of the prefixes in 1 and answer the questions.

a They're going to build another _____ storey car park in the city centre.
What are most city car parks like this?

b The captain took his hands off the controls and put the plane on _____ pilot.
At what point in the flight would / wouldn't the pilot do this?

c The new _____ malaria drug is 99 per cent effective against the disease.
What general name is given to drugs like penicillin which are used to fight particular diseases?

d I have frequently had to pay too much in shops but I have never been _____ charged.
What do you do if you are asked to pay too much or too little in a shop?

e The flight was _____ booked and we had to wait for the next one.
In what other situations can this happen? Why?

f The secretary spilt coffee on the letters and had to _____ type them.
What other reasons might there be for doing this?

g I haven't lost my glasses – I've just _____ placed them.
How could you describe people who do this regularly?

Language in action

Likes and dislikes

Eavesdrop!

Look at the picture and guess the answers to these questions.

- Who are the people?
- Where are they?
- What are they doing?

Listening 1

1 a **11.9** Listen and check your ideas.

b What are these people going to do soon?

2 Work in groups of four. Listen to the conversation again.

Student A Listen and note down expressions one person uses to say they like something.

Student B Listen and note down expressions used to say they dislike something.

Student C Listen and note down expressions used to give preferences.

Student D Listen and note down expressions used to give examples.

Tell each other the expressions you heard. Make lists with the following headings:

- expressing likes
- expressing dislikes
- expressing preferences
- giving examples.

Listening 2

1 **11.10** You are going to listen to two more conversations in which people are talking about their likes and dislikes. As you listen, answer these questions.

▨ Conversation 1 ▨

a What is the subject of the conversation?

b What different types are mentioned?

c What type does each speaker like?

▨ Conversation 2 ▨

d What is the subject of the conversation?

e What does the man like about the person he describes?

f What does the woman dislike about the person she describes?

2 **11.11** Read and listen to the extracts from the conversations on the next page.

a Mark any words or expressions used to:
  - express likes
  - express dislikes
  - express preferences
  - give examples.

b Add the marked expressions to the lists you have already made.

Extract 1

J   Well, I must say I prefer this, something a bit sort of gentle, classical. Puts you in the right mood, doesn't it?

S   This is sort of, a bit lift music, isn't it? Don't you prefer something a bit more …

J   It is a bit muzak, isn't it? Yes, yes. Oh no, I can't stand that either. That's awful …

S   Anonymous …

Ju Mmm, yeah, a bit bland …

J   You're right, you're right. No, no, no, I like jazz, actually. I'm really fond of jazz.

R   Yes, I rather like that. It's good. I particularly like flamenco, though. That's what I like.

J   Oh, do you?

R   Yeah, yeah.

J   Oh, that's exciting.

R   Your Paco de Lucias and all that sort of business, screaming, and wailing. It's a bit like heavy metal, I suppose … without the amplifiers.

S   I'm afraid I really like folk music, I'm afraid …

R   Oh!

S   Do you?

Ju Yeah, Yeah, folk's pretty good.

S   Is it?

Ju Yeah.

J   Oh, no, no …

R   I've never liked that …

J   I never listen to that, no.

S   I mean, not, not sort of not, not, not boring traditional …

Ju Not traditional folk …

S   Not traditional …

Ju … but, yeah, trendy folk …

S   Right, yeah, yeah …

J   No, that's not my thing at all. Oh, gosh, no, no. I think jazz, really. And I hate pop.

Ju Yes …

Extract 2

B   Have I met him?

S   I don't think so, no. Erm, you might have seen him once when you came round to our house. No, he's a really great bloke, he's … what I particularly like about him is that he's, that he's always in a good mood, he's, he's quite difficult to sort of, to, to ruffle, he never gets bad-tempered, the sort of person, you know that you can ring up, erm, late at night and is, and just sort of, you know, pour your heart out to him, he's, he's a great bloke.

B   So, is he your best friend, then?

S   Yeah, I suppose so. He's certainly one of my oldest friends and I suppose if I … it's not quite the same when … you're older to talk about best friends, but he is a very good friend, yeah, yeah.

B   Mm.

S   I mean, just another example. He's, erm, the sort of person, you know, if you, if you break down in your car and you're miles from anywhere and … you can always ring him up and say, you know, 'I'm stuck. Can you help me out?' and if he can, you know, if he can he will …

B   That's really important, yeah.

S   Yeah, yeah.

Features of natural conversation

In Extract **2** the man frequently uses the word *you*. Find three different examples of its use. Explain what *you* means or who it refers to in each case.

Practice

1   **11.12** Listen and repeat these expressions of likes, dislikes, and preferences.

   a   I hate (pop). It's awful.
   b   I can't stand (heavy metal).
   c   I've never liked (opera).
   d   (Folk?) That's not my thing at all.
   e   I'm not that keen on (classical music).
   f   I'd rather listen to (jazz) than (folk).
   g   I prefer (folk) to (jazz).
   h   I really like (reggae).
   i   I'm really fond of (salsa).
   j   I particularly like (flamenco).

2   **11.13** Listen and respond to the questions using expressions **1a–j**.

3   Work in pairs or groups. Ask each other questions to find out if you like the same kinds of music. When you answer, try to use some of the expressions in **1**.

Exploitation

Work in groups. In each situation everyone should express their real likes and dislikes.

Situation 1

You want to go on a day trip together. Try to agree on when to go and what type of day trip you want. When you have made these two decisions, try to agree on precisely where to go and what to do.

Situation 2

You want to go out for the evening together. Try to agree on two different activities, for example, the cinema and a restaurant, or a bar and a disco. When you have decided on the kinds of activities, try to agree which film, restaurant, bar, or disco to go to.

Writing

1 You are going to write a review of a film or an album.

  a First, think about the main differences between expressing general personal preferences in conversation and in a written review.

Spoken language

J   I'm really fond of jazz.

R   Yes, I rather like that. It's good. I particularly like flamenco, though. That's what I like.

J   Oh, do you?

R   Yeah, yeah.

J   Oh, that's exciting.

R   Your Paco de Lucias and all that sort of business … It's a bit like heavy metal, I suppose … without the amplifiers.

Writing

> In my opinion, Paco de Lucia's latest album is not as good as his classic *Entre dos aguas*, but it is certainly worth a listen.
>
> As usual, de Lucia's guitar playing is absolutely superb and his amazing voice adds the passion and excitement typical of flamenco music. Flamenco can be repetitive and unimaginative, but for me de Lucia's music is completely original. He wrote and produced all fourteen tracks on this album, every one is different and I would say brilliant in its own way.
>
> If you are already a fan of de Lucia, you probably bought this one as soon as it came out. If you're new to flamenco, I suggest you go out and buy it today.

  b Underline all the opinion and preference language in the conversation and the written review.

  c In spoken English, speakers tend to overuse words like *good* and *boring* when they give an opinion about something. What alternative words could you use?

▶ **Writing guidelines p.158**

2 Write one of these reviews.

Review 1

Write a short review of your favourite album or an album you have bought recently. Follow this paragraph plan.

1   Give the name of the album and the singer / group and briefly give your opinion.

2/3 Choose two or three things that you like or dislike about the album. Give your opinions and use descriptive language.

4   Make a final comment which summarizes or repeats the opinion you gave in paragraph 1.

Review 2

Write a short review of a film you have seen recently. Follow this paragraph plan.

1   Give the name of the film and the actors and director. Say what kind of film it is and give a brief personal opinion.

2/3 Describe the plot and characters briefly. Then choose two or three things which you liked or disliked about the film. Give your opinions and use descriptive language.

4   Make a final comment on the film summarizing or repeating the opinion you gave in paragraph 1.

3 Exchange your review with someone who has written the same type of review as you.

  a Read each other's reviews and think about these questions.
- Is there an appropriate balance between descriptive and opinion language?
- Is there enough information?
- Do you want to listen to the music or see the film after reading the review?

  b Discuss each other's reviews. Make any suggestions for improvement.

  c Rewrite your review including any improvements.

Unit 11 Summary

In this unit you have worked on the following language points.

- [ ] Causatives
- [ ] Causative verbs and the passive; non-causative use of *have something done*
- [ ] Question tags
- [ ] Word-building: prefixes

- [ ] Expressing likes, dislikes, and preferences
- [ ] Giving examples
- [ ] Writing a review

Tick ✓ the points you are confident about and cross ✗ the ones you need to revise.

Preview

Your thoughts

Work in pairs. Discuss the connection between these illustrations and the title of the unit, *Communication*.

Reading

1 How are these words and phrases related to the theme of communication? Discuss possible connections.

a marriage proposal   voice-sensitive (machine)   chatter   gossip   silence   conversation

2 Now read these short texts and match them with three of the illustrations.

1 *He told Polly he had missed her over the summer and then, quite out of the blue, he asked her if she would marry him. At first she didn't take him seriously, and found it difficult to stop herself giggling. However, Edward was quite serious and repeated his proposal in a distinctly solemn tone of voice. Polly said to herself that being Edward's wife would not be an easy option, but despite this, she told him that she loved him and accepted his offer.*

2 The sure sign of a technology's maturity is its arrival in the kitchen and, hot on the heels of the microwave oven, comes the listening appliance. Many people already talk to their appliances – in puzzlement ('Where's the liquidizer?'), or impatience ('Come on, boil!'), but few expect a reaction. That is now changing, as an American company showed when they demonstrated prototypes of their voice-sensitive oven and fridge. In answer to questions from a digital display, the user replies with something like 'chicken', or '7.30', whereupon the oven will do everything except open the door.

3 How much time did you waste yesterday, chattering? Probably about a quarter of your entire day. And what came of it? Probably not a lot. Most of it was almost certainly gossip. It's an odd thing, language. We find it intensely embarrassing to remain silent in company. We look around desperately for something to say, however meaningless. And apparently there's a curious difference between men's and women's conversations. Harry, it seems, likes to talk about Harry, while Sally talks about Susan. Ah, yes, you say, everyone's stereotypes confirmed. Well, yes, but the interesting question is why this is so.

Person to person

1 Do you agree that men's and women's conversations are different? How would you explain the difference?

2 What kinds of conversation do you enjoy most?

3 Do you find it embarrassing to remain silent in company?

Grammar – Reported speech review

1 a Here are some examples of reported speech. What were the speaker's words?
   1 He told Polly that he had missed her over the summer …
   2 Polly said to herself that being Edward's wife would not be an easy option …
   3 She said that she spent a couple of hours every day talking to the neighbours.
   4 He said that he was going to buy a voice-sensitive fridge the following week.

b Look at the sentences in **1a**. What do they illustrate about reported speech? Think about:
   • tense changes
   • pronouns
   • time references.

2 Look carefully at the verbs in these sentences. How does the verb tense used affect the meaning of the sentences?
   a He *said* he *had missed* her.
   b He *said* he *missed* her.
   c He *said* he *misses* her.
   d He *says* he *misses* her.
   e He *says* he *missed* her.

3 a Here are some ways of reporting questions. What were the speaker's actual words or thoughts in each case?
   1 He asked her whether she would marry him.
   2 He inquired where she wanted to go for the honeymoon.
   3 She wondered why he wanted to marry her.
   4 She wanted to know if he had been married before.

b What do these sentences tell you about word order in reported questions?

▶ **Language commentary p.137**

Check

4 Change these direct speech sentences into reported speech.
   a 'Have you seen Laura recently?' Chris asked Paul.
   b 'Yes, I have,' said Paul.
   c 'I spoke to her on the phone yesterday.'
   d 'I'm meeting her in town this afternoon,' he said.
   e 'Can you tell her to give me a ring?' asked Chris.
   f 'I'll tell her if I remember,' said Paul.

▶ Reported speech: reporting verbs   p.117
▶ Infinitives or gerunds after verbs   p.119

Listening

1 Look at the photograph. The man on the left is Mikhail Gorbachev and the man on the right is Ronald Reagan.

   a What do you know about them?

   b Who do you think the man in the middle is?

   c Why were meetings like this one so important in late 20th-century history?

The Go-between

2 Read this text. Does it give any more information about the answers to the questions in **1a–c**?

> The role of the interpreter in our century has become ever more crucial, though that's only imperfectly understood outside those tiny groups at the summit. Pavel Paleshenko was always one of the most unobtrusive figures, even when he was pictured standing at the shoulders of the two presidents. He was with Mikhail Gorbachev for many years before and after he became the President of the Soviet Union.

3 You are going to hear two people talking about a TV interview with a top American interpreter. Predict how these words and phrases will be used by the speakers.

the United Nations   nervous   proud   concentration
responsibility   international crisis   body language
facial expressions   world peace   brain   instant decision

As you listen

4 **12.1** Listen and check your ideas.

5 Listen to the conversation again. Answer these questions from information in the recording.

   a What is the role of the interpreter in international politics?

   b What is the relationship like between the interpreter and the person they speak for?

   c What are the main problems and rewards of being an interpreter?

Interpretation

1 The interpreter said the president he worked for was *just a normal person*. What do you think he means by this?

2 What kind of *international crisis* could be caused by a translation mistake?

3 How could a politician get across his message without speaking?

Vocabulary

Discuss these questions about the language used in the conversation.

   a What is the meaning of the word *funny* in:
   That's **funny** – There was a programme about international relations on TV last night.

   b Why does John use the words *claimed* and *apparently*?
   … he **claimed** they were good friends.
   … **apparently** his first job was an official visit to Moscow …

   c What does the word *cool* mean here?
   … that first meeting had been pretty **cool** …

   d What is *show-biz* short for?
   … he implied that the president really loved the **show-biz** side of the job.

Speaking personally

1 Would you like to be an interpreter? Why? Why not?

2 Which aspects of the job would you like and which would you dislike?

3 If you could work closely with or for a famous person, who would you choose? Why?

Reported speech: reporting verbs

Exploring concepts

1 a Underline the reporting verbs in these sentences.

1 *… he said he was just a normal person, – he claimed they were good friends.*

2 *… he confirmed that first meeting had been pretty cool, …*

3 *… he admitted he felt quite proud of the part he'd played.*

4 *… he did concede that interpreting at that level takes incredible concentration.*

5 *He explained that … the speakers themselves can use body language …*

6 *… he implied that the president really loved the show-biz side of the job.*

7 *He thought that the president had made a real contribution to world peace.*

b Think about the meanings of the different reporting verbs. What do you think the interpreter's actual words were?

2 Here are some more ways of reporting what people have said.

a How are sentences **5** and **7** grammatically different from the other sentences?

1 Her mother *advised* her to study languages at university.

2 His teachers *told* him to work harder.

3 The police *warned* me not to tell anyone what I'd seen.

4 He left her penniless even though she *begged* him to stay.

5 She *insisted* she had paid for everything.

6 The judge *ordered* him to repay the money he had stolen.

7 He *denied* that he had stolen any money.

b What did the speakers say in each of the sentences in 2a? Think about the meaning of the reporting verbs. For example, to work out the direct speech form of sentence 1, think about different ways of giving advice.
I think you should study languages at university.
You really ought to study languages at university.
If I were you, I'd study languages at university.

▶ **Language commentary p.138**

Exploitation

1 a **12.2** You are going to listen to someone talking about learning a foreign language. Listen to the first part of the interview.

1 Which languages does she mention?

2 Which two phrases can she say in one of the languages?

b Turn the interviewer's questions and Jo's replies into reported speech using the reporting verbs in brackets.

1 **Int** Jo, can you speak a foreign language? (ask)

2 **Jo** No. (reply)

3 **Int** Why not? (want to know)

4 **Jo** I don't know. I tried at school. (say / claim)

5 **Jo** Now, I start off fine, everything is OK, then I get to a stage when I realize that everyone around me is talking in a language (explain)

6 and I don't know what they're talking about. (admit)

2 a Work in pairs. Read the interviewer's rather formal report of the second part of the interview with Jo. What did Jo and the interviewer actually say to each other? Write their conversation.
Student A Write the interviewer's questions.
Student B Write Jo's replies.

I wondered whether Jo blamed her bad ear, or whether it was simply that she didn't have the motivation because she didn't have to speak it very often.
She said that wasn't the case and confirmed that she would like very much to learn another language. She claimed that she loved hearing Italian spoken. She thought it was an absolutely beautiful language and she would love to be able to speak it. When I asked her if there were any other languages she liked, she said that she also liked German. When she had tried to learn it, she had really enjoyed it, but she just couldn't make progress. I asked her why she thought that was, and she said she seemed to have a total blank when it came to learning languages, but she insisted that she had tried.

b Now read your questions and answers together.

c Listen to the second part of the interview and compare it with your version.

3 Write sentences about the following things.

a The best advice you've ever received on three of these subjects.
• driving a car
• cooking
• taking exams
• making new friends
• job interviews
• learning a language

b Some of the things your teachers or your parents used to tell you to do, or warn you not to do.

c Compare your sentences with a partner, then tell each other more about the occasions you have described.

Free speech

4 Tell a partner what you can remember about two of the following.

a The last conversation you had with a member of your family.

b A conversation you overheard in a public place, e.g. on a train or in a shop.

c A recent conversation with someone you work with, e.g. your boss or a colleague.

d The last conversation you had with a child.

Reading

1 What do you think the connection could be between these two photographs? Compare your ideas with a partner.

As you read

2 Check your ideas and answer these questions.

a What kind of text is this? What is its purpose?

b Find verbs in the text which describe the activities in the photographs.

Close up

1.4 What do you think is meant by the term *nitty-gritty*? There are many double words like this in English: *walkie-talkie* and *teeny-weeny* are two more. Do you know any others?

1.6 + 1.14 How are the two words *species* and *crucial* pronounced? Use a dictionary to check.

1.8 What are the meanings of *in* and *out* in the phrase *who's in and who's out*?

1.13 To *witter* (*on*) means to talk in a particular way. Guess the meaning from the context then check in a dictionary. What does the word *on* add to the meaning?

1.28 What is the meaning and pronunciation of *coalition*?

Did you hear about ...?

Research has shown that two-thirds of human conversation is taken up not with discussion of the cultural or political problems of the day, not animated debates about films we've just watched or books we've just finished reading, and certainly not nitty-gritty matters like where our next meal is coming from, but
5   plain and simple gossip.

Language is our greatest treasure as a species, and what do we habitually do with it? We gossip. About who's doing what with whom, and whether it's a good or a bad thing; who's in and who's out – and why; how to deal with difficult social situations involving children,
10 lovers, and colleagues.

So why are we obsessed with gossiping about one another? Are we just natural wasters, of both time and words? Or do we witter on about nothing in particular simply to avoid facing up to the really crucial issues of
15 life? Not according to Professor Robin Dunbar. In fact, in his latest book, *Grooming, Gossip and the Evolution of Language*, the psychologist and anthropologist says gossip is one of these really crucial issues.

Dunbar rejects the conventional view that language
20 was developed by the men in primitive societies in order to coordinate their manly hunting activities more effectively, or even to facilitate the exchange of poetic stories about tribal origins and the supernatural. Instead he suggests that language evolved among women. We don't spend two-thirds of our time
25 gossiping just because we can talk, argues Dunbar – on the contrary, he goes on to say, language evolved specifically to allow us to gossip.

Dunbar arrived at his cheery theory by studying the behaviour of the higher primates like monkeys. By means of grooming, monkeys form coalitions with other individuals on whom they can rely for support in the event of some kind
30 of conflict within the group or attack from outside it.

As we human beings are descended from a particular branch of the primate family, Dunbar concludes that at one time in our history we did much the same. Grouping together made sense because the bigger the group, the greater the protection it provided; on the other hand, the bigger the group, the greater the
35 stresses and strains of living in close proximity to others. Grooming, which stimulates the production of the body's natural opiates, helped to ease those tensions and calm everybody down.

But as the groups got bigger and bigger, the amount of time spent in grooming activities also had to be extended to maintain its effectiveness. Clearly,
40 a more efficient kind of grooming was needed, and thus language evolved as a kind of vocal grooming which allowed humans to bond with ever-larger groups by exchanging information over a wider network of individuals than would be possible by one-to-one physical contact.

The Irish Times

Comprehension

1 What are the traditional explanations for the purpose of human language?

2 How is Professor Dunbar's explanation different from this?

3 How is language more efficient than grooming?

Speaking personally

1 Do you enjoy gossiping? Do you find it relaxing? Does it help you to bond with other people?

2 What are your favourite topics of conversation? Do you talk about different things depending on who you are with?

Infinitives or gerunds after verbs

Exploring concepts

Some verbs are followed by an infinitive (*to* + verb) and others are followed by a gerund (*-ing* form).

*… debates about films we've just watched or books we've just **finished reading** …*

*… on the contrary, he **goes on to say**, language evolved specifically to allow us to gossip.*

1 These verbs are always followed by either the infinitive or the gerund. Write a list for each.

agree	attempt	can't help	choose	consider	decide
deny	dislike	expect	fail	hope	imagine	learn	miss
offer	postpone	pretend	prevent	put off	refuse	resist
risk	threaten				

2 The verbs in sentences **a–e** can be followed by either the infinitive or the gerund. In four of these sentences there is no difference in meaning. In one sentence, the choice of the infinitive or the gerund changes the meaning. What are the different meanings in this sentence?

a I'm not a morning person. I prefer *to work / working* at night.

b He started *to play / playing* tennis when he was seven years old.

c He went on *to represent / representing* his country at the Olympic Games.

d I didn't like *to admit / admitting* that I'd fallen asleep during the film.

e He continued *to read / reading* until he fell asleep.

3 Here are some more verbs where the choice of the infinitive or the gerund affects the meaning. What are the different meanings in these pairs of sentences?

a 1 Thank goodness I remembered *to book* our flight to New York.

   2 I remember *booking* the tickets. I did it by phone yesterday morning.

b 1 On the way home we stopped *to give* our friends a lift.

   2 Many drivers have stopped *giving* lifts to hitch-hikers.

c 1 We regret *to announce* that all flights to New York have been cancelled.

   2 I regret *travelling* by plane now. Flying always makes me feel ill.

d 1 Where have you been? I've been trying *to ring* you all day.

   2 I was in a meeting. You should have tried *ringing* my mobile number.

e 1 Sorry. I shouldn't have said that. I didn't mean *to offend* you.

   2 I'm sorry, but I'm going to say something even if it means *offending* him.

▶ **Language commentary p.139**

Exploitation

1 a Make up different endings to these sentences about yourself. Continue each sentence with an infinitive or a gerund as appropriate.

   1 When I am older I hope …
   2 I'm the sort of person who can't resist …
   3 I've never denied …
   4 Within the next five years I'm going to learn …
   5 I'd always refuse …
   6 When I'm away from home I miss …

   b Compare your sentences with a partner.

Free speech

2 Work in pairs. Using your own experience and ideas, discuss these topics.

   • The best way to give up doing something you enjoy when you know it's not good for you.
   • An occasion when you forgot to do something really important.
   • Something you'll always regret doing.
   • Something you tried to do but failed.
   • Something you expect to happen in your country in the next 25 years.

Compound nouns

1 Compound nouns are made up of two or more words which together function as nouns. Underline the compound nouns in these extracts.
(There are ten compound nouns altogether.)

Example
Football scandal: <u>goalkeeper</u> bribed to lose matches

  a Drug-smuggling: university students confess
  b Church leader mobbed at airport
  c You have complained to the postman and written to your post office, but …
  d Find out more details and ask to be sent a job application form.
  e You are a garage receptionist. One of your responsibilities is …
  f Did they ask him what sort of part he had played in the summit meetings?
  g I've been taken ill … and I believe I've had food poisoning.

2 Referring to sentences **1a–g**, correct these statements about compound nouns.

  a Compound nouns are formed from two nouns.
  b An -s is added to both words to form the plural of compound nouns.
  c The words that form compound nouns are written as separate words.

3 Compound nouns are often used in preference to longer phrases. For example, it is more natural to say *a toothbrush* than *a brush for cleaning your teeth*, and *the town centre* is better than *the centre of the town*.

  a What compound nouns could be used instead of the phrases in *italics* in these sentences?
    1 I've always wanted to be a *reporter for a newspaper*.
    2 On several occasions I've spent the night in a *cell in a prison*.
    3 As soon as I saw the *advertisement in the newspaper*, I wrote off for further information and a *description of the job*.
    4 *Drivers of cars* should take a test every ten years.
    5 *Addiction to drugs* is a problem in most countries of the world.
  b **12.3** Listen and check your ideas.

4 a Listen to the sentences again and repeat the compound nouns. Write them down and mark the stress.
  b Look at the illustrations and answer the questions with a compound noun, using the right stress.

    1 What is this person's job?
    2 What's the name of the thing that you make tea in?
    3 What kind of tree is this?
    4 What's the name of this part of a television?
    5 What day is this for this couple?
    6 What is this?
  c **12.4** Listen and check your answers.

5 Compound nouns formed from an adjective and a noun have a special meaning which is different from the separate meanings of the same two words.
What's in that blue bottle? It's not poison, is it?
Here, *blue bottle* means a bottle which is blue.
That bluebottle is really annoying me. It's been flying round the room for hours.
Here, *bluebottle* means a kind of large, noisy fly.

  a Look at these five pairs and mark the parts that are stressed. (The second in each pair is the compound noun. If you don't know the meaning of any of these compounds, check in a dictionary.)
    1 a black bird / a blackbird
    2 a green house / a greenhouse
    3 a long jump / the long jump
    4 a heavy weight / a heavyweight
    5 a short list / a short-list
  b **12.5** Listen and decide which words from the list you hear.

Language in action

On the telephone

Eavesdrop!

These three people are about to speak on the telephone to people they do not know. Look at the picture and guess the answers to these questions.

- Who are the people going to phone?
- What will the calls be about?
- How are the three people feeling?

Listening 1

1 a **12.6** Listen and check your ideas.

  b What was the exact purpose of each call?

2 Work in pairs. Listen to the telephone conversations again.

  Student A Listen to the person answering the call in each conversation. What telephone-answering expressions do the speakers use? Make a note of them.

  Student B Listen to the person making the call in each conversation. What telephone expressions do the speakers use? Make a note of them.

  Tell each other the expressions you heard. Make lists with the following headings:

  - answering telephone calls
  - making telephone calls.

3 Listen again and make a list of any expressions the speakers use when they are playing for time or can't think of what to say. The most common example is *Er …* or *Erm*.

Listening 2

1 **12.7** You are going to listen to two more telephone conversations. As you listen, answer these questions.

  a Who are the people making the calls?
  b What is the purpose of the calls?
  c What is the mood or attitude of the callers?

2 Listen again and read the extracts from the conversations on the next page.

  a Mark the expressions used to:
  - answer telephone calls
  - make telephone calls
  - play for time.

  b Add the marked expressions to the lists you have already made.

Conversation 1

J … rather ill, erm, and I'd like to make a personal complaint to him.

H I see. If you'd like to hold on just one moment, I'll put you through to his secretary.

J Thank you.

Ju Hello. Can I help you?

J Yes, as I've just explained to your colleague, I'd like to speak to Mr James, please, urgently.

Ju Oh, I'm afraid he's not in today. Can I help you?

J No, you can't. I want to speak to Mr James, the Chairman of the company, please. It's rather urgent. I've been taken ill on one of your airlines and I believe I've had food poisoning. Now, can I speak to Mr James in person, please?

Ju Well, I'm very sorry, he's not in today. Maybe someone else can help you if I can't, but I'm sure if you give me all the details, I'll be able to help you.

J Well, there's nothing more that I can say, other than I've been to my doctor and the tests have shown that I have had food poisoning on your airline. I'd like to speak to Mr James in person and nobody else. Thank you.

Ju Oh, well, I see. I'm very sorry, but erm, I'm afraid you just can't. I can put you through to his Personal Assistant if you really insist.

J Yes, I do. Thank you.

Ju OK, well, if you'd like to hold on.

Conversation 2

K … and I really want to talk to somebody about it.

H I see. Can you tell me when you wrote to us?

K Er, it was, er, it was two weeks ago. And the bill came yesterday, so really you should have, er, you know, sorted it out by now. Er, is it possible to talk to somebody?

H No, I'm afraid not at the moment. Erm, can you tell me how much the bill was for?

K Well, er, er, well it was for £28.30, but I, I really need to speak to somebody, erm, who can do something about this, erm. I'm going to be going away for a week, erm, and I don't want you to invoice me again.

H I see. And you say that you've paid this twice?

K No, I've paid it once but you're, you're invoicing me twice and I can't afford to pay it twice.

H Well, what I can do for you is I can leave a message with the person concerned and make sure that they don't invoice you again. And that the money isn't taken from your account.

K Well …

H Would that be all right?

K Well, that, that seems fine, but I mean, will somebody get back to me and let me know that … will confirm that with me?

H Yes, certainly, but it won't be today.

K When will it be?

Features of natural conversation

1 a The expressions *I'm sorry* and *I'm afraid* are common in polite conversations. Find all the examples of these expressions in the extracts.

b Which of the uses of *I'm sorry* are real apologies? What does *I'm afraid* mean?

2 The expression *I see* is used several times in the two conversations. When is it used and what does it mean?

3 At the end of **Conversation 1**, Julie uses an unfinished conditional sentence as a polite way of telling someone to do something.

OK, well, **if you'd like to hold on.**

a How could she have finished this sentence?

b What other more direct ways of saying the same thing could she have used?

Practice

1 a `12.8` Listen to the telephone answering expressions. Which of the two speakers sounds more polite? How does the other speaker sound?

b `12.9` Listen and repeat the expressions.

2 a `12.10` Listen to the pairs of expressions. Which of the two speakers in each pair sounds determined but polite? How does the other speaker sound?

b Listen and repeat the expressions.

Exploitation

Role play

Work in pairs. Take turns to be the caller, **Student A**, and the person who answers the call, **Student B**. Sitting back-to-back with your partner will make these conversations more realistic.

Situation 1

Student A You regularly receive letters for your neighbours. You have complained to the postman and written to your local post office, but the situation has not improved. You have not received a reply to your letter.

Student B You work in the Complaints Department of the local post office. You are used to dealing with angry customers. Get as many factual details from the caller as you can and remain polite and calm at all times.

Situation 2

Student A You have seen details in the newspaper for a part-time job. You would like some extra evening work, but you are not available at weekends. Find out more details and ask to be sent a job application form.

Student B You work in the Personnel Department of a large company which employs full- and part-time workers. At the moment you are looking for people who can work on three evenings a week and on alternate weekends. You have already had a lot of interested callers.

Student A You are going abroad on business in two days and you have been advised to get your doctor to give you injections to protect you from diseases which are common in the country you are visiting. Phone the doctor's surgery to make an appointment.

Student B You are a doctor's receptionist. The doctors you work for are unusually busy at the moment and you have been told not to accept any more appointments for five days unless they are a matter of life and death.

Writing

1 You are going to practise taking telephone messages.

a First, think about the main similarities and differences between telephone conversations and a written telephone message.

Spoken language

Ju I'm afraid he's not in today. Can I help you?

J No, you can't. I want to speak to Mr James, the Chairman of the company, please. It's rather urgent. I've been taken ill on one of your airlines and I believe I've had food poisoning.

Writing

Phone message	URGENT
For:	Mr James
Time:	Tuesday 17 May 9.25 a.m.
From:	Mrs Radley – passenger
Contact:	5511217
Subject:	Food poisoning
Message:	Mrs Radley demanded to talk to you personally. She claims she was taken ill on one of our planes and believes she has had food poisoning.

b How is the speaker's impatience expressed in writing?

c Why is the reporting verb *claims* used?

d Why are the verb tenses *claims* (Present simple) and *was taken ill* (Past simple passive) used in preference to *claimed* (Past simple) and *had been taken ill* (Past perfect)?

▶ **Writing guidelines p.158**

2 **12.11** You are going to listen to four telephone conversations in which people leave messages. Listen and write each person's message.

3 Compare your messages with a partner.

a Have you used the same reported speech forms?

b How have you conveyed the speaker's attitude in each case?

Unit 12 Summary

In this unit you have worked on the following language points.

- ☐ Reported speech
- ☐ Reported speech: reporting verbs
- ☐ Infinitives or gerunds after verbs

- ☐ Compound nouns
- ☐ Expressions for making and answering telephone calls
- ☐ Expressions to use when you can't think of what to say
- ☐ Writing telephone messages

Tick ✓ the points you are confident about and cross ✗ the ones you need to revise.

Language commentary

Unit 1

▶ Present tenses

a Present simple

In general, the Present simple expresses the idea of permanence. Here are some common uses:

1 to refer to something that is always true.
   *… wood **does not conduct** heat well.*
2 to refer to a regular action or experience (habit).
   *I **attend** two or three conferences a year…*
3 to refer to future time when a timetable or schedule is involved.
   *I **fly** to New York on Sunday.*

b Present continuous

In general, the Present continuous refers to temporary actions or situations. Here are some common uses:

1 to refer to an action that is happening now – at the moment of speaking.
   *He**'s staring** at me and his tongue **is going** in and out.*
2 to refer to an action that is happening around now, but not necessarily at the moment of speaking.
   *I**'m going out** with a boy I was at school with.*
3 to refer to situations or trends that are true at the present time.
   *More and more people **are taking** it (fire-walking) **up** as a regular activity.*
4 with *always*, to refer to irritating habits or frequent but unplanned occurrences.
   *He**'s always losing** his keys.*
5 to refer to future arrangements.
   *We**'re meeting** our friends in Paris next Tuesday.*

Note Certain verbs are rarely used in the continuous form. See Action verbs and state verbs below.

▶ Aspect

Aspect is a term which describes the nature of an action. There are two aspects in English: the continuous (or progressive) aspect and the perfect aspect.

a Continuous aspect

We choose the continuous aspect when we want to make it clear that we are interested in the temporary or continuous nature of an action.
*He **was walking** home yesterday evening (when he was attacked).*
*I**'m reading** a book about computers (and I have got 20 more pages to read).*
*This time next week, I**'ll be sunbathing** on a beach in Australia.*

b Perfect aspect

We choose the perfect aspect when we want to show that a completed past action still has a connection with, or a relevance to, the present.
*I**'ve walked** home every night this week (and now I feel much healthier).*
*I**'ve read** three books about computers (so now I know a lot about the subject).*
Or a connection with, or a relevance to a more recent past time.
*By the time he was six, Mozart **had composed** many pieces of music.*

c Simple verbs

Verbs which are not continuous or perfect are called simple verbs. The simple form of a verb does not indicate a particular way of thinking. It conveys facts about the past or the present.
*I **walked** home yesterday evening.*
*I always **drink** coffee for breakfast.*

▶ Action verbs and state verbs

a Action verbs

Action verbs express the idea of activity or change.
*As I was driving home my car **skidded** and **crashed** into a tree.*
Here *driving, skidded,* and *crashed* are action verbs.
Action verbs are used in all forms.

b State verbs

State verbs refer to conditions rather than actions, and to situations which stay the same, or which only change slowly.
*Although I **have** lots of acquaintances, I **don't know** many people really well.*
*I **understand** Russian, but now I **want to** learn to speak it.*
Here *have, know, understand,* and *want* are state verbs. State verbs are not normally used in the continuous form.
There are five groups of state verbs.

Being	appear* seem exist* consist of involve look* mean resemble weigh*
Having	own belong contain hold* include* possess have involves
Opinions	agree believe consider* disagree doubt expect* hope* imagine*/ know presume* realize* suspect* think* understand
Feelings	dislike envy fear hate* like* love* mean* mind regret* respect trust
Senses	feel* hear taste see* smell*

*These can also be action verbs.

c Verbs with both state and action meanings

Some verbs with more than one meaning can be state verbs and action verbs. When they are used as action verbs, they can be used in the continuous form. (Here are some examples.)

1 weigh   I **weigh** 120 kilos. (This is how heavy I am.)
            The shopkeeper is **weighing** the fruit.
            (He is finding out how heavy it is.)
2 appear   He **appears** to be much happier than he was.
            (He seems happier.)
            He is **appearing** in Hamlet at the National
            Theatre. (He is acting in Hamlet.)
3 consider   Most people **consider** work to be important.
            (They think or believe this.)
            I am **considering** changing jobs.
            (I am thinking about the possibility.)
4 have   My sister **has** flu. (She is ill.)
            My sister is **having** lunch. (She is eating food.)

Unit 2

▶ Past simple and Past continuous

a Past simple

The Past simple is used to refer to:
1 completed actions or events that happened at a particular time in the past.
   *One Friday morning I **went** into a phone box, **rang** the fire brigade …*
2 completed actions or events which took place over a specified length of time in the past.
   *I **worked** in New York from January to May last year.*
3 actions that were habitual or repeated over a period of time.
   *He **looked** after me whenever my mother was at work.*

b Past continuous

The Past continuous is used to refer to:
1 actions or events in progress when another action took place.
   *She found the drink the next day when she **was doing** the housework.*
2 temporary actions which provide background information to a past event.
   *One particular afternoon I **was watching** television …*
3 two or more continuous actions in progress over the same period of time.
   *He **was dozing** in an armchair while I was playing with my toys.*
4 repeated actions which form a background to an action or event.
   *(At that time) I **was taking** medicine twice a day.*

▶ Past perfect

a Form

There are two forms of the Past perfect:
1 the Past perfect simple.
   *We arrived at the station ten minutes after the train **had left**.*
2 the Past perfect continuous.
   *I went to bed early last night. I'**d been travelling** since dawn.*

b Continuous

1 This is used to stress the continuity of an action.
   *I went to bed early last night. I'**d been travelling** since dawn.*
2 It also shows that an action was still in progress and had not been completed at a particular time in the past.
   *I'**d been waiting** for the train for over an hour when they announced that it had been cancelled.*
   This means I was still waiting when the announcement was made.

c Use

The Past perfect is used to:
1 clarify the order in which a number of past events happened. (They are often used with time conjunctions, like *when, after, as soon as* etc.).
   *When I'**d finished working**, I had breakfast.* (Here the use of the Past perfect shows that the speaker finished working and then had breakfast.)
2 say what was completed before a specific past time.
   *By seven o'clock this morning, I'**d done** three hours work.*
3 explain past events or situations.
   *I'**d eaten** hardly anything the day before, so I was really hungry.*
4 provide background information to past events or situations.
   *It **had been** a tiring day. I'**d been** working since five a.m. By midday, I was almost asleep.*

Note
1 In everyday use, once the sequence of past events has been established by one or two Past perfect verbs, speakers often use Past simple verbs.
   *The accident **happened** at three o'clock in the afternoon. I remember the day very well. We'**d left** home early and **had spent** the morning exploring the area. We **stopped** in a village and **had** lunch at a small hotel.*
2 Another common use of the Past perfect is in reported speech.
   Actual words: *I **wrote** to you last week.*
   Reported speech: *He said he **had written** to me the previous week.*

▶ used to / would

Both *used to* and *would* are used as alternatives to the Past simple, especially when we are remembering past habits and states or comparing the past with the present.

a *used to*

1 *used to* can refer to:
   repeated past actions that no longer happen, or that did not happen in the past but happen now.
   *In my parents' house, I **used to** suffer from repeated bouts of bronchitis … (But I'm better now.)*

2 past conditions or states that no longer exist, or that did not exist before but exist now.
   *She **used to** have long blonde hair.* (Now her hair is dark or short.)
   *I didn't **use to** like classical music.* (But I like it now.)

b *would*

would can refer to habitual past actions (like *used to*), but it cannot be used to refer to states.
*My grandfather **would** often talk about his childhood.*
NOT *My grandfather **would** have long hair and a beard.*

Note
1 *Used to* is like a regular Past simple verb.
   *I **used to** ride a bike.* (statement)
   *I didn't **use to** ride a bike.* (negative)
   *Did you **use to** ride a bike?* (question)
2 There are three negative forms of *used to*.
   *I **didn't use to** believe in ghosts.* – most common
   *I **used not to** believe in ghosts.* – less common / more formal
   *I **never used to** believe in ghosts.* – more emphatic
3 *used to* can only refer to general past time, not specific lengths of time in the past.
   *We **used to** live in Greece.* NOT *We **used to** live in Greece for ten years.*

Unit 3

▶ Futures – *will, going to*

a *will* + infinitive

The *will* future is used to express:
1 predictions or expectations.
   *Over the next 50 million years the continents **will break up**.*
2 future facts or certainties.
   *I'll **be** 22 next Friday. Can you come to my party?*
3 offers and spontaneous decisions about the immediate future.
   *Don't worry about catching the train. I'll **take** you home.*
4 promises and threats.
   *I'll **write** to you every single day.*
   *If you don't leave immediately, I'll **ring** the police.*

b *going to* + infinitive

The *going to* future is used to express:
1 predictions based on present evidence or prior knowledge.
   *We know from measuring the temperature that sea levels are **going to rise**.*
   *My sister is **going to have** a baby.*
2 future plans or intentions.
   *I'm **going to stop** listening to weather forecasts.*

c Other ways of expressing future ideas
1 The Present continuous is used to refer to definite future arrangements.
   *I'm **getting** married next Saturday.*
2 The Present simple is used to refer to a future timetable or schedule.
   *My plane **leaves** at three o'clock this afternoon.*

▶ Future continuous and Future perfect

a Future continuous

The Future continuous is used:
1 to predict actions or events in progress at a particular time in the future.
   *This time next year I'll **be studying** at university.*
   *In twenty years' time, he'll probably **be running** his own business.*
2 to predict probable future trends.
   *Fewer people **will be paying** tax.*
   *In the 21st century more and more people **will be working** from home.*

Note By contrast, the Future simple (*will*) predicts future facts.

3 to refer to fixed, decided plans, or actions that will happen in the normal course of events.
   *I'll **be seeing** Paul this evening. I'll tell him you called.*
   ***Will** you **be writing** to your sister this weekend?*

b Future perfect
1 There are two forms of the Future perfect: simple and continuous.
   *I'll **have finished** this book by tomorrow.*
   *On 23 April we'll **have been living** here for ten years.*
2 The Future perfect is used to refer to actions or events which will be completed before a particular time in the future.
   *By 2100 nations as we now know them **will have broken up**.*
   *When she retires next year, she'll **have been working** for the company for over forty years.*

▶ The language of contrast: *but, however, although*

We can use a number of words and phrases to express contrast.

a *although / (even) though*

These can be used to start a sentence or between clauses in a sentence.
***Even though** scientists have proved the earth is round, some people still think it's flat.*
*Some people still think the earth is flat, **although** scientists have proved that it's round.*
In conversation *though* is sometimes used at the end of a sentence.
*I've got a terrible headache. I'm still going to work, **though**.*

b *but*

But can introduce words, phrases or clauses.
*The challenge is not to cover 100m in the shortest time, **but** to cover it in one hour.*
*Some people think the earth is flat, **but** I know it's round.*

c *however*

However is more formal than *but*. It can be used in different sentence positions but it cannot link clauses in the same sentence.
Nadolny believes in slowness. **However**, *he insists that speed has its place.*
Nadolny believes in slowness. He insists, **however**, *that speed has its place.*
Nadolny believes in slowness. He insists that speed has its place, **however**.

d *in spite of / despite*

These are used to refer to a contrast that is surprising in view of what has already been said or shown.
In spite of / Despite *all the evidence, some people still think the earth is flat.*
In spite of / Despite *having* almost no money, we enjoyed our holiday.*
In spite of / Despite *the fact that we had no money, we enjoyed our holiday.*

Note *in spite of and *despite* can be followed by a noun or the *-ing* form of a verb.

e *instead (of)*

Instead introduces a contrasting alternative. It can be used in different ways.
Stop doing lots of things at once; **instead**, *do one thing at a time …*
Instead *of doing a lot of things at once, do one thing at a time.*
Stop doing a lot of things at once. Do one thing at a time, **instead**.

f *not*

Not expresses a definite, black-and-white contrast.
This year we're going to Italy for our holidays **not** *Spain.*
It is sometimes followed by another word or phrase to emphasise that contrast.
Not *everyone has two holidays a year.* **In fact / Actually** *most people don't even have one.*

g *rather than*

This is similar in meaning to *not*.
Slowness **rather than** *speed, patience rather than power, are the qualities needed to win …*

h *while / whereas*

These words are used to refer to a balance between contrasting facts or ideas. Both words can start a sentence or link clauses.
While / Whereas *most people prefer summer, my favourite season is winter.*
Most people enjoy sunbathing, **while / whereas** *I prefer sightseeing.*

Note *On the other hand* is similar to *while* and *whereas*, but (like *however*) it cannot link clauses in the same sentence.
I have to work long hours in my new job. **On the other hand**, *it's well paid.*

▍Unit 4

► Rules, needs, duties, and advice

Many of the verbs which are used to express rules, needs, duties, and advice are modal verbs. Here is a summary of their uses.

a *must*

1 *Must* is used for rules, law, or obligations and expresses the authority or strong feelings of the speaker or writer.
If you threaten your child, you **must** *carry out the threat.* (The speaker firmly believes this.)
All passengers **must** *wear seat belts.* (This is a law.)
I **must** *write to my sister.* (This an obligation I feel.)
2 *Must* can also be used to express feelings of enthusiasm or seriousness.
I've been shopping all day. I **must** *show you what I've bought.*
You **must** *believe me – it's the truth.*

b *have to / have got to*

Have to / have got to are also used for strong rules, laws and obligations. But unlike *must*, they express the authority of a third person, rather than the speaker. The speaker passes on the message.
Sorry, but you **have to** *wear a seatbelt in the car.* (I am not telling you to do this – I am just reminding you about the law.)
I've got to write to my sister. (This is a family duty – I am expected to write.)
Parents **have to** *send their children to school.* (This is an obligation imposed by society.)

Note *Have got to* is more informal than *have to*.

c *need to*

1 *Need to* is used to express an internal necessity rather than an obligation or a desire.
We're really tired – we **need to** *rest.*
To stay healthy people **need to** *have a balanced diet.*
2 *Need* can be followed by an *-ing* form verb instead of a passive verb.
The cat **needs** *feeding.* (The cat needs to be fed.)

d *ought to*

Ought to expresses moral obligation or responsibility, and is often used to give strong advice or to remind someone (including yourself) about a duty.
You **ought to** *set a good example (to your children).*
I know I **ought to** *tidy my room, but I haven't got the time.*

e *should*

Like *ought to*, *should* can be used to express moral obligation and to give advice, but is not quite as strong as *ought to*.
You **shouldn't** *ask your child to make decisions.*
You **should** *consult people before you make important decisions like that.*

f *want to*

Want to expresses a desire rather than a need.
*We **want to** play with our daughter when we get home but we're too tired.*

▶ Modal verbs: prohibition / no obligation

These negative forms express prohibition or absence of obligation.

a *mustn't*

Mustn't is used to express these ideas:
1 prohibition.
   *You **mustn't** drive without a licence.* (It is against the law.)
2 strong advice or warnings.
   *You **mustn't** look directly at the sun.* (I'm advising you for your own good.)
   *You **mustn't** say anything to anyone or we'll all be in terrible trouble.* (This is a warning.)

b *don't have to / needn't*

These both express lack of obligation or necessity.
*You **don't have to** say anything to anyone – you have the right to remain silent.* (There is no obligation to speak. You can if you like – It's your choice.)
*You **needn't** say anything to anyone. I'll do the talking.* (It's not necessary for you to speak.)
*You **needn't** phone Julia.* (It isn't necessary to phone her, because I've already phoned her. OR Julia's here, so you can talk to her.)

Note *Need* is an ordinary and a modal verb. There is no difference in meaning in the present, so you can use *Don't need to* + verb or *needn't* + verb.

c *needn't have / didn't need to*

These two forms have very different meanings.
1 *Needn't have* means it wasn't necessary but it happened anyway.
   *He **needn't have** come to meet me from school but he did because he enjoyed the walk.*
   (He came to meet me even though it wasn't necessary.)
2 *Didn't need to* means it wasn't necessary, so it didn't happen.
   *He **didn't need to** come and meet me from school, because he knew I was coming home with a friend.*
   (He didn't come to meet me, because it wasn't necessary.)

▶ Modal verbs: speculating about past events

These verbs are all used to speculate about, or explain past events.

a *must have / can't have*

Both express near certainty about something that happened or didn't happen in the past.
*Neanderthal Man **must have been** very artistic. The caves they lived in were covered in colourful drawings.*
(The colourful drawings are almost certain proof that these people were artistic.)

*Neanderthal Man **can't have been** very artistic. The walls of the caves they lived in were bare – there was no sign of any drawings.* (The lack of drawings on the cave walls is almost certain proof that these people were not artistic.)

b *may have / might have*

Both express possibility or uncertainty.
*The Cro-Magnons **may have killed** off Neanderthal Man.* (But we can't be sure – this is just a possibility.)
*They're late. I hope they're OK. I suppose they **may / might have missed** the train.*

Note *Might* suggests greater uncertainty or a weaker possibility than *may*.

Unit 5

▶ Conditionals

There are five common conditional sentence patterns in English, each with its own meaning and sequence of verb tenses.

a Zero conditional

The zero conditional refers to what (always) happens under certain conditions.
*If I **get** money for my birthday, I **put** it straight in the bank.* (This is what I do every birthday.)

b First conditional

1 The first conditional refers to possible, or likely future situations.
   *If I **win** the lottery, I'll **spend** all the money on a luxury holiday.*
   (I think it is quite possible that I will win.)
2 This form can also express warnings, threats or promises.
   *If you don't **look** after your money, you **may end up** in serious trouble.*
3 It can also be used to give instructions.
   *If you **see** my brother, **tell** him to phone me.*

c Second conditional

1 The second conditional refers to possible but improbable future situations.
   *If I **won** the lottery, I'd **spend** all the money on a luxury holiday.*
   (I think it is unlikely that I will win.)
2 The second conditional can also refer to unreal or impossible situations.
   *If I **were** a man, I'd **have** a beard.* (But I'm not!)

Note It is also possible to say *If I was …* In formal English *were* is more correct.

d Third conditional

The third conditional refers to imaginary past situations and is used to speculate about how past events or actions might have been different.

*If I'd **won** the lottery, I **might have** bought a new house.*
*If only I **hadn't lent** you my CD, you **wouldn't have** heard that song.*

▶ The verb *wish*

The verb *wish* is followed by these verb patterns to refer to different situations.

a *wish* + Past simple / Past continuous

This is used to express wishes about present situations or states. These constructions are often used to show dissatisfaction or a desire for things to be different.

1 It can refer to situations or states that cannot possibly change.
   *I **wish** I didn't have such big feet.*
   *I **wish** I wasn't the oldest child in my family.*
2 It can also refer to situations which could possibly change in the future.
   *I **wish** I had enough money to buy an Armani shirt.*
   *I **wish** you were coming on holiday with us.*

b *wish* + Past perfect

This is used to express wishes or regrets about something in the past which cannot now be changed.
*I **wish** I **hadn't** cut the label off (my jeans) now.*
*I **wish** I'd got a job instead of going to university. I don't enjoy studying.*

c *wish* + would

This is used to express annoyance or impatience about things outside the speaker's control. It is often used for complaints.
*I **wish** that dog **would** stop barking. (It's getting on my nerves.)*
*I **wish** you'd drive more carefully. I'm frightened of having an accident.*

Note
1 Some other ways of expressing regrets are:
   a *regret + -ing*
      *I really **regret drinking** / **having drunk** so much coffee at bedtime.*
   b *I'm sorry*
      *I'm **sorry** I didn't phone you earlier.*
      *I'm **sorry** I can't come to your party.*
   c *if only* can be used instead of *I wish*.
      *If **only** I didn't have such big feet. (I wish I didn't have …)*
      *If **only** I could come to your party. (I wish I could …)*
2 *I wish I would* is not possible, because this is within the speaker's control to change the situation. This conversation shows the alternative:
   John *I **wish** you'd stop smoking. It's giving me a terrible cough.*
   Paul *I **wish** I could stop. I know it's an unhealthy habit.*

▶ Mixed conditional sentences

Whereas third conditional sentences refer entirely to past situations, mixed conditional sentences are used to relate something that did or didn't happen in the past to a present situation.
*If my parents **had had** more money, I'd probably **be** more worried about what I wear now.*
*If I **hadn't accepted** a lift in your car, I **would be** lying in hospital now.*

Note Grammatically, mixed conditional sentences combine a third conditional *if*-clause with a second conditional main clause.

▶ Past verbs with present or future meaning

Past verb forms do not always refer to past time. They sometimes refer to the present or the future. This is usually when something unreal, imaginary, or improbable is being referred to. Here are some uses:

a in second conditional sentences.
   *If you **talked** to the other animals, you'd probably find they feel the same way …*
b to express a desire for things to be different.
   *I wish we **had** more time.*
   *If only I **didn't** feel so guilty.*
c with *I'd prefer / I'd rather*.
   *I'd rather you **didn't** stare at me like that.*
   *I'd prefer it if you **smoked** outside.*
d to refer to unreal or imaginary present or future situations.
   *Suppose / Supposing you **had** enough money to give up your job?*
   *Imagine / Pretend you **didn't** have to go to work.*
   What if we said we were poor students?
   1 *She looks as if she **was** about to fall asleep, but she's probably thinking about something important.*
   2 *It's time we **went** to bed.*
   3 *We've **got** to get up early in the morning.*

Note
1 This is similar to a second conditional *if*- clause.
2 *As if* and *as though* + past verbs are used to describe what a situation seems like but isn't. These phrases can also be followed by the present.
   *You look **as if** you are about to fall asleep. (The speaker thinks the person is about to fall asleep.)*
3 The use of the past verb in *It's time we went* suggests that this is what we ought to but may not do. The alternatives are statements of fact.
   It's time (for us) to go to bed.
   It's time for bed.
4 Using the Past simple or Past continuous can make questions or requests sound less direct and so more polite.
   *I **thought** you might like to come round for the evening.*
   *I **was wondering** what you were doing at the weekend.*

Unit 6

▶ Present perfect

The Present perfect is a present tense which is used to show a connection between the present and the past. The action may or may not be completed.

It's been a great day, but now I'm really tired. (Today isn't over yet.)
She has left her job and broken off her engagement. (So, now she's unemployed and is no longer about to get married.)
Having a baby has changed the way I look at everything. (Now everything seems different.)
He's given me the sack. (Now I have no job.)

Note By contrast, the Past simple is used to refer to completed actions or events that happened at a particular time, or over a particular period in the past. *Last Saturday morning I left home at six o'clock and drove into town. She lived in Japan for seven years.*

▶ Present perfect continuous (1)

There are two forms of the Present perfect: simple and continuous.

a Present perfect simple

The Present perfect simple is used to refer to:
1 something which began in the past, is still true now, and could continue into the future.
   The village has stood there for 400 years.
   I've had a cold for three days.
2 something which happened in the past but in an unfinished time period, like this morning, today, or this year.
   We've travelled 2000 kilometres this week – so far.
3 a completed past action, activity or experience, without specifying when it happened.
   I've found that they also have substantially lower blood pressure.
   He's climbed Mount Everest. (It could be yesterday or ten years ago.)
4 a recent past event which has an effect on the present.
   She's broken her leg. (The effect of this is that she can't walk.)

b Present perfect continuous

The Present perfect continuous is used to:
1 emphasize the duration of a past action over a period of time up to the present.
   I've been doing housework all morning.
2 emphasize the repetition of a past action or activity up to the present.
   Scientists have been visiting this remote mountain village regularly.
   I've been studying the children and the grandchildren of the over-85s.
   I've been coming to Spain for holidays since I was fifteen.

Note With *since* and *for*, the following verbs can be used in the Present perfect simple or continuous with no real difference in meaning.

drive	live	rain	smoke	stay	study	wait	work

We've lived in Athens since June last year.
We've been living in Athens since June last year.

▶ Present perfect continuous (2)

1 The Present perfect continuous is used to emphasize the duration of a recent activity responsible for a present situation. It focuses on the activity itself rather than its completion.
   He's been repairing his car all day. (That's why he's tired and dirty.)
   Compare these two sentences:
   My hands are dirty, because I've been cleaning out the attic. (Here it is the process, not the completion of the activity that is important.)
   I've cleaned out the attic. Doesn't it look tidy?
   (Here the fact that the activity is completed is what is important.)
2 The Present perfect continuous can also make a statement sound more polite or sincere. It is used like this in fairly formal social situations and depends on the speaker making the listener think that something has been in their mind continuously for a period of time leading up to the moment of speaking.
   I've been going to ask you for ages, what …?
   I've been hoping you'd ring.
   I've been meaning / intending to write, but …
   I've been so looking forward to meeting you.
   It also implies that what follows is something serious.
   I've been wanting to tell you this since we met …
   I've been waiting for the right moment to say this …

Unit 7

▶ can, could, be able to

a can / can't

Here are some common uses of *can* and *can't*:
1 to talk about abilities.
   They can and do still speak their own language.
   I can't swim very well.
2 to talk about possibilities.
   It can be very hot in Madrid in July.
   Sorry, but I can't come to your party on Friday.
3 to talk about permission.
   Can I leave, please?
   You can't smoke in here. You'll have to go outside.
4 to make offers and requests.
   Can I give you a lift to the station?
   Can you tell me the time, please?

b *could / couldn't*

Could / couldn't can refer to the past, the present, and the future. Here are some uses:

1 to talk about general past abilities.
   *When I was four I **could** speak three languages fluently.*
2 to talk about future possibilities.
   *Be careful! Anything **could** happen.*
   (*can* is not possible here.)
3 to ask for permission.
   ***Could** I borrow the car for the evening?*
4 to make offers and requests.
   ***Could** I help you with that case? It looks very heavy.*
   ***Could** you tell me the where the nearest post office is, please?*

Note *Could* is more formal than *can* in offers, requests, and permission.

c *be able to*

1 *Be able to* is used to talk about abilities when the appropriate form of the modal verb *can* does not exist.
   *I'm afraid I won't **be able to** come to work today – I'm ill.* (Future)
   *I haven't **been able to** find any of the missing letters.* (Present perfect)
   *I enjoy **being able to** ride a horse.* (*-ing* form)
   *I'd like to **be able to** play the guitar well.* (Infinitive)
2 It is also used as a formal alternative to *can / could* when referring to abilities and permission, but not possibilities.
   ***Are** you **able to** attend the conference?*

▶ Ability and inability

a *Could, couldn't*

1 In the present *can* and *can't* are used to refer to general abilities.
   *I **can** swim but I **can't** ride a bicycle.*
2 They are also used for specific abilities.
   *Look, I **can** open this door. It isn't locked.*
3 In the past the negative *couldn't* is used for general and specific abilities.
   *I **couldn't** swim until I was seventeen.* (General ability)
   *I **couldn't** get to sleep last night. I was worried about work.* (specific ability)
4 But the affirmative form *could* is only used for general abilities.
   *By the age of three I **could** read the newspaper.* (general ability)
   You cannot use *could* for a specific past ability.
   (You cannot say: *I **could** get to sleep quickly last night.* Instead, you must use *be able to* or one of the alternatives in **b**.)

b Other ways of referring to specific past abilities

1 *was able to* + infinitive
   *Eventually I **was able to get** out of the burning house.*
2 *manage to* + infinitive
   *After lying awake for three hours I eventually **managed to go** to sleep.*
3 *succeed in* + *-ing* form
   *He was in prison a week before he **succeeded in escaping**.*

Note *Manage to* and *succeed in* suggest that the action was in some way difficult to do.

c *Can / could* with verbs of perception

Can / could are often used with verbs of perception.

feel	hear	remember	see	sense	smell
taste	understand				

*I **can** smell something burning.*
*I **could** hear someone shouting.*

▶ Articles

a Definite article – *the* – summary of uses

1 common knowledge
   When both the speaker and the listener know what is being referred to.
   *Ever since **the** accident, I've had back pains. How about you?*
2 repetition
   When this thing or person has been mentioned before.
   *A 26-year-old man is being questioned by police in connection with a series of recent burglaries. **The** man was arrested in a London hotel late last night.*
3 uniqueness
   When there is only one possible thing or person being referred to.
   *I'd love to go to **the** Moon.*
   This includes superlative constructions.
   *She's **the** best swimmer in the world.*
4 In *the …the …* comparative constructions.
   a This construction relates one action or situation logically to another.
      ***The** more you eat, **the** fatter you get.*
   b Various grammatical patterns are possible, but a comparison in the first part of the sentence must be balanced by a comparison in the second part. Neither part of the sentence makes sense without the other. Use any of these patterns as the first or the second part of a *the … the …* sentence.
      The + comparative adjective / *The* + comparative adverb / *The more* + noun / *The less* + uncountable noun / *The more* + clause / *The less* + clause / *The fewer* + plural countable nouns.
      ***The more intelligent** people are, **the more quickly** they understand ideas.*
      ***The harder** you work, **the more** money you earn.*
      ***The fewer** people know, **the happier** I'll be.*
      ***The more** you worry, **the less** you'll get done.*

Note A few *the … the …* expressions can be used without verbs.
1 A *Can I bring some friends to your party?*
   B *Yes, of course, **the more the better**.*
2 A *Shall I pay you straight away?*
   B *Yes, **the sooner the better**.*

5 Other uses
   a some geographical names
      oceans, seas, rivers, mountain ranges, groups of islands
      the *Pacific Ocean,* **the** *Dead Sea,* **the** *Nile,* **the** *Andes,*
      the *West Indies*
      Some countries and groups of countries.
      the *Netherlands,* **the** *Yemen,* **the** *United States*
   b adjectives referring to groups of people, including
      nationalities
      *Robin Hood robbed **the rich** and gave to **the poor**.*
      ***The French** are better cooks than **the English**.*

b Indefinite article – *a / an* – summary of uses
   1 non-specific reference. Any one, it doesn't matter which one
      *I'm going out to buy **a** cabbage.*
      *Is there **a** bank near here?*
   2 first mention of something specific
      *I met **a** university professor on **a** train yesterday.*
   3 single – one, not two, three, or four
      *I lived in Brazil for **a** year.*
      *Can I borrow **a** pound until tomorrow?*
   4 classification, including jobs
      *I'm **an** architect.*
      *Tyrannosaurus Rex was **a** dinosaur.*

c Zero article – summary of uses
   1 with uncountable nouns referring to something in general
      I like fruit juice, but I prefer wine.
      Some of Alexandra's paintings are about friendship and peace.
   2 with plural countable nouns referring to something
      in general
      Children love animals.
   3 with some phrases relating to places, institutions,
      or situations
      He'll be back from lunch at about 2 o'clock.

lunch	school	home	work	prison

   Note The meaning changes if you add *the* to these expressions:
   He's gone to hospital. (= *He's ill, he's a patient.*)
   *He's gone to **the** hospital.* (= *He's not a patient, he may be visiting.*)

   4 in some two-noun phrases
      He's getting better day by day.
      They went dancing night after night.
      They always walked home hand in hand.
      I've never seen eye to eye with my brother.
   5 in *by* expressions related to methods of transport
      A *Shall we go by car?*
      B *No, it'd be quicker to go by train or plane.*

   Note *It's usually quicker to go into town **on foot**.*

Unit 8

▶ Relative clauses

Relative clauses give extra information about people, things, possessions, places, times, and reasons. They are linked to the rest of the sentence by relative pronouns or other relative words.
*Dallas, **where John F. Kennedy was assassinated in 1963**, is the capital of Texas.* (place)
*The person **who is alleged to have shot him**, Lee Harvey Oswald, was himself shot and killed two days later.* (person)

a Non-defining and defining relative clauses
   There are two kinds of relative clauses.
   1 Non-defining relative clauses give extra information which is not essential to the meaning of the sentence.
      *Doctor Brown, **who has worked in the practice for thirty years**, will retire next year.*
      *The accident, **which happened in dense fog**, was caused by reckless driving.*
   2 Defining relative clauses give extra information which is essential to the meaning of the sentence. They make clear which person or thing is being referred to.
      *The man **who got the job** lives in London.*
      *The car **which was used in the robbery** had been stolen.*

b Relative words
   1 If the relative word gives information about place, time, or reason the relative words are: *where*, *when*, and *why*.
      *Bridget grew up with actors. That's **why** she chose a film career.*
   2 If the relative word gives information about people or things or is a possessive, the choice of relative word depends on these factors:
      a whether it is the subject or object of the sentence.
      b whether it refers to a person or thing.
      c whether the relative clause is non-defining or defining.

   Non-defining relative clauses

	Person	Thing
Subject	*who*	*which*
Object	*who(m)*	*which*
Possessive	*whose*	*whose* (*of which*)

   Note *That* can never be used in non-defining clauses.

   Defining relative clauses

	Person	Thing
Subject	*who that*	*which that*
Object	*who(m) that* (no word)	*which that* (no word)
Possessive	*whose*	*whose* (*of which*)

   Note
   1 As a subject, *who* and *which* are more usual in writing. When referring to things, *that* is more usual in speech.
   2 As an object, the relative word is frequently omitted, particularly in spoken English. *Whom* is formal and is used mainly in writing.

c Punctuation

1 Punctuation is important in non-defining relative clauses. There is a comma before the relative word and at the end of the relative clause, unless this is also the end of the sentence.
Joseph Kennedy, **whose** *grandparents were poor Irish immigrants,* *was the head of the Kennedy clan.*

2 In defining relative clauses there is no punctuation.
The Kennedy family achieved a prominence which was unique in American politics.

► Relative clauses (2)

a The relative word *which*

1 The relative word *which* can refer to things in defining and non-defining relative clauses.
It was the pullover **which** *started the whole thing.*

2 *which* can refer to a whole clause in non-defining clauses.
Luciano has also come to include friends and colleagues in the business once they have demonstrated a solid commitment to the firm, **which** *is why he is unconcerned about the group's future ...*

3 In defining relative clauses *which* can be replaced by *that*.
It was the music **which/that** *spoiled the film for me.*

4 In non-defining relative clauses *which* cannot be replaced by *that*.
Harlow, **which** *used to be a village, is now a big modern town.*

b Relative words and prepositions

1 When relative words occur with prepositions, the choice of relative word depends on these factors:
   a whether the clause is defining or non-defining.
   b whether it refers to a person or a thing.
   c whether the register is formal, neutral or more informal.

Non-defining relative clauses with prepositions

	Formal	Informal
Person	*(to) whom*	*who ...(to)*
Thing	*(in) which*	*which ...(in)*

Defining relative clauses with prepositions

	Formal	Informal
Person	*(for) whom*	*(no word) ...(for)*
Thing	*(by) which*	*(no word) ...(by)*

2 The preposition can occur in two places:
   a before the relative pronoun. This is more usual in formal English.
   The Dorchester Hotel, **at** *which the meeting will be held, is in central London.*
   The man **to** *whom we spoke was a well-known footballer.*
   b at the end of the relative clause. This is more usual in neutral or informal English.
   The hotel (which) we stayed **at** *was very comfortable.*
   The man (who) we spoke **to** *had been a professional golfer.*

c *What, whatever*

1 When the word *what* means *the thing(s) that*, it is used as a relative word. Unlike other relative words, however, it does not refer back to a noun but acts as a noun + relative together.
I'll never believe **what** *he tells me ever again.* (= the things that)
What *you believe is up to you.* (= the things that)

2 *Whatever*, which means *anything that*, is used in the same way.
whatever *you decide, I'll stand by you.*
You can have **whatever** *you want.*

► Emphasizing words and structures

Here are some words and structures used to emphasize information.

a The auxiliary verbs *do/did*

1 The auxiliary verbs *do/did* can be used in the Simple present and Simple past tenses for emphasis. They can be used to show that the speaker feels strongly about what they are saying.
I think being an only child **does** *make you very spoilt and intolerant.*

2 Or they can be used to introduce contrasting information.
I know you don't believe me but I **did** *try to contact you. Honestly!*

Note In speech, these auxiliary verbs must be stressed.

b Emphatic pronouns

The emphatic pronouns *myself, yourself, himself, herself, itself, ourselves, yourselves, themselves* can be used to emphasize a personal pronoun or noun.
The restaurant was very nice but the food **itself** *was nothing special.*

c *Very, really, indeed*

1 *Very* and *really* can be used in front of an adjective or adverb to give emphasis.
The exam was **very / really** *difficult.*

2 *Indeed* can be used after a phrase with *very* for extra emphasis.
We're all very different **indeed.**
It was very late **indeed** *when they arrived.*

d *On earth / ever*

The phrase *on earth* and the word *ever* can combine with the words *what, when, why, where,* and *how* in questions where the speaker wants to emphasize that they have no idea of the answer. These emphasizing phrases are interchangeable.
Why **on earth** */ Why* **ever** *do you want to do that?*
*What***ever** */ What* **on earth** *does Karen see in him?*

Unit 9

► Time and reason clauses

Time clauses give information about when something happened, happens or will happen in the future. Reason clauses tell us why.

a Time words and phrases

The following words and phrases can introduce a time clause:

1 *when*
   Fiona teaches in a secondary school **when** she needs extra money.
   When I eventually mention it, teaching colleagues say, 'Oh, you don't look like one of those.'

2 *as*
   This is used to show that two actions happened at the same time.
   As he walked down the street, he thought about everything that had happened.
   It can also be used to show a link between two events:
   As it got colder, people started to complain even more.

3 *as soon as*
   This emphasizes that one thing happens immediately after another.
   Gypsy parents withdraw them (their children) from school **as soon as** they reach secondary age ...

4 *before* and *after*
   After Richard finished / had finished university, he did his military service.
   Emma takes the dog for a walk **before** she goes to school.
   After Guiseppe leaves school, he'll go to work for his father.

5 *until*
   I didn't leave the house **until** it stopped raining.

6 *while*
   This shows that something happens over a period of time.
   While I was at university, I did a lot of sport.
   With the Past continuous it shows that two actions went on at the same time.
   While I was studying hard every evening, Andy was going out with friends.

Note In time clauses which refer to the future we use present verbs. The future *will* is never used in these clauses.
*When I **get** back, we can discuss it.* NOT *When I **will** get back,...)*

b Reason words

The following words can introduce a reason clause. They are interchangeable.

1 *because*
   Some people become New-Age travellers **because** they have strong green beliefs.
   Because they want their children to get a proper education, many parents decide to come off the road and move into houses ...

2 *as*
   ... **as** she needs to supplement her income, Fiona occasionally puts on smart clothes and teaches in secondary schools.

3 *since*
   I won't tell you **since** you don't seem to be interested.

c Position of clauses

1 Time and reason clauses can come before or after main clauses. When they come before the main clause, a comma is put at the end of the clause.
   As soon as she left, everyone started talking.

2 When they come after the main clause, there is no comma.
   We switched on the lights **as soon as** it got dark.

► Participle clauses

In written English, participle clauses are sometimes used instead of relative clauses, result clauses, time clauses, and reason clauses. They can also be used instead of two main clauses joined by *and* or *but*. Participle clauses can come before or after the main clause.
Present participles are the *-ing* form of the verb.
He got out of the car, **slamming** the door behind him.
Perfect participles are formed with *having* + past participle.
Having already **eaten**, I wasn't very hungry.

a Participle clauses instead of other types of clause

1 instead of relative clauses
   Major roads out of the city become clogged with motorists **heading** for the countryside.
   (Instead of ... motorists **who are heading** for the countryside.)

2 instead of time clauses
   Travelling around Paris in August, I couldn't help noticing how quiet it was.
   (Instead of **When / while I was travelling** around Paris in August, I couldn't...)

3 instead of main clauses joined by *and* or *but*
   Parisians avoid city locations for their holidays, **heading** instead to mountain retreats ...
   (Instead of ... holidays **and head** instead to mountain retreats ...)

4 instead of reason clauses
   Not **needing** to explain their every move to their parents, young Madrileños stay out till all hours.
   (Instead of – **Because / As** they don't need to explain their every move to their parents, young Madrileños stay out till all hours.)
   Having done well in end-of-year exams, lucky children are sent to holiday camps.
   (Instead of – **Because / as** they have done well in end-of-year exams, lucky ...)

5 instead of result clauses
   Some food shops close, **making** day-to-day life more complicated.
   (Instead of ... shops close, and **so** day-to-day life is made more complicated.)

b Time relation between clauses

We can only use the present participle when the action in both clauses happens at the same time. When we want to emphasize that the event in the subordinate clause happened before the event in the main clause, we must use a perfect participle.
Having forgotten to take my umbrella with me, I got wet.

Note The subject of the participle must also be the subject of the main verb.
Looking at my watch, I realized I was going to be late.
The following sentence is not possible.
Looking at my watch, someone stole my briefcase.
When the subjects of the two clauses are different an alternative construction must be used.
While I was looking at my watch, someone stole my briefcase.

▶ Cause and effect

These verbs and verb constructions can be used to express cause and effect.

a *make*

The verb *make*, which means *to cause to (be)*, is used in two different ways.
1 *Make* + object + infinitive (without *to*)
   *Travelling by train always **makes** me feel tired.*
2 *Make* + object + adjective
   *Dull weather **makes** me depressed.*

b *cause*

The verb *cause* is used in two different ways.
1 *Cause* + object
   *Working too long at a computer can **cause** repetitive strain injury.*
2 *Cause* + object + infinitive
   *Recent advertising campaigns have **caused** me to think twice about drinking and driving.*

c *bring about* + object

*The food shortage helped to **bring about** the fall of the government.*

d *lead to* + noun or noun phrase

*Marrying too young may **lead to** divorce.*

e *result in* + noun or noun phrase

*Increased competition has **resulted in** decreased sales.*

▐ Unit 10

▶ Passives

a Definition and form

1 Passive verbs are formed using part of the verb *to be* + a past participle. Compare an active with a passive sentence:
   *His boss **forced** him to resign.* (active)
   *He **was forced** to resign by his boss.* (passive)

2 Passive sentences sometimes, but not always, mention an agent, that is the person who does the action – the 'doer'.
   *He was asked to leave **by the authorities**.* (with agent)
   He was asked to leave. (no agent)

b Reasons for using the passive

These are some of the reasons for using passive rather than active verbs. (Often there is more than one reason.)
1 to focus on the person or thing affected by the action rather than on the 'doer' of the action
   *He had **been educated** by private tutors, not in normal schools.*
   *He thought **he might be asked** for his birth certificate.*
2 when you don't know or don't want to say who did the action
   *The information **had been passed** to the press.*
3 to make what you say or write sound less personal and more formal
   *He **was asked** to leave by the authorities.*

c Leaving out the agent

Common reasons for not including the agent in passive sentences are:
1 the agent is not important.
   *I've just **been told** I've got an interview this morning.*
   (Here the fact of getting the interview is more important than knowing who passed on the information.)
2 it is obvious who the agent is.
   *Twenty bank employees **have been arrested** on fraud charges.*
   (Only the police arrest people, so we do need to include this information.)
3 the identity of the agent is unknown or a secret.
   *The headmaster **was informed** that Brandon Lee and Brian McKinnon were the same person.*
   (Maybe the informer was anonymous or maybe the headmaster promised not to reveal his identity.)
4 the agent is no-one in particular or people in general.
   *The president **wasn't recognised** in his casual clothes.*

▶ Passive constructions

a Reporting people's words and thoughts

Certain passive constructions are frequently used, especially in writing, to report people's words, thoughts, expectations, or beliefs.
*Scientists ... **are believed to be** interested in this feature.*
*Three people **are said / thought to have been** involved in the accident.*
*It **has been claimed** that computers will be able to think in the future.*

b Reasons for using passive constructions

1 to express doubt about the accuracy of the information we are passing on, to avoid taking responsibility for the truth of what we are saying or writing.
   *Norns **are said to be able to** sneeze like humans ... (... but I think this is very unlikely!)*

2 to make what we say or write sound less personal or more formal.
*Twenty passengers **are thought to have been** injured in the accident.*

3 to hide or protect a source of information.
(This explains why these expressions appear so frequently in newspaper reports.)
*It **has been reported** that the a prominent politician is about to resign. He **is said to be** living in a secret location somewhere in Spain.*

c Alternatives

These are some other ways of saying you are not sure about the truth of the information we are passing on.

1 *Apparently*
Apparently *Annabella is leaving her husband … (but we'll have wait and see.)*

2 *According to*
According *to some politicians, there's going to an election next year… (but you can't always trust what politicians say, can you?)*

3 *They say*
They say *that the company's going to close down … (but we've heard rumours like that before.)*

4 *to be supposed to*
*She's **supposed to** have had thousands of pairs of shoes … (but I think that's probably an exaggeration.)*

▶ The pronoun *it*

The impersonal pronoun *it* is used in many different constructions.

a to avoid repetition

Like other pronouns *it* can be used to avoid repetition of a noun.
*I enjoy my job. **It**'s very interesting but I also find **it** very tiring.*

b for emphasis

it is also used to show the listener or reader that the word or phrase that follows is important.
***It** was my mother who first realized I was artistic.*
Here *my mother* has more importance than in the more neutral sentence.
My mother first realised I was artistic.
***It** was only after careful thought that they decided to emigrate to Australia.*
(This emphasizes that they thought carefully before making their decision.)

c to introduce a subject which comes later in the sentence (preparatory subject)

***It** was great to see you.* (The subject = *to see you*.)
***It** was a terrible shock to hear about your accident.* (The subject = *to hear about your accident*.)
(These are more usual than: *To see you was great.* and *To hear about your accident was a terrible shock.*)

d to introduce an object which comes later in the sentence (preparatory object)

*I find **it** difficult to imagine living in space.*
(The object = *to imagine living in space*.)
*The government has made **it** clear that taxes will have to rise.*
(The object = *that taxes will have to rise*.)

e in expressions referring to certain conditions

***It** was really windy yesterday.* (weather)
***It**'s nearly midnight.* (time)
***It**'s 17 March tomorrow.* (date)
***It**'s about 400 kilometres from London to Manchester.* (distance)

f as the subject of verbs which refer to appearances

***It** looks as if it's going to rain.*
***It** appears that he can't even remember his own name.*
***It** seems as though everything is going wrong for me this week.*

Unit 11

▶ Causatives

a Form and use

1 Causative verbs are formed with *have / get* + object + past participle.
*He **has** his teeth **checked** every six months.*
*I **had** my car **serviced** yesterday*
***Have** you **had** your hair **cut**?*
*I'm going to **have** my bedroom **painted** black.*

2 Causative verbs refer to actions which a person arranges for someone else to do rather than doing themselves.
*I always used to repair the car myself, but these days I **have it repaired** at the local garage.*
*We're going to **have the house painted** – it's too much for us to do ourselves.*

b *Have / get something done*

have something done and *get something done* are sometimes interchangeable although *get* is usually more informal.
*I **have / get my house redecorated** every two years.*
*If you keep getting headaches it might be an idea to **have / get your eyes tested**.*
However, in some contexts the two forms are not interchangeable.

1 In the Present perfect tense only *have* is possible.
***Have** you had your windows cleaned recently?*

2 To show that an action is or was urgent, *have* is possible but *get* is more usual.
*I really must **get** (**have**) my car serviced soon.*

3 For imperatives (eg. orders) *get* is used.
*'**Get** your hair cut!' the sergeant shouted at the soldier.*

Note There is an alternative personal or 'active' construction with *get*.
*I **got** the mechanic to check my brakes.*
Here the speaker arranges for a particular person to do the job.

▶ Causative verbs

a Causative verbs and the passive

Passive and causative verbs are similar in meaning but have a different focus.

*Alex's flat **was redecorated** last month.* (passive)
*Alex **had his flat redecorated** last month.* (causative)

In both sentences the focus is on what was done rather than what someone did (active voice). However, in the causative sentence the emphasis is on the fact that the person mentioned was responsible for arranging (but not doing) the action.

b Non-causative use of *have something done*

1 The structure *have something done* is also used to refer to events like accidents or disasters which happen to someone but which are outside their control. In these cases, it has the meaning of *have an experience.*
   *We **had our roof torn off** in the storm. (We experienced our roof being torn off.)*
   *He **had his telephone disconnected** because he didn't pay his bill.*
   *Hugh **had his car stolen** at the weekend.*

2 These ideas can be expressed in the passive with a similar meaning.
   *Our roof **was torn off** in the storm.*
   Causative verbs, however, can emphasize the dramatic nature of the event.

▶ Question tags

a Use and pronunciation

Question tags are questions that can come at the end of sentences in speech and informal writing. There are two main uses of question tags.

1 To ask other people if they agree with us. In this case, the question tag is said with falling intonation.

2 To check that something is true. In this case, the question tag is like a real question and is said with rising intonation.

b Form

1 If the main clause contains an auxiliary verb, the question tag contains an auxiliary verb.
   *She**'s got** three sisters, **hasn't** she?*

2 If the main clause contains the verb *be*, the question tag contains the verb *be*.
   *That**'s** what you're here for, **isn't** it?*

3 If the main clause is in the negative then the question tag is positive.
   *We still **can't** believe he's gone, **can** we?*
   *He **never** apologizes, **does** he?*

4 Normally, if the main clause is in the affirmative then the question tag is negative.
   *Now you **know** more about Elvis than anyone else in the world, **don't** you?*
   *He **doesn't** exactly sing it though, **does** he?*

5 If the main clause contains a non-auxiliary use of *have*, the question tag contains *do, does,* or *did.*
   *Stefan **has** a shower every morning, **doesn't** he?*
   *You usually **have** lunch with Alan, **don't** you?*

6 If the main clause contains *let's,* the question tag contains *shall.*
   ***Let's** take a break, **shall** we?*

7 If the main clause doesn't contain an auxiliary verb, the question tag contains the auxiliary *do.*
   *Patrick **left** early, **didn't** he?*

8 If the main clause contains an affirmative imperative, the question tag contains *will* or *would.*
   ***Close** the window, **would** you?*
   ***Tell** me again, **will** you?*

9 If the main clause contains a negative imperative, the question tag contains *will.*
   ***Don't** forget to send me a postcard, **will** you?*

10 If the main clause contains *nobody, somebody* etc. the question tag contains *they.*
   ***Nobody** phoned for a taxi, **did** they?*

11 If the main clause contains *nothing,* the question tag contains *it.*
   ***Nothing's** wrong, is **it**?*

12 If the main clause contains a modal verb, the question tag contains a modal verb.
   *You **can't** speak Swahili, **can** you?*

c Question tags and requests

We can make requests less formal by using question tags.
*You couldn't give me a hand, **could you**? (Could you give me a hand?)*
*You don't mind if I smoke, **do you**? (Do you mind if I smoke?)*

▌Unit 12

▶ Reported speech

a Form

1 **Statements**

Direct	Reported
*'I**'m leaving** you,' she said.*	*She said she **was leaving** him.*

2 **Questions**

Direct	Reported
*'Where **will you go**?' he asked*	*He asked her where she **would go**.*
*'Do you **love** me?' he asked.*	*He asked if / whether she **loved** him.*

3 **Commands**

Direct	Reported
*'Get lost!' she **said**.*	*She **told** him to get lost.*

1 **Tense changes**

a If the reporting verb is in the past, the direct speech verb is often moved back a step in time.

Direct	Reported
'I **spend** a couple of hours every day talking to neighbours'.	She said she **spent** a couple of hours every day talking to the the neighbours.
'Being Edward's wife **won't** the easy option.'	Polly said to herself that being Edward's wife **would not** be an easy option.

Note Past perfect verbs in direct speech do not change in reported speech.

Direct	Reported
'I**'d seen** her somewhere before.'	He said he**'d seen** her somewhere before.

b The original verb tense can be kept if the reporting verb is in the present.

Direct	Reported
'I'm **leaving** you.'	She says she's **leaving** me.

c The original verb tense can be kept if we want to emphasize that what was said by the speaker is still true.

Direct	Reported
'I**'ll always love** you.'	He said he**'ll always love** me.

d These modal verbs change in reported speech.

may – might   can – could   must – had to

Direct	Reported
'I **may** not feel like it.'	She said she **might** not feel like it.
'**Can** we talk about this again?'	He asked if they **could** talk about it again.
'I **must** see you again.'	He said he **had to** see her again.

e These modal verbs do not change.

might   ought to   could   should   would

Direct	Reported
'I **ought to** prepare for my interview.'	He said he **ought to** prepare for his interview.

2 **Pronouns**

Some personal pronouns change depending on who is reporting.

Direct	Reported
'I'm leaving you.'	She said she was leaving **him**. OR She said she's leaving **me**.

3 **Time and place references**

Direct	Reported
'I saw her **yesterday**.'	He said he'd seen her **the previous day / the day before**.
'I'm leaving **today**.'	She said she was leaving **that day**.
'Stay until **tomorrow**.'	He asked her to stay until **the next day / following day**.
'I'm going **here** and **now**.'	She said she was going **there** and **then**.
'When are you **coming** back?'	He asked her when she was **coming** back.

4 **Determiners**

Words like *this, that, these, those* may change to *the*.

Direct	Reported
'Who's this letter from?'	She wanted to know who **the** letter was from.

▶ Reported speech: reporting verbs

These are the most commomnly used reported verbs.
He **said** he was feeling tired.
She **told** me she'd spent all day working.
They **asked** (him) whether he could drive a car.

Note The verb *tell* must be followed by a personal object pronoun.

However, other verbs can often express the purpose of the original direct speech better than *say*, *tell*, and *ask*. Here are some common alternatives.

acknowledge   admit   agree   announce   argue   claim
complain   confirm   decide   deny   doubt   emphasize
explain   hope   imagine   imply   inquire   insist   predict
reply   report   state   think   wonder

There is also a group of verbs which follow the same grammatical pattern as reported commands: reporting verb + object + *to* + infinitive.

advise   ask (polite command)   beg   forbid   instruct   order
persuade   warn

The policeman **told me to drive** more carefully.

There are three ways of using the verb *suggest* as a reporting verb.
He **suggested** (that) they (should) try again.
He **suggested** (that) they tried again.
He **suggested** trying again.

Note You cannot say *He suggested to try again.*

► Infinitives or gerunds after verbs

Some verbs are always followed by an infinitive (*to* + verb) and others are always followed by the gerund (*-ing* form). Except in a few cases, there are no rules to help you work out whether the infinitive or the gerund follows a particular verb.

a Verbs followed by the infinitive

1 Verbs + *to* + infinitive

afford	agree	arrange	ask	appear	attempt	choose
decide	expect	help	hope	intend	learn	manage
offer	pretend	promise	refuse	seem	want	

*When he was only 15, Steven Spielberg **decided to become** a film director.*

2 Modal verbs + infinitive (without *to*)

can	could	may	might	must	should	would

***Can** you **see** my brother? He **should be** here by now.*

b Verbs followed by the gerund

1 Some verbs expressing likes and dislikes.

can't stand	dislike	don't mind	enjoy	fancy

A *'Do you fancy going to a disco tonight?*
B *'No, I **can't stand dancing**.'*

2 Other verbs with the infinitive or gerund.

admit	avoid	can't help	consider	deny	finish	give up
imagine	involve	keep	mind	miss	postpone	put off
prevent	report	resist	risk	suggest		

*I **can't help thinking** about those animals in tiny cages at the zoo.*

c Verbs which can be followed by either the gerund or the infinitive

1 Many liking or disliking verbs are most commonly followed by the gerund but can also be followed by the infinitive, sometimes with slight changes of meaning.

hate	like	love	prefer

*I **hate travelling** by sea.* = Travelling by sea is something I don't enjoy.
*I **hate to tell** you this, but I've crashed your car.* = I regret to say.
*I **like / love to dance**.* = Dancing is something I do by choice.
*I **like / love dancing**.* = I enjoy dancing.
*I **prefer to write**.* = So I am going to write – this is my decision.
*I **prefer writing**.* = I would rather write – I enjoy it more.

Note If these verbs of liking or disliking are preceded by *would*, they are always followed by the infinitive.
*I'd **love to go** on holiday. I'd **like** you **to come**. I'd **prefer to fly**.*

2 The choice of the gerund or the infinitive makes little or no difference to the meaning of these verbs:

begin	can't bear	continue	intend	start

*Spielberg **started to make / making** films at the age of 12.*

3 Verbs of perception can be followed by either a gerund or an infinitive (without *to*).

feel	hear	see	smell

If these verbs are followed by an infinitive, the speaker experienced a complete action.
*He **saw** the plane **land**.* (He saw the landing from beginning to end.)
If these verbs are followed by a gerund, the speaker may only have *experienced part of the action*.
*He **saw** the plane **landing**.* (He may have seen the plane coming down, but not actually hitting the runway and stopping.)

4 The choice of the gerund or the infinitive changes the meaning of these verbs completely.

forget	go on	mean	remember	regret	stop	try

a *forget*
*I'll never forget **going** to the cinema for the first time.* (I recall this occasion.)
*Luckily, I didn't forget **to buy** the cinema tickets.* (I did what I had to do.)

b *go on*
*Nobody was listening but he still went on **talking**.* (He didn't stop.)
*After lunch we went on **to talk** about the economy.* (The next thing we talked about.)

c *mean*
*I'm going to finish this even if it means **working** all night.* (involves)
*I didn't mean **to fall** asleep, but I was just so tired.* (intend to)

d *remember*
*I remember **booking** the tickets.* (I can recall this action.)
*I remembered **to book** our flight.* (I did something I was supposed to do.)

e *regret*
*We regret **to inform** you that the match has been cancelled.* (We are sorry for something that is going to happen.)
*There was so much traffic. I regret **going** by car.* (I am sorry for what I did.)

f *stop*
*A lot of people have stopped **smoking** recently.* (finished / given up)
*We got lost so we stopped **to ask** the way.* (interrupted one activity to do another)

g *try*
*I've been trying **to talk** to you for days.* (attempting to do something difficult)
*Have you tried **talking** to him? He usually listens.* (doing something to find out if it is helpful or useful)

Tapescripts

1.1

Speaker 1

I've done over twenty walks now and have never been hurt. The reason for this has nothing to do with the old idea of 'mind over matter'. It can all be explained by the laws of physics. A normal fire-walk is made of red-hot wood or charcoal and it's a well-known fact that wood does not conduct heat well. Because of this, your feet are safe. More and more people are taking it up as a regular activity. It's exciting and it makes them feel good. It's certainly made me more confident.

Speaker 2

I attend two or three conferences a year in different parts of the world. It's the preparation and the waiting that really get to me, I always feel nervous for several days in advance, but once I'm up there with the lights on me, I forget my nerves and concentrate on what I've got to say to my audience.

Speaker 3

Whenever you're near the creatures, it's extremely important to watch their body language carefully for danger signs. For example, at the moment he's coming slowly towards me. He's staring at me and his tongue is going in and out. He may be hungry and looking for food, so I have to watch out. Sometimes he moves backwards, his neck becomes s-shaped and he breathes heavily, or hisses. In this case, he's probably frightened and so may attack in self-defence.

1.2

/s/	/z/	/ɪz/
types	buys	rises
writes	rides	catches
asks	runs	washes
		damages
		kisses

1.3

1 What are you studying?
2 What are you studying?
3 Where are you studying?
  Where are you working at the moment?
4 Where have you been recently?
  What have you done this week?
5 Where do you live?
  Where do you work?
  Where do you study?
  When did you start there?

1.4

Speaker 1

Of course there's no doubt about it – it is a risky business, but I try not to think about the risks – I mean they're always there at the back of my mind, but you've just got to get on with it, haven't you? Most of the work is pretty routine – not specially exciting or dangerous. When you are faced with a life-and-death situation, you haven't got time to think – you just get in there. If there are people inside the building, your job is to get them out safely – the smoke and flames are obstacles to overcome. Afterwards it hits you – when you get home and relax when everything's peaceful – that's when I think about what might have happened.

Speaker 2

For as long as I can remember I've been obsessed with kicking a ball about – it's all I ever really wanted to do. When I signed up at sixteen, I thought the worst that could happen would be that I'd waste a couple of years of my life. No one ever tells you about the risks you run – mental and physical – when you play the game at international level, though I don't suppose it would have made any difference if I had known. This is the third time I've been into hospital for operations on my legs – and it probably won't be the last.

Speaker 3

I started off in Cambodia and I've recently finished a spell in the Middle East. Of course it's dangerous work and we're all well aware of the physical risks involved. I've been arrested more times than I can remember. Usually they ask you a few questions, chuck you in a cell overnight, then the next morning you get your camera back with the lens missing – without the film of course – and then they let you go. If you take on a job like this, you've just got to accept that certain risks are involved, but they're calculated risks. As far as I'm concerned, what I do is worth taking risks for. The world needs to know what's going on in these places.

Speaker 4

The most important thing is to keep a cool head – I'd say the risks are fairly low – of course it can be nerve-racking and you worry about the car, but the vast majority of learners are ultra cautious and they hardly ever go over the speed limit. I've had a few minor accidents over the years, but that's all. And of course these days you've got dual control cars – so that means there's even less to worry about.

1.5

J OK, Liz, so what are we going to do? We've got less than a day left.
P Er …
L I've told you what I think, John. We can get Paul to do it. That way there's less chance of serious problems later.
P Can I just say …
J Hold on, Paul, what sort of problems are you thinking of, Liz?
L Well, mainly another injury to Rob, of course.
R I'd go along with that. The last thing I want is three more weeks in hospital.
P Excuse me, could I …
L Yes, that would delay the rest of the shoot by goodness knows how long. And that all adds to the expense.
R I have to agree, John – we're already over budget.
J I'm not so sure, people really believe it's you, you know. If they found out it wasn't, …
P I'd just like to say …
J I haven't finished yet. Look Rob, people really believe you take the risks, you know.
R I suppose so. Liz?
L In the end it's up to you, Rob. I can only give you advice. The film industry can't afford to lose you just yet, you know.
P Can I just get a word in, please? It's me you're talking about, you know – I may not be a well-known star like Rob but I am …

1.6 includes 1.7 (see p.12)

Conversation 1

K Couldn't I have just one str … one colour in the room, if I was going to say go for a … for a strong colour on the curtains? Wouldn't that be enough? Wouldn't …
R I think, I think that would be better.

J It might look a bit strange if you've just … got one sort of colour, don't you think?
R Not necessarily.
J I think it could be like a little rich gem in here with all sorts of deep vibrant colours, like a fruit cake.
K Oh, I don't know about that. I don't know that I could live in it.
J Don't you like that?
K Ooh …
R Well, as you say, a room this size.
J Right. What would you do?
R Well, … I'd …
S I'd … Sorry.
R I tend to go along with the neutrals, but with a splash of … strong, strong …
J Something bright …
R … strong … but not make that the overall theme … you know …
J Mmm – I see your point. Mmm …
R … you know.
S Yeah, I agree with you, I think, I think. The other thing I think about is, strong colours is they're likely to date.
J Mmm …
S I mean I wouldn't …
R Yeah, that's a good point …
S I mean, I wouldn't want to redecorate in less than about ten years.
J A Victorian house would have had very deep and rich colours for – years and years and years. It's a very classic look for that period.
K But it's very difficult to get anything to match though, isn't it?…
R Absolutely. Absolutely.
K … if I go for very strong colours.
J No, not strong primary colours, but deep colours, deep rich colours, you see.
K Mmm. I don't know.
J Don't you think?
K No, I don't think so.
R Don't know.

Conversation 2

T Yes, I know, but the point the point is we work our guts out for this place and they're just constantly leaning on us all the time. It's more work, it's more money, it's more hours, it's more admin.
J Oh Tony, Tony, be reasonable.
T This is getting ridiculous.
R Wait a minute, wait a minute. You know, I mean if everyone could bring their car in, nobody could park in there anyway because …
J Exactly!
R … there'd be too, too many cars.
J Absolutely. Absolutely right! Absolutely! So that's going to give you a great opportunity of a guaranteed place to park.
T Where's the money going to go to? What's it going to be used for?
J Well, I suppose they're going to have a security man there so that your car at least it'll be safe – it's not on the road, Tony.
T Oh come on, I mean, … it's, the, there're gates, the gates are normally closed – that's no particular problem anyway, is it?
R But that can be decided later.
T This is just one way of ripping off the staff.
J Oh no, that's not true.
T It is!
J No, I don't agree. Oh come on, Roger, you know you're nearly there. It is …
T Twenty quid a year, well all right, but a hundred, a hundred is absurd.
J Oh twenty's nothing. What's that going to do?

T   Yes, but think how many people there are. If everybody's chipping in twenty quid, that's plenty of money to pay a security man or one or two people to run round with walky-talkies and this sort of silly equipment.
J   A hundred is nothing if you work out how much that is a quarter. What do you pay in the multi-storey?
R   It's really nothing for over a year, I mean what is it? Two pounds a week?
J   Exactly! How much do the meters cost?
R   Yeah, what is it? Two pounds an hour or something in a meter?
J   You're right, you're right.
T   Well that's, all right, yes …
R   I understand why they're charging …

1.8 (see p.12)

1.9 (see p.12)

1.10 (see p.12)

2.1

/d/	/t/	/ɪd/
longed	laughed	needed
loved	knocked	wanted
gazed	kissed	added
judged	watched	waited
tried	stopped	
	washed	

2.2

I have a secret power. I can make objects vanish into thin air. I can put keys, pens, or glasses on to surfaces or into drawers, and a few seconds later they have disappeared. Unfortunately, I don't have quite so much control over the re-appearance of these objects.

Sometimes my secret power makes an object invisible, so that it only looks as if it's disappeared – after a few days, weeks, or months, it becomes visible again, and there it is, exactly where I first put it. Once I spent a whole day looking for an important document that I knew I'd left in an obvious place on the table. Although I couldn't see the document, it was there. Medical experts might say this was a case of temporary blindness, but, er, I'm not so sure.

More often, objects disappear on special parts of the house. They particularly like hiding in my daughter's bedroom. She can never understand how my hairbrush or T-shirt materialize in her room. Another favourite hiding place is my car. Objects I'm certain I left on top of the fridge turn up under the driver's seat.

My most remarkable experience was when the last remaining key to the kitchen door disappeared and we had to leave the door unlocked and banging in the wind for several weeks. One day, as I was unpacking the food I had just bought at the local supermarket, I discovered the missing key under a bag of potatoes. I have to say I was puzzled by this, but grateful, of course, to be able to lock the door again.

When I first became aware of my talent, I was not altogether happy about it. I began to envy people whose keys always hung on special hooks and whose papers were always neatly put away in cupboards and drawers. Then I realized that the tidiness of these people's houses reminded me of old-fashioned museums with their carefully labelled exhibits.

In my opinion, a good house is an unpredictable house, with objects in all kinds of unexpected places.

It's nice to be able to open a kitchen cupboard without having the slightest idea of what's inside.

Another advantage is that unpredictable houses don't appeal to burglars. In the last few months every house in my street has been burgled except mine. Admittedly I don't have a video or a hi-fi system but I feel the unusual combinations of objects in my house might have made the burglar think that my house had already been broken into.

It is true that the pleasure of finding things is far greater than the inconvenience of losing them. The things I find are hardly ever the things I'm looking for. While I was looking for a screwdriver recently, I found my daughter's birth certificate which I'd been searching for for months. On another occasion, while I was looking for my glasses, I came across a sandwich I'd lost the previous weekend.

The happiness you feel when you find a missing object is worth every minute of the time you've spent searching for it. Of course, even as you smile to yourself, you know that the object will not be staying for long.

2.3 (see p.17)

2.4 (see p.19)

2.5

A   Well, that's everybody. What do you reckon?
J   Personally, I wouldn't even consider Jackie or Rachel – they just wouldn't fit in, but I quite like the look of Christina and I'd say Robin sounds OK from his letter.
A   Charlie?
C   It's difficult to say. Several of them sound OK from their letters.
J   So, you're not keen on Christina or Robin?
C   I didn't say that.
A   So, what do you think?
C   I don't have any very strong feelings, really.
J   But we've got to decide this together. There's no point in one of us being unhappy – I mean we'll probably have to live with our choice for the next six months at least.
A   How do you feel about having another man about the place Charlie?
C   I don't really mind. I wouldn't be jealous if that's what you're getting at.
J   Come on, Charlie – no one's suggesting that. We just want your opinion, that's all. It's difficult enough deciding who to interview. We need all the ideas we can get.
C   But it's not up to me to decide, is it?
J   Why not?
C   Well, it was you two who found this place originally, wasn't it? It's up to you.
A   Look, Charlie, you've been here for over a year now, you and Jo have been going out together for half that time and you pay a third of the rent. It's your decision just as much as it is ours.
J   Well, if you ask me, I think we should talk to Christina, Robin, and possibly Ed.

2.6 includes **2.7** (see p.22)

Conversation 1
B   Well, how much money have we got?
J   What is it?
T   About seventy quid, wasn't it?
J   Is it? Have you any ideas, Roger?
R   No, nothing, no, nothing springs to mind, no.
T   I think we ought to get a picture or a print,

something, you know, something she can actually put on the wall – it'll be there to remember us by.
B   Well, she's keen on art. I mean she went to that art course this, this year, so …
T   That would work, yeah. What sort of things does she like, then?
B   Well, I don't know. It'd be nice to get something original, but I don't know if we've got enough money for that.
T   No, seventy quid's not much for an original, is it?
R   No, it's not much for that.
J   I suppose so. Might be able to get a nice piece of pottery, though, or glass, or something like that.
T   Yeah, there's quite a good place down, is it down the end of … the High Street somewhere …?
J   That's right, that's right, they're lovely.
T   … that's very often got some stuff there.
B   She's got quite a lot of pottery already, I mean …
T   Oh, has she?
B   Well, she's … it's quite a small house – a bit limited space really.
J   Roger, come on, what do you think?
R   No, I can't really think.
B   You know her well, you know her well, I mean.
R   I really don't have any strong ideas on it, I mean … I don't think pottery or glass, as you say, she's got a lot already.
B   … Well, why don't we have a … ? Why don't we … ? Why don't two of us go down and have a look at that shop that you were mentioning … ?
J   That's a good idea.
B   … and just what there is.
T   That the Gallery?
B   Yeah.
T   Yeah, all right.
B   We could come back and report and see what there is, but I mean … Roger are you going to come down?
J   Oh come on!
T   Yeah, come on down …
R   No, really, really, I'll leave it up to you, honestly. I don't, I really don't have any strong ideas, I mean I'll go along with what you, what you decide.
J   But you made a big contribution, Roger. You know you should.
R   No, I'll go along with what you decide.

Conversation 2
B   What do you suggest, then?
J   Well, I think we should go round, look at a lot of places – something of interest, something sort of … that will er, um, educate you.
B   Like what, for example?
J   Well, bit of um, historical sightseeing er … maybe somewhere like erm Cambridge or a … to a nice er … castle somewhere.
K   Oh … I …
B   Oh, I don't know – sounds like hard work, all that walking around and things – I'd rather something a bit more rela … relaxing. Erm …
J   Well, … I'd, well … I don't really like the idea of that very much – not really.
K   What, going to the health farm?
J   No, no. I think if you want something relaxing, perhaps we ought to do something a bit more active, but relaxing.
B   Yeah, but with the health club you can do both, I mean you can do exercises in the gym, you can do aerobics, or you can do swimming, or you can just lounge around and do nothing.
K   Mmm, sounds all right.
B   What do you think?
K   Well, you know, it's … we're going away. I don't mind really where we go or what we do.
J   Well, don't you think you might waste your weekend if you were just lazing around?

K Well, I don't know. It's difficult to say, I mean once we get there we might find that, you know, there's all sorts of things we could do.

B Well, in the end, I mean, I don't suppose I really mind, I mean, you know, whatever you two decide, I mean, if we can all decide ... if two of us decide on something ...

K Yeah, fine, that's OK with me.

J Well, how about ... Well, I think perhaps then we ought to then choose a neutral erm ... one that we all ...

B Karen, can you suggest something?

K Well, I'm quite happy with any of these suggestions really, I mean the health, the health club, that sounds fine.

B Yeah, but Julie's not keen on that, so ...

2.8 (see p.22)

2.9 (see p.22)

3.1 (see p.25)

3.2

T Look, there's a really interesting programme on tonight – it's called *Visionaries* – it's about the future.

D What time's it on?

T Eight-thirty – oh, it's just started. I'll switch it on.

'... then the most important natural threat we should be concerned about is asteroids or comets. In the next 100 years there's a one in a thousand chance of a kilometre-sized object hitting the Earth. The effect would be devastating – probably half the population would die. '

D Half the population?

T Yeah, that's incredible, but I definitely won't be worrying about comets in a hundred years' time.

D I wouldn't be so sure. Some scientists are predicting that we'll all be living to the age of 130 or more.

T Oh, that's scary.

'... even more exciting than that, we'll start seeing intelligence in computers – not the kind of intelligence people claimed for *Deep Blue* when it became the world chess champion. No, I mean genuine intelligence. By about the year 2200 humans will almost certainly have merged with computers, though I have to say I don't like the idea much. In fact it'll be very embarrassing, because it means we won't be the most intelligent beings on the planet ...'

T What does he mean 'we'll have merged with computers?'. That sounds terrifying!

D I don't know – it sounds like science fiction to me.

T Perhaps he means we'll be spending more and more of our time working on computers – you know, we'll be more dependent on them.

D I'm not so sure – it doesn't sound as simple as that. You know, like nowadays people have pacemakers fitted to control their heartbeat – well, maybe in a hundred years' time, we'll all have been fitted with other kinds of devices, like those virtual reality helmets you wear on your head.

T You mean like some kind of brain implant. So we'll all be walking around with computer chips in our brains – telling us what to do.

D Yeah, and what to think.

T That sounds horrendous.

'The impact of information technology means enormous change. In the fairly short-term, half of the entire workforce will be working from home,

for at least part of their time. It also means that there will be massive unemployment, and so fewer people will be paying tax. It is my estimate that by the year 2100 nations as we now know them will have broken up and been replaced by smaller economic units – regions, states possibly, or even independent large cities. I see no reason, for instance, why London should not become independent. '

D Incredible – I don't believe any of it.

T It's too frightening even to think about.

'This means, of course, that there'll be first- and second-class citizens. The identity card of the future will be a credit card, and the better your credit, the higher up the citizen ladder you will be.'

D I haven't even got a credit card so where does that leave me, I wonder?

T Better off than me! I've got a credit card, but at the moment I'm nearly up to my limit.

D I've had enough of this – I'm turning it off.

3.3 (see p.27)

3.4 (see p.29)

3.5

W So, Stuart, let's go over this again, shall we? Mr Johnson phoned you at three-thirty yesterday afternoon? Right?

M Yes.

W And what did you do?

M I took his telephone number.

W What did you say to him?

M I said someone would ring him back.

W And did they?

M Did they what?

W Did someone ring Mr Johnson back?

M I don't know.

W What I can't understand, Stuart, is why you told him someone would ring him back. Why didn't you deal with it then and there?

M Mainly because I didn't really know what he was talking about, I suppose.

W So why on earth didn't you pass him on to someone who could deal with his problem?

M Because I don't actually know who does what around here yet.

W Well, you should know by now – you've been here nearly a month.

M Sorry. It won't happen again.

W I hope not. Anyway, to get back to Mr Johnson. What exactly did he want?

M I'm not sure – I didn't ask him.

W Why not?

M Well, he didn't really give me a chance – that's why. He just kept saying it was a disgrace and that he'd had an account here for nearly forty years and it was the first time anything like this had happened and he wanted to speak to the manager.

W So why didn't you pass him on to me?

M I didn't want to bother you.

W OK, OK. Perhaps you could find out if anyone has phoned Mr Johnson back. On second thoughts, phone him back yourself.

M What, now?

W Yes, now!

W2 Sorry to interrupt, Mrs Harper, but a Mr Johnson has just rung to say that as no one's phoned him this morning he's taking his account elsewhere.

W Oh no! Well, I suppose it's not really surprising in view of ...

M Shall I still phone Mr Johnson?

W Of course. Why not?

M I just thought that if he's taking his account ...

W Phone him now! See what you can do!

M Right, OK. Oh yes, before I forget, Mrs Harper, I'm, er, I'm going to a party tonight. Would it be OK if I came in late tomorrow morning?

W No, it would not be OK. You're here on time or you can start looking for a new job. OK?

3.6

B Yeah, uh–huh ...

T What on earth for?

B Well, I mean, the main reason is, I mean, on terrestrial television, you've just got five channels, erm, if you've got satellite, then you get about forty.

S But why d'you want more, more channels?

B Well, there's more choice, you know, you've got lots of films, you've got sport, lots of live sport.

T You'll never have, you'll never, never have the ... all the time to watch all that TV

B No, but, but you, I mean you've got more choice, so you can watch, you can choose what you want to see, I mean a lot, now a lot of the time there's nothing you want to see at a time you want to see it, there's much more choice. You can see films when they're out much more quickly, erm ...

T Do you really think you're going to have the time to sit down and go through all the choices and do all the recordings and watch the recordings afterwards? Come on, you'll never make it.

B No, I mean a friend of mine's, a friend of mine's got it and he's really pleased with it, you know, and I've watched it and I think it's really good – it's not that expensive either.

T I don't understand why it's, you know, why it's so popular, why it's the thing to have. Four channels of terrestrial TV is fine.

B Well, five, Tony. Well, for the simple reason that it's, it just gives more choice, that's all. And I mean, I think it's really good for the sports, you know, because you can't get live sports now on a lot of, erm terrestrial television.

S There must be another reason than sport, though, because there ... there's quite a lot of sport on television already.

B Well, yes, certain sports ...

T Too much sport ...

S Too much, yeah.

B It depends, you know, there are certain sports you, you can only get if you've got satellite ...

S By the way, did you see the tennis yesterday?

T Tennis?

S Yeah.

T Yeah. Who won?

S Erm ... Can't remember who won ...

3.7 (see p.32)

3.8

1 A Why on earth are you here?
  B Mainly because we had arranged to meet.

2 A Why did you lie to me? There must be a reason.
  B The main reason was I thought you'd be angry.

3 A Can you tell me exactly why you came?
  B For the simple reason that I wanted to see you again.

4 A What I don't understand is why you didn't phone.
  B The phone was broken. That's why!

5 A Why didn't you tell me?
  B Well, you see, I thought you'd be upset.

1   Oh, by the way, I've invited John.
2   Oh yes, I nearly forgot, the meeting's been cancelled.
3   Just to change the subject for a minute, I saw Pete the other day.
4   Going back to what you said about David, I'm sure he wouldn't mind.
5   Incidentally, I'll be at a meeting all day tomorrow.

4.1 (see p.35)

4.2

Speaker 1

I remember my grandad really well – although he died nearly twenty years ago. He was one of the kindest people I've ever known – he never got angry or shouted at me or anything like that, you know, and he'd often take my side in arguments I had with my Mum and Dad. When I was about seven or eight, he came to meet me from school and walk home with me even though he had rheumatism in one of his knees. I mean, he needn't have done that – I could easily have got home on the bus. And it was him that started me off smoking – he got through about forty a day and he used to give me the odd cigarette when I was quite young – you know about ten or eleven, and said I mustn't tell anyone. That made me feel really grown up. My Mum always said he spoiled me, and looking back, it's fairly obvious I was his favourite grandchild – he had seven altogether – but I was his first and I suppose that made me sort of special. People have always said I look like my grandad. In fact, my Mum even says that I remind her of him when he was the age I am now – that's a strange thought, isn't it?

Speaker 2

My mother's amazing – she'll be ninety this year and she's incredibly independent – in fact, she still lives on her own, cooks all her own meals, and that kind of thing. She has loads of visitors, though, and a nurse who comes in every two days or so to check she's all right. She's not that good on her feet and she moves around pretty slowly, but at least she lives in a bungalow, so she doesn't have to climb any stairs. When she was in her mid-eighties, she went to live with my youngest sister and her family, but she couldn't stand them fussing around her all the time, so after a couple of years she moved back into a place of her own – the place she's in now. As I say she's got lots of friends who pop in regularly, so she's never lonely and she doesn't have to do too much for herself. She spends most of the time listening to the radio – mainly the news and talk programmes. She's got a TV but she still thinks of it as a new invention – and she's never really got used to watching it regularly.

Speaker 3

There's Nanna, my great-grandmother. She's my mother's grandmother. She's ninety-two but she's still pretty fit, she still goes on walking holidays with her youngest daughter – my great-aunt –and until recently she drove everywhere in her own car. Unfortunately, she's got problems with her eyes now and the doctor's said she mustn't drive any more. From the personality point of view she's amazing too – probably the most patient person I've ever known. You know, when we were younger she'd spend hours playing games with us, reading us stories, taking us for walks –anything we wanted to do really. She couldn't be more different from her eldest daughter, my Grandma, who's nearly always grumpy – she never has any time for us – not even now we're older. The thing is she paints in her spare time – and as far as she's concerned we're just in the way. But Nanna – she's just amazing for her age.

Speaker 4

My grandparents are really young – they're both forty-nine and they hate being called Grandma and Grandad – so we have to call them Aunty and Uncle. It still surprises everyone 'cos most people our age have got grandparents in their late fifties or early sixties at least. Some people assume they're our parents – that makes them feel really good! They live on the coast, so we quite often go and stay with them especially in the summer when we can go down to the beach. They're both great swimmers – when he was younger grandad was quite famous apparently, and he still swims every day in the summer and once a week all through the winter. We get on pretty well with them, but they're always having arguments with Mum and Dad about how we should be brought up. They think Mum and Dad are too easygoing – Grandma thinks we have far too much freedom.

4.3 (see p.37)

4.4 (see p.39)

4.5 (see p.40)

4.6

adventure   adventurous   fame   famous   humour   humorous   mystery   mysterious   nature   natural   nerve   nervous   profession   professional   religion   religious   season   seasonal   tradition   traditional

4.7

A   OK, so that's agreed then. Let's move on to the next item on the agenda, shall we? I think we all agree with the suggestion, don't we, that in future all requests for time off should be made in writing and made six months in advance of the proposed starting date? Fiona?
F   Yes, I think that's perfectly reasonable. After all, we're a growing business – these things need to be formalized more than …
D   That's right. I mean, it was OK when we only had ten or so staff, for people to ask their manager a couple of weeks before they wanted to go. It's a much more serious matter with a staff of over three hundr …
R   I think there's a danger of too much bureaucracy here, Andrew. I remember, when I first started here nearly forty years ago, me and a mate of mine in accounts decided to go to Greece – it was, you know, a spur-of -the-moment decision, and I was quite happy to …
A   Can we stick to the point, Richard? Things have moved on since you first started here.
R   I can still see the look on my boss's face when I said I was taking a couple of weeks off. But he didn't really mind – everything was much easier …
F   Look, Richard, we're supposed to be talking about a new system which will be fair to everyone.
R   As far as I can remember, we left on the Friday night. I put a few clothes in a rucksack and we were off.
D   I'm sorry, Richard, but we're not here to talk about the good old days. If we're going to survive and grow in a competitive world, we've got to move with the times. You know the company motto – 'Plan or perish'.
R   I can remember as if it were yesterday. We went by train to Brindisi in Italy and then got a boat across …

4.8 includes **4.9** (see p.42)

Conversation 1

R   Well you're lucky – 'cos I, I work on my own now, so …
K   Ah, do you? – so it must be very different.
R   Well, it's a bit, bit lonely at times, you know, but er …
K   That was one of the best things, I think, erm, just that there were so many people that you could get on well with.
R   Yeah, well, I can remember those impromptu drinks and things we used to have …
K   Well, there was always so many things to do, weren't there, I mean you could always just sort of nip round the corner and go out for a drink or …
R   'Cos it was so central.
K   That's right.
R   But it's a bit difficult now.
K   Is it?
R   Yeah, well …
K   I suppose if you …
R   It's only me.
K   Yeah, that's true …
R   Nip out with myself round the corner, but … I'll never forget the time we all went to the restaurant together … about ten of us, weren't there?
K   Oh, that was wonderful, wasn't it? Yeah, I really enjoyed that. It just doesn't hap … , the people I work with now are not the same, I mean they're a lot older …
R   They don't like …
K   Well, they just have different interests, erm, and it's a lot harder to sort of get people together …
R   I mean, that's the problem when you work with a lot of people – sometimes it clicks and sometimes it doesn't click and er, you know, you're lucky if it does, and you're in a group of people that you can do those things – those those times were good, I'll never forget those times – it was a good period.
K   Mmm it was.

Conversation 2

R   What about teachers – did you have any strange teachers?
J   Oh, yes, – they were all Miss somebody or another and they were very fierce …
R   I can remember one – he was a French teacher – he used to put … if you did something wrong he'd put his hands all over your face and – but he was a heavy smoker and it used to choke you …
J   Oh, how awful.
R   It was either that or he'd hit you with a book – strange people.
J   Oh, no, I can't remember anyone as terrible as that – we used to get some funny punishments, though, from our teachers. Did you?
H   What sort of punishments?
J   Well, I used to talk too much, and I used to have to stand in the corner on my chair …
H   That's very Victorian …
J   I can remember doing that an awful lot.
R   One used to make us bang his head, bang our head, bang our head on the blackboard …
J   Oh, no – that's awful …
R   Yeah, he, he wouldn't do – he'd make us do it.
J   He'd make you do it yourself?
R   Yeah, auto-punishment.
J   Oh, dear.
H   We used to get chalk flung at us.
R   Oh, yeah …
H   Yes.
J   That's not very nice, is it, really? Oh, dear …

R   And uniforms. Did you, did you have to wear uniforms?
J   Yes, we did, that's right.
R   I used to hate uniforms.
H   Our school was very strict on uniforms.
J   Yes, and we couldn't wear our skirts too short.

4.10 (see p.42)

4.11 (see p.42)

5.1

Lucie and Matthew married fairly recently. They've been together now for two years and they are expecting their first child. They met when Matthew shared a flat with Lucie's friend, Jane. Lucie says her friends didn't expect her to go for someone like Matt. He was older than her and he was divorced. But she thinks he's very typical of the kind of men she likes – older and professional. Matthew feels they get on well because they want the same things out of life.

Matthew and Lucie look as if they come from well-off backgrounds. Their choice of holidays and the desire for children are an excellent fit. If Matthew's idea of a perfect weekend is watching football, it's just as well Lucie likes staying at home doing nothing, otherwise she might get bored or nag him to take her out.

Nelson and Ruth met through a friend and have been together for seven years. They think they make a good couple because, although they are very different, they are both easygoing and give each other a lot of space.

Both Ruth and Nelson have artistic, creative personalities which seem to complement their home and working lives. Even though Ruth comes from a large family, neither Ruth nor Nelson really seem to want children. I suppose Ruth could see Nelson's need to save as meanness, but she may also find that this more cautious approach is a useful curb for her own concerns, as she worries when things are not under control. Holidays will have to be quite carefully negotiated.

Pip and Helen got married after four years together. They met when Helen was a hairdresser – Pip says she deliberately gave him a bad haircut so he had to go back to have it recut, but Helen denies this. According to Pip, they're best friends, but they're careful not to crowd each other. Helen mentions their sense of humour as being important.

Pip and Helen look happy and relaxed. Loyalty is top of their list, so this looks like playing an important part in their relationship, as do creativity, the countryside, and the company of friends. It seems that children will be something for the future, as neither is ready yet. The desire for exotic travel is shared though there may be disputes over modes of transport.

5.2 (see p.45)

5.3 includes **5.4**

A   Did anyone see that article in the paper the other day about brand names?
C   Not sure – what did it say?
A   Well, it said how important brands are to young people.
P   It sounds pretty boring to me.
J   What sort of brands?
A   Well, you know, clothes, drinks, food, cigarettes – things like that. It said that lots of young people need them to create an identity for themselves.
P   Sounds really heavy.
A   No, it wasn't – it was interesting.

C   I think there's something in it. I remember when I was about thirteen, I wanted a pair of Levi jeans. I mean they had to be Levi's. I went into this shop and they had Wranglers but not Levi's – I remember storming out and then getting home feeling depressed. I wouldn't go out with my friends until I'd actually got some real Levi's – they had to have that little orangey label.
J   That was like me when I was only about twelve – everyone had Nike shoes – so that's what I wanted. I didn't care whether they were comfortable or not – or what my Mum and Dad thought about them – as long as they had that Nike symbol on them – that was all that mattered.
P   My parents were always broke, so I got what I was given. If they'd had more money, I'd probably be more worried about what I wear now. As it is, I don't really care.

5.4
C   It's a bit the same with drinks – I mean Coca-Cola and Levi jeans are fairly similar, aren't they?
P   'Cept you can't drink jeans!
C   You know what I mean, Pete. I wish you'd stop being so childish. Jeans are a sort of uniform – if you're young and you don't drink Coke, there must be something wrong with you.
P   I don't drink Coke and there's nothing wrong with me.
A   Well, you're not exactly young, are you? Anyway what do you drink?
P   Fanta, Seven–Up – I'm just not keen on Coke. And I really like the Fanta adverts on telly.
A   Exactly – it's all a question of image.
P   Rubbish.
J   It's not rubbish, Pete. Image is important. Think of how many people want a Mercedes or a BMW – they're status symbols.

5.3 continued
P   I don't see what cars have got to do with drinking Coke.
A   Anyway, this article I was reading said it isn't just kids that are obsessed with brands – it said that strong brands reflect people's deepest emotions – like people are attracted to Volvo cars because they have a safe dependable image.
C   It's funny though – 'cos you can buy things without really being aware of their image. I mean, last year, I bought myself a new coat in Harrods. It wasn't particularly expensive – but every time anyone saw the Harrods label inside, they'd say – 'Oh, you're going up in the world', or 'Has someone died and left you some money?'. Irritating remarks like that. I really regret buying it now. I wish I'd gone to Marks and Spencers' instead – you know, somewhere more ordinary like that.
J   When I bought my Armani shirt – I knew how people would react – so as soon as I got it home I cut the label off.
P   Blimey! I wish I had enough money to buy an Armani shirt – I wouldn't cut the label off – I'd make sure everyone could see it.
J   Actually, to be honest, I wish I hadn't cut the label off now – it's not quite the same somehow.
A   Look, you lot, stop side-tracking me. What was I saying? Oh, yeah, this article also said that brands give young people something to believe in – it makes them feel more adult.
C   It's a bit like The Body Shop – I know loads of teenagers who buy soap and stuff there because they believe that the Body Shop cares about animals and the environment.

5.5 (see p.47)

5.6
1   Unfortunately, I can't take you anywhere at the moment. I've had my licence taken away for dangerous driving.
2   I know I'm stupid – I should never have started smoking – now I can't stop.
3   Yes, I'd love to work abroad now – I shouldn't have refused that job in Malaysia when they offered it to me.
4   I hope it tastes all right. I never went to cookery lessons when I was at school.
5   I'd like to, but I can't swim. Everyone else I know learned when they were four or five years old.
6   Sorry I can't, I'm completely broke. I spent most of it on an expensive French meal.

5.7
A   OK, so let's try that again. The car will stop here.
B   Where?
A   Here. Exactly where I'm standing now. OK?
B   Yeah, OK.
A   The front door will open and one of the detectives will get out and take a good look round.
B   So that's when I start to walk forward, is it?
A   No, you don't start wa …
B   I'm nervous just thinking about it.
A   Try not to worry.
B   I can't help it.
A   Anyway, when the detective is satisfied everything's safe, he'll open the back door and that's when you start to walk forward.
B   In other words, I don't move until the door's open?
A   Right. Oh, and don't forget, you won't be wearing jeans tomorrow, so you'll need to allow a little more time to reach your meeting point. Does that make sense?
B   Yes, that's fine. I'll just need to practise walking in the dress a bit before tomorrow.
A   Right, so, then, at the meeting point you look her in the eye, smile, and present her with your gift. Right?
B   I just hope nothing goes wrong.
A   Don't worry. Everything will be just fine.

5.8 includes **5.9** (see p.52)

Conversation 1
H   Right, Julie, you'll find a lot of this job is to do with answering people's queries. People will come in with lots of different queries and they'll expect you to know the answer to them. Now, I know that's not always possible, but you've really got to just try and answer, erm, everything that you can and if you don't know the answer, then you'll have to find out the answers and get straight back to them.
J   Erm – Do you … Do you mean that, erm, we, we can't or that I can't ask other people? Will there be somebody else about apart from you that I can ask?
H   Well, it depends on the time of day really, erm, I'll be here most of the time so you don't have to worry about that. Sometimes there will be questions which I can't answer, so we'll really have to find out the answers together, because you never know what people are going to ask you.
J   So what you're saying, is I've got to learn as I go along.
H   Yes, that's right. A lot of it is is just learning, as you say, as you go along. You will also be asked by people for various documents – erm – now, you'll find in the file over in the corner that I have put a lot of specimen documents there – they are

also on the computer, but the file will just give you the layout of the documents.

J   Yes ...
H   Is that all right?
J   Erm, yes, I think so. Erm, I think I'd like to, erm, do as much as I can of, of speaking to people, erm, so I can learn what to do.

Conversation 2
K   Right, OK.
B   ... and, erm, the ones in the kitchen – they need watering every other day really.
K   Oh – right, OK.
B   Is that clear?
K   Yeah, I think so – that's fine. Yeah.
B   I mean, it's not the end of the world, but ... there are more important things. Erm, the washing machine ...
K   Right ...
B   ... erm, just be careful that you close the door properly.
K   Right – what, what, what do you mean?
B   Well, er, I've had a few problems with it, so just make sure it's properly closed.
K   Er, OK.
B   ... and, erm, try to avoid using that long programme.
K   Do you mean I shouldn't use it?
B   Well, it might be better if you didn't, yeah. Aha.
K   Right. OK. Fine.
B   OK, and erm, I've given you some keys,
K   Yes.
B   All right. Check when you leave that the back door's locked.
K   Right, OK.
B   And one of the keys is a bit dodgy ...
K   Right ...
B   ... erm – you've got to sort of put it in quite, er, erm, hard and then turn it – so if you, if you don't get it the first time just try again.
K   Right. OK.
B   Are you all right with that?
K   I'm fine, yeah. That's fine.
B   Erm. Right. Do you just want, just to, just see if there's anything else?
K   You mentioned something about the cleaner.
B   Yeah.
K   When does she come in?
B   She comes in on Mondays – all right?
K   Right.
B   All right? She's got her own key so you don't need to worry about her.
K   Right. So, do you mean – do I have to lock up after she's gone or will she ... or do I have to stay while she's there?
B   No, no, no, no, not a problem – I mean she'll probably come when you're out anyway, and I mean, she can arrange to come on another day if it suits you better ...

5.10
1   Right. / All right. / OK. (I'm not sure. Falls then rises)
2   Right. / All right. / OK. (Do you understand? Rise)
3   Right. / All right. / OK. (I understand. Fall)

5.11
A   You need to feed the dog once a day. All right?
B   OK.
A   The dog food's in this cupboard.
B   All right.
A   And remember to change the water. OK?
B   OK.

5.12 (see p.52)

5.13 (see p.52)

6.1 (see p.55)

6.2 (see p.57)

6.3

P   Good morning to you all. If I sound slightly out of breath, it's because I've been running around the studio trying to find my notes for today's programme! That's better. Now, I have with me in the studio two senior citizens: Mary Craig, who is a hundred and two, and Edward Macintosh, who's a hundred and one. Welcome to you both. I've been so looking forward to meeting you. Could I start by asking you, Mary, what you remember about your hundredth birthday?
M   Oh, I had a wonderful day. I had a special lunch at a nice hotel in town and then I spent the afternoon and evening with my family and friends. Everything went so well.
P   And a, er, telegram from the Queen?
M   Oh, yes, in fact I had three telemessages – one from the Queen, one from the mayor of the town where I live, and one from the Minister for Social Security.
P   Edward, what was it like for you – crashing through the hundred barrier?
E   Fantastic – because we all had free drinks! We had a lovely get-together and I had two hundred and twenty-five letters, postcards, and telegrams – two hundred and twenty-five.
P   Sounds wonderful. You certainly both look very relaxed and happy. Tell me – what's good about living so long?
M   Well, one of the things I think is you live a selfish sort of life. You've only got yourself to think about. You do what you want, you eat when you want, you go to bed when you want. There's nobody there to ask what time you're coming home – you're free. And of course you can travel.
P   When did you start travelling?
M   Oh, I've been travelling ever since my husband passed away – I started in my seventies. I had a world cruise in my nineties. I've had other cruises to the Mediterranean and the Caribbean, and in September I'm going on a cruise along the Rhine.
P   You've done a fair amount of travelling too, haven't you Edward?
E   Well, when I lost my wife in 1970, I sold my hotel and started travelling. I've been round the world – in both directions – I've been to America, Canada, Australia, Morocco, ... I've been all over.
P   Do you think that people today are happier than you were in hard times?
M   Well, they don't appreciate things so much as we do. As far as young people are concerned it's easy come, easy go. You see, we had to make do and mend in our young days. There was no help, nothing.
P   Do you think that has made you appreciate what you've got now, Edward?
E   Of course I do. Children get taken to school in a bus now. I used to walk four miles to go to school.
M   Well, the tragedy now is that parents daren't let their children walk to school. It's not safe any more. They can't be independent. I think the young have a very difficult time nowadays. At a very early age they get introduced to drugs – and we never had that worry. It was a much easier life when we were young. We were always kept on the straight and narrow.

P   You two are speaking what many people would say are words of wisdom. Do you think you are wiser now that you are older?
E   Oh, sure, you go on learning no matter how old you are – you go on learning. I learn something every day, every month, every year.
P   Mary?
M   No, I'm sure I'm not wiser. I've been going to various adult education courses recently. I'm still trying to learn things, because I like keeping my brain ticking over, but most of it goes in one ear and out of the other. I enjoy it at the time but my memory's terrible – I just don't remember things. I can't remember names or names of places – it drives me mad. People think I'm going soft in the head.
P   I'm sure that's not true. We're sitting here having a perfectly normal, intelligent conversation. By the way, I've been meaning to ask you this: do you find generally that people of your own age are better company than younger people – people like me, for example?
E   Oh, no, not at all. I'd much rather talk to younger people – not teenagers or school children – I mean sensible people, business people. I'd rather talk to them than the elderly people where I live. The thing is, we think a lot but we don't say very much.
P   And finally, looking towards the future, I was wondering whether you still have any goals – any special things you want to do?
M   Well, I take any opportunities that come along, but no, there's nothing I really want to do now. I just live from day to day. I have a great-grandson who's getting married the day before my hundred-and-third birthday and I'm having a champagne lunch party – that's what I'm looking forward to at the moment.
P   Edward?
E   No, no, no special goals – but I still want to do a little more travelling before I finish – I like travelling. And I've made up my mind I'm going to live to be a hundred and ten – so I'm looking after myself.

6.4 (see p.59)

6.5
1   I heard the weather forecast but I didn't know whether to believe it or not.
2   She didn't know where her glasses were so I had to read the letter to her.
3   When I travel by plane, I prefer to sit in an aisle seat.
4   Four days ago I was fined for speeding.

6.6 (see p.60)

6.7

M   What's the matter, Daniel?
D   I'm really fed up with people thinking I'm under age. That's the second time today. It's really getting me down.
B   Well, you must admit you do look pretty young.
D   Yeah – OK, I may not look eighteen, but surely I look older than fourteen. It really annoys me.
M   Don't let it worry you. You got what you wanted didn't you?
D   I did in the end, but not until I'd shown him my driving licence.
L   That's OK then, isn't it?
D   No, it isn't. I think the whole system is really

stupid. It's OK to leave school, become a soldier and fight for your country and die if necessary – when you're sixteen, but you can't vote in elections and you can't even buy yourself a drink until you're eighteen. It really irritates me.

M That's because people under sixteen haven't got a clue what elections are about.

D How can you say that? We've been talking about politics since we were about twelve.

B Relax.

L Calm down.

D I'm quite calm. All I'm saying is that it isn't logical. I mean you can go into a pub when you're fourteen, but what's the point of that if you've got to wait for four years before you're allowed to buy a drink?

L He's right. There are some really silly laws. The one that really gets me is that you can't get a part-time job until you're thirteen.

D Everyone does though, don't they?

M That's because no one bothers checking how old you are when you go for that kind of job.

L Exactly! That's what I mean – it's a really silly law.

6.8 includes **6.9** (see p.62)

Conversation 1

Ju ... break reduced from twenty minutes to ten minutes.

All What? I beg your pardon. What do you mean?

B What was that? Could you say that again?

Ju Well, we're going to have our coffee break reduced from twenty to ten minutes.

R You're joking!

J That makes me really angry. Why?

Ju Well, I wasn't told officially, but that's what I've heard and I think it's right.

R Oh, that's outrageous ...

Ju I know, I, well ...

J I can't believe it. Who said ... ?

R That's not enough time to get your sugar in the cup. That's ridiculous.

Ju No, I know, no ...

J Ten minutes, we don't even get back – just haven't got the time for that ...

Ju Well, it's just a money-saving exercise, isn't it?

R Whose, whose brainwave was that?

J Yes.

Ju Well, I don't know. I don't know where it came from.

J Oh, that's so infuriating. Barbara?

B I mean, don't get so worked up about it. I mean, you know, I mean, we've got to be a bit more flexible, perhaps. I mean ...

R Flexible?

B Ten minutes is, ten minutes is ...

J Barbara ...

R Ten minutes is nothing.

B Well ...

J We can't even get back here in ten minutes.

R You can't even get out of your seat in ten minutes.

J No, that's right.

Ju And not to be consulted ...

J Oh, this is ridiculous. I want to speak to someone about this.

B Well, I think you're getting a bit worked up about it ...,

Conversation 2

J ... and he's making me so angry ...

B Just calm down, it's not as bad as all that ...

J Oh, it is, it really irritates me ...

S Yeah, take it easy. What he actually ... What actually happens?

J Well, he's a radio ham and he sets up his radio and he's got a huge aerial in the garden and you can hear him trying to contact other people in other

countries like Australia where it's daytime, but of course it's night time at our place, so all we hear through the walls is him calling and, and, and talking to people in other countries where it's daytime and he's making me so cross.

B Have you spoken to him? Have you tried to reason with him?

J Well I've tried, yes. I've tried, and he says, 'Oh yes, hmm, hmm, hmm,' and then the next night it's the same thing.

B Well, I can understand your point of view, but I mean, I don't think, I mean, there are worse things.

J No, there aren't – it's making me lose nights and nights of sleep and I'm really, it's really getting me down. I don't know what to do any more, I really don't know what to do. I have tried talking to him.

S Well, neighbours can be pretty awful. I mean, we've, we got, the people next door to us, erm. We went ... I went out one morning and they, they, were in the process of building a wall between our house and theirs – they hadn't even asked us whether they could or not.

J Oh, you see, that's what's so irritating – people don't care.

S It's just so infuriating.

B Yeah, but I mean, you've got to, got to live with each other, you know, I mean ...

J Well, not at night time ...

6.10 (see p.62)

7.1 (see p.65)

7.2

Speaker 1

It was so bright I really thought they'd switched on floodlights outside the hotel. Luckily I was still awake. As soon as I pulled back the curtains the heat hit me; all I could see was a wall of flames just a few centimetres from the window. I didn't realize until later that the floor below me was on fire. I moved back into the room. I'm sure there'd been no alarm but I could hear banging noises and people shouting.

Someone knocked on my door – I opened it and a man grabbed my hand but I pushed him away and went back into my room – panic isn't logical – I can't believe it now, but I left with my shoes, a toothbrush, and a straw hat of all things.

The corridor was full of people hammering on doors and screaming. Someone yelled at me, 'Drop your things and run!' So I ran with the others to the end of the corridor away from the smoke to a staircase – I had to stop there to pick up my hat.

Anyway, at the bottom of the staircase there was a door. The man in front of me pushed and pulled at it but it wouldn't open. He turned back – you could see the blind panic on his face. We couldn't move, there were so many people. He tried again and finally succeeded in opening the door. We ran barefoot across the car park and scrambled over a two-metre-high fence. Eventually we were able to make it round to the front of the hotel. It was an amazing sight – windows were being smashed, people were jumping from the first two floors, others higher up managed to climb down on knotted sheets. One girl escaped by smashing the window with her shoe and jumping out; another had her life saved by a man breaking her window with a hammer from outside.

Fire engines kept arriving. One of them raised its ladder and moved towards a room on the top floor where there was someone sitting on a window sill. Then the ambulance came and six of us were taken to hospital.

Speaker 2

We were flying along quite normally when I decided to roll the plane – it was an old two-seater air-force jet. It's a fantastic feeling flying upside down at 400 kilometres an hour. The next second, my brother's ejector seat had broken away from the plane and shot through the cockpit, and he was falling from 1,000 metres. The air was rushing in and for a moment I couldn't breathe. It was a few seconds before I managed to regain control. I looked down and watched my brother pulling at the rip-cord of his parachute but for some reason it didn't open. I just watched him fall – I was sure I'd never see him alive again. I circled round for six or seven minutes, looking for the parachute, but there was nothing. Finally I headed back to the airfield. The return flight was horrific – I was convinced that I'd lost my brother. When I landed and found out he was alive – it was incredible. I went straight to the hospital and there he was, sitting in an armchair with a brace round his neck, joking with the nurses. His first words were, 'Where have you been?'

Later he told me that the torn parachute had slowed him down just enough and he'd had a soft landing on a grassy bank. Amazingly, he could still walk, and was already on his feet when the rescuers arrived.

7.3

I turned off the main road on to a dirt track – it was narrow and bumpy with hedges on both sides. I drove quite slowly – then I noticed I was coming to a bridge over a stream. I could see that the road went steeply up to the bridge and dropped steeply again after the bridge. My car is very long and the bottom is close to the ground, which means that if you go over a bump it's easy to scrape the bottom. I knew by looking at the bridge that I couldn't get over it without damaging the car. I'd have to go back. The problem was, because the road was so narrow I couldn't turn the car round. The only option was to reverse the way I'd come. I remembered that about 500 metres back there was a farm entrance where I'd be able to turn. I started reversing but by then there was another car behind me – of course he couldn't overtake me so he had to reverse too. It was just as narrow and bumpy going backwards and there was an added problem: because of my bad neck I couldn't reverse quickly. Eventually I managed to reverse into the farm entrance and after a lot of to-ing and fro-ing I succeeded in turning the car round and driving forwards again. What a nightmare!

7.4 (see p.69)

7.5

Father Are you sure you're doing the right thing, Martin?

Martin No, I'm not sure, but I want to give it a go. I've always been attracted to Africa.

Father We don't think you should do it till you've finished university. That's what most people do.

Martin I know that – but these people need help now; they may not be here in two years' time. Anyway, on the whole, I think it's better to do these things when you're young. You tend to get set in your ways when you're older.

Father I don't call twenty-one old, Martin.

Mother We're only thinking of what's best for you, Martin.

Martin I know you are, but you don't know what's best for me. That's the whole point.

Mother I mean, have you really thought this through? How are you going to cope with the heat – and apparently it gets very cold at night. And what about eating? Where will you get food?

Martin Stop worrying, Mum. I'll survive. I mean, it's not as if I'm going to some remote village in the jungle.

Father And what about wild animals? There are still quite dangerous animals in some parts of Africa, and terrorists.

Martin What do you mean, terrorists?

Father Well, you hear cases of foreigners being kidnapped and held hostage by terrorists, don't you? Surely it would be more sensible to go somewhere nearer home.

Martin Look, I know what the dangers and the difficulties are going to be, but these people need help now and I'm going to do what I can to help.

7.6 includes **7.7** (see p.72)

Conversation 1

S   How much are you trying to lose?

B   About seven kilos.

K   In, in a couple of weeks?

B   Well, I hope so, yes.

J   Oh, I don't think you should do that. That'd be really bad for you.

B   Well, I mean, if I can't lose seven in a couple of weeks. I've got three weeks before I go on holiday. You know, I've, I've just, just got, I can't, ... I look awful in my swim ... swimming costume, I mean, I can't, ... I wouldn't dream of getting into a bikini.

K   The trouble is if you lose weight that quickly, you, you, you're bound to put it back on again.

J   That's right. And I don't think you should eat just eggs, I mean, that's not a balanced diet.

B   But that's only today. Tomorrow I can have bananas and then the next day it's carrots and then the day after that it's grapefruit, so I mean it is a mixture.

S   Oh, come, just think about it. Bananas for a whole day of bananas. Are you going to be able to stand that?

B   Yeah, I can put up with that for ...

K   Shouldn't you be thinking about, doing things like exercise, not just about diet?

J   That's a good idea.

B   Well, you know, I mean, I haven't really got much time for that, you know. I'm just too busy. What time have I got to exercise?

K   Oh, I don't know, it just seems much more sensible to just, be ... just eating ...

J   That's all the good advice you always do read about, isn't it? You know, exercise as well as diet.

S   Yeah. Most peo ... most people who are thin, or reasonably slim, are like that because they take exercise, I think, as a rule, anyway.

K   Or I think what you were saying about balance, I think that's generally right. You've got to have a balance of everything.

J   I mean, just think about it for a minute, you know. If you, if you're just stuffing yourself with eggs one day and grapefruits the next, your body's going to react in very strange ways.

Conversation 2

R   It's not going to be, any, any really any more expensive than, than a normal car.

J   Oh, I wouldn't if I were you, you know – I'd really think again and perhaps buy a new car, I mean ...

R   No, that's the whole point of a classic car is that it's not new, that, it's, it's something, something they ... you can't get any more ...

J   Well, you know ...

R   It's like buying a piece of history ...

J   Yeah, but I think you're making a big mistake, because if you're going to use it for travelling to and from work, I mean, is it really suitable for that

sort of thing?

R   Well, I'm not going to use it to and from work every, every day perhaps, maybe during the summer, but erm, I'm not going to sort of ...

J   I wouldn't if I were you, you know, it could be very difficult on the roads in traffic jams and all that sort of thing.

R   Yeah, but it's a car, it goes, that's what it was made for.

J   Mmm, mmm, I mean, what can I say to persuade you? I mean what, what, have you really thought it through? Have you thought about where you're going to park it, for inst ... You can't park it on a street.

R   I've got a ... I've got a garage. I've got all that lined up ... , it's, it's, it's OK.

J   And what about during the daytime when you're sort of parking near work for instance?

R   That's fine. You have to ... Life's a risk. You have to take a risk. If somebody hits it they hit it. But I mean you can't, you can't not do something ...

7.8 (see p.72)

8.1

1   Henry Fonda, who was Jane's father, had a long and distinguished film career.

2   The film which won him an Academy Award was *On Golden Pond*.

8.2

1   I'm twenty-six. I live with my mother and father. There's just me. They tried to have another child but my mother miscarried and she couldn't have any more children. I think being an only child does make you very spoiled and intolerant. But you do become more of an independent person when you're an only child. You tend not to follow the crowd or rely on what other people think, and you make up your own mind about things and take your own decisions. That's probably because there's no one there to say 'Why on earth do you want to do that?' or 'Maybe you should, you know, do something else'. It might have been nice to have had a brother or sister when I was young. Someone to play with.

2   I'm the middle sister. I've got an elder sister, she's eighteen months older than me – and a younger sister – she's three years younger than me. We're all very different indeed but we get on really well. My elder sister's got a very forceful personality and she does everything at a hundred miles an hour. She really knows what she wants and she goes for it, whereas my little sister is really laid back. She's a bit like a hippy – she's into environmental issues, and is a vegetarian and all that sort of thing. And I'm a bit ... em ... a bit of a loner, I suppose. I keep my feelings to myself really. And even though I'm really close to my elder sister, I don't confide in her. I'm just reserved, I suppose.

3   There are just the two of us. Just my sister and I – Michelle – she's two years younger than me. We get on well but there's always been a certain amount of rivalry between us – on my sister's side, anyway. When we were young, she always wanted to do better than me, so if I got second prize at something she wanted to get first. She was very competitive.

I think myself that when you're the elder child you always feel in some way responsible for the other person. Well, I certainly did. My sister was perfectly capable of looking after herself but just because I

was the elder child I felt I had to look after her. Chelle didn't really care about what my Mum and Dad thought – if she decided she wanted to do something, basically she went ahead and did it and she got into trouble quite often. I always tended to do the right thing.

8.3

B   Jenny was always successful and did well. Mum and Dad were always so proud of her, especially Dad, and I wanted them to be proud of me too. When I was younger I always seemed to fail at things. And my father would sort of say, 'I might have known it, Ben's in trouble again', and that sort of stuff. So later on, the main thing for me was not to be a failure. If I thought I might fail at something, I wouldn't even try it – I'd leave it alone. Even now, you know, I'm still afraid to take risks sometimes in case I fail, because then it's like, 'Oh, Ben's messed up again'. I've tried loads of things and I've had lots of different experiences. In fact, I'd say I've actually done more than a lot of people I know and I'm sort of beginning to feel more confident, you know – I can say like, 'Well, actually, I've done that, I've done that, I've done that'. I may not go to the top in it, but compared with a lot of other people, I've been incredibly successful. But then, when I've got to that point, I've thought, 'Oh the next stage is quite a big step, I might fail', so I've said to myself, 'Right, I'll give that up and I'll try something else instead'.

In the end, I suppose there was only enough money and time in our family for one, and that was it, so rather than try and compete I'd just give up. It wasn't necessarily the right thing to do but I could never have beaten Jenny, so I didn't even try. In comparison with a lot of people, you know, we're pretty competitive in our family, believe me, but you don't go and try and beat someone if you know you can't win. That's how I felt anyway.

J   It's easy enough now to look back and see how it affected the family, but it was different at the time – I just couldn't see it, 'cos when you're in the middle of it, I mean, you're young. I suppose you tend to be quite selfish. I think a lot of athletes are very selfish. They have to be, because they always have to do what they need to get the best performance. And Dad was always there for me, 'cos he was so determined that I was going to win and do the right things and compete at the very highest level. He used to make sacrifices without even realizing they were sacrifices. Mum and Dad hardly ever used to, you know, go out for a meal together or do any of the normal family things. Ben didn't have Dad there to take him to football practice or do any of the things fathers do with their sons. The thing is, all those sacrifices were for me and most of the time I wasn't even aware of them – you know – life was going on as usual and Mum was making sure that I'd a clean kit and that dinner was on the table and I was in bed at the right time. She was brilliant, my Mum. I mean she was always my best friend, my Mum.

8.4 (see p.79)

8.5 (see p.79)

8.6

Jackie was very young indeed when she got married – just seventeen. Now, she herself admits it was a mistake. 'I really did think it would work. My parents did warn me that I was too young but I didn't listen.' So whatever went wrong? 'I do love Dave,' said Jackie, 'but we've changed. We both want very different things from life now.'

8.7

BM Now, how can I help you, Mr Bennett? I don't normally deal with these matters myself you know.
C No, I realize that. I'm very grateful. Thank you for seeing me.
BM Yes?
C Well, actually I was ... It's a bit awkward. You see I borrowed some money from you last year and I ... well, I was wondering ... do you think you could extend the repayment period?
BM Are you trying to tell me that you are unable to keep up with the interest payments, Mr Bennett?
C No! No! Well, not exactly. It's just that one of our machines has broken and we really need to replace it, otherwise we'll get behind with the orders.
BM What sort of business do you run, exactly?
C It's a family business. Bags, purses, belts, that sort of thing – leather goods.
BM I see. And the original loan was for £10,000?
C That's right.
BM I'm afraid that's not possible, Mr Bennett. It's quite out of the question.
C Well, could you possibly increase my loan?
BM How much would you need?
C £2,000 would be enough.
BM Oh, certainly. No problem, provided you can keep up with the payments.
C That won't be a problem.
BM Excellent. Well, I can authorize that now if you'll just step into the bank, Mr Bennett. Mr Smith will give you the relevant forms to fill in.

8.8 includes 8.9 (see p.82)

Conversation 1

H Might be possible, Tony. It depends how long you would want me to work for, though.
T Well, is there any chance of working, er, a couple of evenings and maybe Saturday, or some time at the weekend, perhaps?
H I'm not sure if I can do that.
T Er ... Are you sure? 'Cos really we need to get it now. We need to get it finished by Monday and it's going to be very difficult to get it done, you know, just in the normal working hours.
H I would if I could, Tony, but it very much depends on when you would want me to work.
T Well, how about, erm ... How about tomorrow evening? Say till about six or six-thirty, something like that, and maybe Saturday morning? Is that any good?
H I'm afraid I can't do the weekend. No. I can do tomorrow evening, but not the weekend.
T Would it be possible to do a couple of evenings then? Say tomorrow evening and Thursday evening?
H I'm afraid not. One evening would be all right.
T Erm ... Hmm. Any chance of working through till say about seven then?

Conversation 2

H Hello.
K Hi! Is that Heather?
H Yes, it is.
K Hi there. It's, er, Karen here. How are you?

H Oh, fine, Karen.
K Erm ... Heather, I know this is really short notice ... erm ... Would it be possible ... em ... to borrow your car this evening?
H Oh, Karen, I'm sorry. I'd lend it to you if I could, but I've really got to go to a meeting tonight.
K Oh, right. Erm ... Oh, OK. Well, thanks anyway.
H All right ...
K Thanks. Speak to you soon.
H Yes, OK ...
K OK, bye.
H Bye.

Conversation 3

T 722342.
K Oh hi! Er ... Tony?
T Oh, hello Karen, hi.
K How ... How are you?
T Well, thank you. You?
K Oh, that's ... yeah, I'm fine actually ... yeah. How's work?
T Oh, you know. It's not so bad but ... We get by ...
K Oh great, great. Em, Tony, I've got a bit of a problem ... em ... I really need to get hold of, em, a car this evening and, em, I was wondering, er ... Is there any chance of, em, possibly bor ...
T Oh, Karen, I'm sorry. It's in the garage at the moment. I took it in for an MoT this morning and there's some work to be done on it.
K Oh, that's bad timing.
T Sorry. Er ... no good tomorrow night?
K No. It's, it's tonight ... Oh, well ...
T OK. Yeah, I'm sorry I can't.
K OK, well, thanks anyway ...
T OK.
K OK.
T Bye now.
K Bye.
T Take care.
K I will. Bye.

Note An MoT (Ministry of Transport Test) is an annual safety test for all British cars over three years old.

Conversation 4

S Hello?
K Hi, Simon. It ... It, it's Karen here.
S Oh, Karen, hi.
K How ... how are you?
S Oh, not so bad ... you know ... long day, busy day.
K Er, oh, right. Em?
S Tired.
K Em. Em ... Simon? Is it ...? em, I really, I've got a bit of a problem. I need to, em, I need to get hold of a car this evening. Em ... I need to give a friend of mine a lift and I was wondering, would it be possible to borrow your car at all?
S To, to borrow mine?
K Yeah ...
S Em ... I'm not sure, really. When do you want it?
K Well ... about seven, really, this evening.
S This evening? That's about in an hour and a half's time.
K Well, yeah, I know it's short notice. Em ...
S I've got to ... the thing is, I've got to go and pick up ...
K Right.
S ... my daughter from the station ...
K Right. What, what? Would, would, would, er ...
S I know, I mean it's, it's possible, em ...
K Yeah? I mean, I could, I could come round. I mean it, it, maybe I could make it a bit later. Seven-thirty?
S ... That might be OK actually, seven-thirty ...
K Yeah?
S I'm picking her up about twenty-past seven.
K Right.
S It takes about another fifteen ...
K Right.

S I could ... It's possible ...
K Yeah, I mean, I'd have the car back to you by at least ten ...
S This evening?
K Yeah, oh yes, yeah ...
S OK, em, all right.
K Yeah? Oh, that's brilliant.
S Yeah, fine, OK ...
K Oh, thanks ever so much!

8.10 (see p.82)

8.11 (see p.82)

8.12 (see p.82)

8.13

1 I'm afraid that's not possible.
   I'm afraid that's not possible.
2 It's quite out of the question.
   It's quite out of the question.
3 I would if I could.
   I would if I could.
4 I'm afraid not.
   I'm afraid not.
5 I'm sorry.
   I'm sorry.
6 I can't.
   I can't.

9.1

Part 1

Good afternoon. In today's programme we'll be looking at the subject of cars and young people and considering just how safe a combination they are.

First, some statistics. According to recent research, young people – that is people between the ages of seventeen and twenty-five – are involved in nearly a fifth of motoring accidents. What is significant about this figure is that only one in ten of all drivers are in this age group. This means that a young man aged, say, twenty, is nine times more likely to die in a road accident than his father.

Researchers have also looked into exactly what makes someone a safe or an unsafe driver. They tested young people's skills as well as their attitudes to driving. The results are disturbing to say the least. Apparently between 30 per cent and 40 per cent of young drivers were found to be potentially dangerous. In many cases, it is not because they lack the necessary driving skills but because they choose not to use them. In what is a fairly common situation where a teenager is in a car with a group of friends, it is more likely that they will be driving to impress their friends, rather than to be safe. This, of course, means that they often end up taking unnecessary risks, which can lead to accidents. Andrew Graham, a driving instructor, says:

In my experience, and colleagues of mine say the same thing, both the young and the old overestimate their ability behind the wheel. Erm, actually their ability to judge situations is not as good as they like to think, though I should add, how good a driver you are has more to do with attitude than your age. Older drivers on the whole are more careful and take fewer risks. They are more aware that the car is potentially a lethal weapon. Young people, on the other hand, tend to think of themselves as being in some way immortal.

Part 2

Here are some views on driving which you phoned in to us. First, Jane Haycock, aged nineteen, from Croydon.

I'm really glad I've got a car. I passed my test second time round and I've been driving for two years now. Driving has made me more independent and it's really necessary for going out and socializing. I wouldn't feel safe out on my own at night waiting for buses, and taxis are quite expensive here.

I've been very lucky really. I've never had a bad accident – thank goodness – but I find it quite difficult to concentrate for a long time when I'm driving. If I'm not careful, I find myself looking around and not watching the road. I think my bad habits probably all come from being a passenger in other people's cars.

I'm probably a more aggressive driver then my parents – I mean, I try not to drive too fast and I never, never drink and drive, but I'm not as patient a driver as my Mum. The way I see it, safe driving is about your attitude as much as your ability to handle a car. I mean, you can't do without the skills, because you've got to be able to react instinctively in any situation you find yourself in – but it's attitude that makes some people drive like maniacs and overtake every car in sight. I know quite a few boys like that. They drive dangerously just to impress their friends. I don't usually drive so fast if there are other people in my car.

Now let's hear what Dan Masters, aged twenty-two, from Philadelphia has to say.

Everyone, but absolutely everyone, has a car in the States. It's really important. Unless you live in a big city like New York or San Francisco there isn't really much in the way of public transport. So you need a car to get around. In LA, you're likely to get picked up by the police if they see you on foot.

I think people of my age are much more aware of the dangers than people of my parents' generation. For example, me and most of my friends stick to soft drinks if we're driving, whereas my dad and lots of older drivers I know think it's OK to drink a bit if they're driving. I think that's fairly typical.

Young drivers always seem to get the blame for causing accidents. That's not fair. Sure, young people drive fast but driving slowly causes just as many accidents as driving fast – and elderly drivers, boy can they go slow! They sometimes seem completely unaware of what's going on around them. One nearly drove into the back of me when I was stopped at a junction the other day! Amazing.

And finally Gabrielle Richards from Doncaster.

I have a Citroen 2 CV. It's twenty years old! I've had it for a year. My parents bought it for me when I passed my test. I've had the odd accident – nothing big – when I've driven too close to parked cars but apart from that nothing – touch wood! I'm very safety-conscious and I always feel responsible for my passengers especially as there are no safety belts in the back. I never drink alcohol if I'm driving and I wouldn't get in a car with anyone that had been drinking. And I'd never speed. Someone I know was injured in an accident involving two young drivers who were racing each other. I don't usually have problems with other drivers. They never act aggressively towards me when I'm in the Citroen but I have noticed a more negative attitude when I've borrowed my father's Golf GTI. Some men, particularly older men, don't like to see a woman overtake them. Some of them get very aggressive. They drive up really close behind you and flash their lights. It makes me furious. I'm sure they wouldn't do it if I was a man.

9.2

A   How far is it?
C   From here?
A   Of course. Where else?
C   Well, I don't know.
N   Erm, it, it's about 400 miles, I think.
D   Surely it must be more than that, Nick. It's about 400 miles from London to Glasgow to start with.
C   Well, anyway, it's a long way.
A   That's a big help, Chris.
D   Oh, stop being so stupid, you two. We'll never get anything sorted out at this rate.
A   OK. Point taken. Any ideas on the best route, Nick?
N   Oh, erm, have we actually decided to drive up?
A   Haven't we? I just assumed that we were.
N   Well, I mean, once we get to – what's the name of the place?
D   Ullapool.
N   Ullapool.
C   Where is Ullapool?
D   It's on the north-west coast of Scotland.
N   ...Once we get there, we've still got to get a ferry across to Stornoway.
C   Couldn't we just fly to Stornoway? From London?
D   There aren't any direct flights. And, anyway, I'm sure it's bound to be mega expensive.
A   And we'd still need a car once we were there. I don't imagine the bus service would be very good.
N   Would it be an idea to fly up to Glasgow and hire a car there?
D   Yeah, that's a good idea, Nick. I'm pretty sure there are cheap flights so long as you book in advance.
A   I still think driving up in my car would be a better option. If we flew up we'd have to go into London, and that isn't cheap. How much is a return fare to London?
N   Don't you think it'd be a better idea to actually sit down and do some sums before we start?
D   Definitely.
N   We need to find out the cost of driving up in Andy's car, which uses leaded petrol, and compare that with the price of flying up to Glasgow and hiring a car for ten days.
D   We'd also need to add the cost of a night's accommodation.
A   We could always sleep in the car.
C   Sleep in the car? No way. It'll be bad enough sitting in the car all that time.
D   Yeah, I'm not keen on that idea either.
A   Are you sure you want to come, Chris? I mean you don't have to you know. It is supposed to be a holiday.
D   Is that the time? I'm going to be late. Sorry, but I've got to go ...
N   Well, look, since Diana's got to go, erm, shall I make a few enquiries, find out a few prices and then we can get together next month and decide.
C   Great idea, Nick!
D   Mm. I'm not sure we should leave it till next month, especially if we do decide to fly.
A   OK. Next Friday?
N   Yeah.
D   Yeah, that'll be fine. Look, I really must go or I'll be late.

9.3 includes 9.4 (see p.92)

Conversation 1

J   I think we could make it a mixture of both, couldn't we?
R   Possibly.
R   Yeah.
J   I mean, would they like to ... you know...for instance have a trip into Birmingham, don't you

think that would be nice? We could see the galleries and er ... the theatre.
K   Well, but the best galleries are ... it's got to be London, really.
R   Well, that is true, yeah. I mean London's got the ... well, I
K   But don't ...
R   wouldn't say best ... biggest.
K   Yeah ...
R   Anyway ...
J   Well, there must there must be another way of doing it really because I mean they're going to be studying in London anyway ...
R   Yeah.
J   ... so, it's not sort of not like having a holiday or a break, is it?
R   Well, look, I've em, ... you know, got to go, so, er... well, what do you think?
J   Oh, right, erm ...
R   What do you think?
K   Well, what about we try and combine both? I mean ...
J   Yeah, I think that's a good idea.
K   Is it a nice idea to try and do a bit of both?
R   Yes … mmm ...
J   Mmm, mmm, mmm ...
K   Some place in London and a bit of, sort of natural ...
J   And some countryside or something, er ... yes, the Welsh hills. Would that suit you?
R   Well, yeah, I'd go along with that, yes.
J   Yeah, all right then.
R   So, I mean, we could ...
J   Just a few days in each, sort of thing. Would that be a good idea?
K   Might be a good idea ...
R   Yes. So, I mean, we can continue this maybe ...
K   Well, it'd be nice to make a ...
J   Yeah ...
K   ... you know, a sort of decision today really ...
J   Yeah, I think it would be a good idea to do that ...
K   What would you ... what do you want to do? Where would you take them?
R   Well, I think outside of London. I think they see enough of London, anyway ...
J   Mmm, I'd agree with that.
K   So where? Where would you go?
R   York, as I said, Edinburgh, somewhere like that. Anyway, look … erm ... you know ... can we carry on with this maybe ...?
J   Yeah, yeah we'll have to have to think about the cost you know. And if it's going up as far as Edinburgh, I think ...
K   But there's also time as well ...
J   Mmm.
K   I think Edinburgh's just too far.
J   Mmm.

Conversation 2

J   Oh, no!
S   What?
J   Well, it's stopped.
R   Oh, no.
J   Em, oh, dear.
R   Try the buttons. Try the buttons.
J   Yeah, press that ...
R   Try the buttons.
J   Press the red one.
S   What? This one?
J   Yeah. Oh.
R   Well, that's the alarm, well we saw it ...
B   Well, there's a telephone there. Why don't you try that?
J   Oh, yes. See if you can ... er ...

S No, I can't. The, the, the little door seems to be stuck.

R Oh, no!

J Wouldn't it be a good idea to try and get that little door open? Has anybody anything we could …?

S Mmm … we could try. Have you got something?

B Oh, I wouldn't do that!

K No. Don't fiddle with it.

B I wouldn't, I wouldn't do that …

S Why?

B Well, you don't know, I mean …

R Just, just, play, play with the buttons.

S Well, wouldn't that be a way of letting anybody know …?

K Yeah, they'll know … Why don't we just, just wait? I mean it's only just … you know …

B We could, em, bang on the door? Sing and shout?

J Actually, this has happened before so, hmm it's, nothing new.

S Is it?

J So perhaps if we just wait …

S … How long have you been in here before?

J Well, it's happened once or twice, you know. Oh, a few minutes … a few minutes.

S Oh, it's not too long.

K It'll go in a minute. We'll be all right.

S What about that? There's that little hatch thing up there.

J Oh, no.

S I mean, we could go … I mean … how long have we got in here before the air runs out?

B Oh, well, not, not yet. I mean we could always, erm, just sit, sit down?

K Yes, yes that's …

S A bit like giving up!

J A bit dirty on the floor, though, em…

S Fag ends.

J What about the buttons for opening the doors? If you, if you push that one…

R Well, that's what I said. Play with the buttons.

J Yeah, yeah, good idea.

S Perhaps, perhaps we should try and pull the doors apart.

R No, don't do that. You might see something up there.

B Well, I mean, I think we should just wait a few minutes.

9.5 (see p.92)

9.6 (see p.92)

9.7 (see p.92)

9.8 (see p.92)

9.9

a Would it be an idea to invest the money?

b Don't you think it'd be a better idea to spend it all on a big party?

c We could always spend it on more lottery tickets.

d Don't you think it'd be a better idea to share it out and then everybody can decide to spend it how they like?

e We could always give it to a charity, like Save the Children, or something.

10.1

This is the story of an incredible deception which started out as a desire to help people. Brian McKinnon desperately wanted to become a doctor. In 1980 he was accepted at Glasgow University to study medicine, but a few months into this demanding course he caught a mystery illness and had to spend much of his time in bed. Subsequently he failed his exams and was asked to leave the university.

In 1984 he went back to Glasgow University as a librarian, hoping to be able to transfer back to medicine. When that failed, he began a degree in experimental pathology, still hoping to switch back. After four years, however, it became clear that he wasn't going to achieve his ambition, so he left without graduating. At the age of twenty-seven, as determined as ever, Brian McKinnon went to Canada and started a pre-medical course. However, that route too was blocked when he realized that his immigrant status would prevent him from completing his studies. So he came home from Canada to visit his sick father – an event that was to change his life.

During their last conversation McKinnon asked his father whether he thought he'd ever be able to do anything meaningful with his life. His father replied that he had never lost confidence in his son. That conversation convinced Brian that the only thing to do was to re-invent himself and go back to school.

His only real worry was whether he could pass for a seventeen-year-old boy. He believed he could. But this incredible plan became even more bizarre when Brian realized that the only school that would let him in with minimum documentation was in his old home area. He had to go back to the school he'd left thirteen years before.

He went along, with bogus documentation under the name of Brandon Lee, and enrolled. It was nothing very sophisticated – just a letter from his father who he said was a professor and another letter from a tutor in Canada. The headmaster of the school remembers a very articulate, friendly young man who arrived at the school for interview with excellent credentials. He said he had been touring the world with his mother who was an opera singer and because of this he had been educated by private tutors, not in normal schools.

Brian McKinnon later admitted that he had found walking through the school gates an intensely nerve-racking experience. He was acutely aware of the fact that at any moment a question could arise that he wouldn't be able to answer. He thought, for example, he might be asked for his birth certificate. He remembers meeting one of his original teachers. He says he simply kept his head down, and looked shy.

10.2 (see p.95)

10.3

Part 1

In today's programme we're going to look at ways in which the human brain processes visual information. But before we do that, let's look at some of the impossible objects artists have created by bending the rules.

For the next few minutes, you'll need to refer to the illustrations.

We're all so used to two-dimensional drawings of solid objects that we don't give them a second glance, but look at these drawings.

First of all there's the *blivit*, so called because it asks you to believe it. This is a classic 'impossible object' from the early 1960s. The separate parts of the drawing make sense, but when the two ends are seen together things begin to fall apart. What is the middle prong of the fork attached to and how could the three nuts be made?

Then there are the *baby blocks*, which can be seen as a pile of boxes standing on the floor or hanging from the ceiling. If you can't see the two different images, try turning the page through forty-five degrees.

Thirdly, there's the *staircase to nowhere*. The eye sees the obvious fact that the steps must be coming out of the hole in the ground. But the first storey cannot be flat.

Then there's the *mad spiral*. Here it is the illusion that all the angles are right angles and all the lines are straight lines that gets you into trouble.

Last of all, and perhaps the most famous, is the *tribar*, which was invented in the 1950s. Each part is correct, but the whole triangle will get you in a twist.

Part 2

Why are our brains fooled by these impossible figures? When we look at any picture, the brain instantly processes the visual data and allows us to see the three-dimensional object on a flat surface, although we know it cannot actually be there. That illusion is commonplace – and is very useful to us. The art of painting depends on it for a start, as does any activity where we need to convey a sense of three dimensions on a piece of paper.

But our brains didn't evolve to appreciate paintings, or blueprints for that matter. They evolved to make life-saving judgements in a world where it was vital to interpret visual information very fast.

It is our brains, however, that sort out the information, not our eyes. Light from the outside world hits the retina, but the patterns of brightness mean nothing without the power of the brain to process these signals. That's quite a trick on the part of the brain. Scientists have made artificial retinas – for collecting information from light. But it seems that interpreting the patterns is much harder. Programmers have found it extremely difficult to 'teach' even super-computers to recognize quite simple images.

So it's not surprising that the human brain can be fooled. Where and how it is fooled is a subject that interests psychologists studying how perception works. But people have been playing around with ambiguous figures for far longer than psychologists have been explaining them. Designs incorporating *baby blocks* are found on the floors of churches dating from the 10th century. The first person to write about ambiguous figures was L.A. Necker, a Swiss professor, who described the *necker cube* in 1832. This is simply a cube, drawn from an angle and without perspective, and it has the same effect on our perception as the *baby blocks*. The 'front corner' can become the 'back corner' and vice versa.

As 19th-century interest in perception grew, more ambiguous figures were developed. One major, if elementary, discovery was the effect of shadow – a picture of a sun-lit hill appears to be a hollow when turned over – and the crucial role light and shade play in art. In effect, visual clues are interpreted by the brain in a programmed way – which can be tricked remarkably easily.

It is a small step from the *necker cube* to the truly impossible *tribar*. More subtle than the blivit, the tribar has three linked sections; any two of the links make perfect sense. It is only when the eye follows the loop all the way round to the third link that the inconsistency leaps out.

Put the *necker cube* together with the *tribar*, add skilful photography, and you get the apparently three-dimensional dog kennel. Created by the American William Wick back in the early 1980s, it too is impossible. The clues the brain uses to reconstruct a solid image from a flat picture have been cleverly manipulated and added to real three-dimensional elements, until the mind cannot cope with all the contradictions it is being asked to accept.

10.4

MD Natalie, come in, sit down, what can I do for you?
N No, I won't sit down, thank you, Mr Roberts. I've just come to give you this.
MD Oh, what is it?
N It's my resignation. Open it and read it now if you like.
MD Natalie, I'm sure we can work this out.
N No, no. I've decided. I've got a job in New Zealand. I'm starting next week.
MD New Zealand? But, but, what if you don't like New Zealand?
N I'm sure I will. Everyone says what a wonderful place it is.
MD If it's a question of money, ...
N It's nothing to do with money, Mr Roberts.
MD Martin, please. Call me Martin. Is it the people you're working with, then? I'm sure we could work out ...
N No, I get on fine with all my colleagues. I'm sorry, but it doesn't matter what you say, I'm not going to change my mind.
MD I was thinking of offering you promotion within the next month or so.
N Look, Mr Roberts, you won't change my mind.
MD But all your family's here. What would you do if you were in New Zealand and your mother or your father was ill?
N Martin, it's no use. My mind's made up. I'm going.
MD It's us, isn't it?
N I'm sorry, I have to go.

10.5 includes 10.6 (see p.102)

Conversation 1

J Well, I was, you know, getting a bit bored and feeling a bit staid in the same work, so I thought – well, a complete change, so ...
B Have you tried any teaching before? I mean, what ...
J Well, they, they will give us ... erm ... a bit of training I think beforehand.
B Well, what happens if you decide you don't like it? I mean it seems a bit of a risk to take to give up a good job.
J Yes, I know, but I've, I've been doing this for, you know, a number of years now ...
T What are you going to do about living there? I mean, what happens, ...
J Well ...
T ... what happens if you can't find anywhere to live?
J Well, I think they're going to try and help us to find somewhere and erm, yes, so I'm really excited – it's going to be a great opportunity.
T What are you going to do about the language?
J Ah, yes, well, I shall ...
T You don't speak Czech.
J No – awful, I shall ...
B It's quite a difficult language.
J Yeah, I think so, mmm, I'll have to get some lessons sorted out, won't I?
T Sounds a bit ...
J Aren't you excited? Don't you think it's great?
B Well, I mean ...
T Well ...
Ju I just wish I had your confidence.
J Oh, but it's nothing. I mean, if you want to have a change in life, why not do it?
B Well, I mean, it just seems a big risk to me to take – I mean you've got a ... I mean, I know it's not an exciting job, but it's a permanent job and ...

J Well, yes ...
B You know, it just seems an awful big risk, I mean, what, just what happens if it doesn't work out?
T And what do you do about friends? You're leaving all your friends here. Think about that.
J Well, I shall make new friends and, I mean, I'm outgoing and sociable and I shall meet an awful lot of new people in the school I'm going to.
T I'm not so sure. Sounds a bit risky to me.
J No, no, they're a very nice lot. I've, I've talked to them quite a lot and I've, I've talked to some other people who've been there and they're very enthusiastic about it so, you know, I've got to make a move, really I've, well, I've made my mind up – I have to have a change in life, I think.
B Well, I think you should really, you know, think twice before you take it – it's a big decision.
J Well, it is a big decision and I have been thinking about it for, well, to be honest ...

Conversation 2

S What's so good about the country?
Ju The best thing is, is the lack of people really – the, the city's too full. It's not natural for people to live in the city.
R Yes it is, it's, it's, it's exciting, there are things to do, I mean, the country – slow death.
Ju Yeah, but then you can choose, you can choose to go into the city to do the pastimes you want and then you just escape to the peace and quiet of the country.
S Yeah, what happens if it's, like the weekend and you think – what can I do at the weekend? There's nothing to do, is there? What do you do?
Ju Oh, you read and you go for walks and you listen to music and just listen to the, the countryside and it's all quiet.
R I mean, what would you do if you ... suddenly had an emergency, you, you got ill or ...
Ju Oh, well, it's not, it's not out in the outback, there are ... we still get sort of ... the emergency services ...
R Sounds like it.
S You hear terrible stories of people getting stuck when they're ...
R Yeah, I mean in winter.
S Yeah, cut off ...
Ju Well, yes, you can get cut off, yes, yes, I have heard stories of that, but that, that's just a small price to pay for, for just a life.

10.7 (see p.102)

11.1

I Why do you do this job?
A It's a question of money really. To make money. For one photo you can get 60,000, 70,000 if you take in all the worldwide sales.
B There's a definite buzz to it. The most exhilarating moment is quite literally the second that you stop taking the photos. At that precise moment, that's it. You've achieved what you set out to do. Obviously, there's a great sense of satisfaction when you see the results as well.
I Do you develop the photographs yourself?
B No, I have them developed. I'm not all that technically minded. A friend of mine does that. Obviously, it has to be someone you can trust.
I How do you get your photographs?
B You drive around. You look at various restaurants in certain areas of town that you know are frequented by celebrities. You go there and you have a look to see if there are any interesting cars, i.e. any chauffeurs that you know drive certain

people about, any number plates that you recognize. And if there are, then you wait.
A Sometimes you get a tip-off from a chauffeur or a waiter. You slip them a few pounds and they tell you who's there, what time they're likely to leave, whether they'll be coming out the back door or the front door – that sort of thing.
I What kinds of things are you prepared to do to get a photograph? How far are you prepared to go?
A Well, the end result you are aiming for is a sellable picture so you'll go as far as you feel you need to go. If necessary, I'll climb up trees, hide behind bushes, whatever. Sometimes it means actually going into people's gardens, but that's usually quite difficult because of the security systems.
I So you trespass on private property?
A It isn't trespass to me. I'm only doing my job.
I Do you think that the general public supports what you do?
B If there wasn't such a great demand from the public, we wouldn't be supplying this type of picture, we'd all be doing something different.
A I go all over the world doing this job. I've asked people if I can use their gardens or their front rooms and I never ever remember anyone saying 'no'. I don't remember anybody looking at any pictures and saying, 'This is wrong'. All I remember everybody saying is, 'Can we have more?' The world wants to see the pictures. We're just doing what most photographers do all the time.

11.2

J That's very interesting. I didn't know that. How long have you been an Elvis fan, Mr McDonald?
C Just call me Chuck, will you? Mr McDonald sounds awful formal. Let me see now. Must be going on for forty years now.
J And you consider yourself his number one fan?
C Me and my boy both. This is Elvis Junior.
E Howdy.
J Pleased to meet you.
C Called him after the King – Elvis Aaron Presley McDonald. You know he was just a kid when the King passed on. Now, you know more about Elvis than anyone else in the world, don't you?
E Sure do.
C You got a question about Elvis? He knows the answer. His music, his movies, anything and everything.
J Amazing. When did you decide to open your house to the public?
C I decided to open up my home to the public few years ago. I had so much stuff it just seemed a shame not to let the other fans share it. My wife left me not long after that. It kind of got to her in the end I suppose. She told me she'd had enough, packed her bags and left.
J Do you regret that?
C My wife leaving me? Or opening up the house?
J Both.
C Hell, just one of those things. Anyway, let me show you round. That's what you're here for, isn't it? I put all my newspaper cuttings in these here files – not just articles – anything at all that even mentions his name goes in here. And at the last count I had 1,350 files.
J Wow.
C Well, that's not such a lot when you think I've been collecting stuff for the last 36 years. Over here I've got all his albums. These ones are the original ones I bought when they first came out but I've got tapes and CDs and all the cover

versions too. On those shelves over there are videos of all his films, excerpts of his concerts. Now this, this is one of my most prized possessions. It's signed to me. See? I put it in a gold frame to go with the gold and blue satin drapes.

J Very striking.

C They were his favourite colours. Course I keep the drapes closed all the time just like he did. He hated sunlight – even went so far as to paste tin foil over his windows. I took this photograph at the last concert he gave – had it enlarged.

J It's come out really well, hasn't it?

C I'm pleased with it. These plastic bags here are full of ribbons and flowers from his funeral wreaths. Did you know it took 100 vans to transport the wreaths?

J Really?

C Yeah. More than when Kennedy died. Saddest day of my life that was, the day he passed on. We still can't believe he's gone, can we?

E Sure can't.

C Matter of fact I was at 'Graceland' day before he died. Who'd have thought? Now in here is the TV monitoring room. Elvis Junior is in charge of this. As you can see there are four TV monitors, four VCRs. The TVs are on 24 hours a day. Elvis Junior looks through the TV listings and we tape anything that makes any mention of the King. In that trunk there we got details of all the Elvis impersonators. Do you know there were 30,000 at the last count, including a parrot with a miniature jump suit and a microphone fixed to its feathers. Matter of fact we've got him on videotape doing 'Blue suede shoes'. He doesn't exactly sing it, though, does he?

E It's kinda more like a squawk.

C Yeah. It's an absolute hoot!

J Did you ever meet Elvis?

C No. Greatest sorrow of my life is that I never actually met the King. I got real close to him eight times but there was always too many folks between us. Never did get to reach out and touch his hand. Never did. Real shame that. Real shame.

11.3 (see p.109)

11.4 (see p.109)

11.5

1 Don't tell Jessica.
2 You will remember.
3 Matt looks happy.
4 You didn't remember my birthday.
5 You don't smoke.
6 Nothing's broken.
7 You've got my number.
8 Nobody else knows.
9 Let's decide tomorrow.
10 Someone's told you.

11.6

1 Don't tell Jessica, will you?
2 You will remember, won't you?
3 Matt looks happy, doesn't he?
4 You didn't remember my birthday, did you?
5 You don't smoke, do you?
6 Nothing's broken, is it?
7 You've got my number, haven't you?
8 Nobody else knows, do they?
9 Let's decide tomorrow, shall we?
10 Someone's told you, haven't they?

11.7

1 You can't come back tomorrow, can you?
2 You couldn't help me with my homework, could you?
3 You wouldn't be able to come a bit later, would you?
4 It wouldn't be possible for you to work late tomorrow, would it?
5 You don't mind if I invite Tom, do you ?

11.8

trained / untrained
literate / illiterate
mature / immature
efficiency / inefficiency
approve / disapprove
legally / illegally
dress / undress
responsible / irresponsible
agree / disagree
relevant / irrelevant
practical / impractical
experienced / inexperienced

11.9

A Let's have a look at the programme, then. Oh, no. I don't believe it! He's playing Stevenson again!

B He's not, is he? After last week?

A Couldn't score if his life depended on it.

C No, I've never liked him. I can't understand why we bought him.

B How much did we pay for him?

A Three million or something like that.

B Three million!

A And Davidson! How many goals has he scored this season?

C Two. And they were before Christmas!

A I don't know what Kennedy's thinking of. If it was up to me I'd have Thompson and Sanchez play. Wouldn't you?

B I'm not that keen on Thompson. Take last week for instance when he came on as substitute.

C Be fair! He was only on for ten minutes.

B No, I'd rather have Jackson.

C You're joking, aren't you?

B No, I'm being perfectly serious. The thing I like about Jackson is that he gives 100 per cent.

C He's useless.

B And what I particularly like about him is that even when he's not playing all that well he still causes the opposition problems.

C He's useless.

B All right, who would you play then?

C Well, Somerville, for example.

B Somerville isn't fit yet. You could bring him on as a sub but you couldn't play him for a whole game, not yet.

11.10 includes **11.11** (see p.112)

Conversation 1

J Well, I must say I prefer this, something a bit sort of gentle, classical. Puts you in the right mood, doesn't it?

S This is sort of, a bit lift music, isn't it? Don't you prefer something a bit more …

J It is a bit muzak, isn't it? Yes, yes. Oh no, I can't stand that either. That's awful …

S Anonymous …

Ju Mmm, yeah, a bit bland …

J You're right, you're right. No, no, no, I like jazz, actually. I'm really fond of jazz.

R Yes, I rather like that. It's good. I particularly like flamenco, though. That's what I like.

J Oh, do you?

R Yeah, yeah.

J Oh, that's exciting.

R Your Paco de Lucias and all that sort of business, screaming and wailing. It's a bit like heavy metal, I suppose … without the amplifiers.

S I'm afraid I really like folk music, I'm afraid.

R Oh!

Ju Do you?

Ju Yeah, yeah, folk's pretty good.

S Is it?

Ju Yeah.

J Oh, no, no …

R I've never liked that …

J I never listen to that, no.

S I mean, not, not sort of not, not, not boring traditional …

Ju Not traditional folk …

S Not traditional …

Ju … but, yeah, trendy folk …

S Right, yeah, yeah …

J No, that's not my thing at all. Oh, gosh, no, no. I think jazz, really. And I hate pop.

Ju Yes …

S What? Ordinary pop?

J Oh, ordinary pop. I think Radio …

S Radio …

J One …

S … that sort of …

Ju Oh, no. Well, Radio One doesn't play pop.

J Doesn't it?

Ju No.

J You see, I don't even listen. I only listen to Radio …

S So what sort of thing's pop?

Ju Well, sort of a bit sort of bland and sort of, oh I can't think of anybody in particular.

R Bland?

Ju Yes. I can't think of anything worse than just some sort of little pop tune … like Boyzone and that sort of thing, that sort of pop.

J Oh, I don't even know the names of them. Oh, it's awful, isn't it?

Ju Oh, yes. They're all a bit young.

R Not my cup of tea.

J No, no. Don't like that at all.

Conversation 2

B So who's this person here?

S Oh, him? Erm, that's Jonathan.

B Jonathan? That …

S Yeah, I've known him for years. He's a … he's been he's a very good friend … yes.

B Have I met him?

S I don't think so, no. Erm, you might have seen him once when you came round to our house. No, he's a really great bloke, he's … what I particularly like about him is that he's, that he's always in a good mood, he's, he's quite difficult to sort of, to, to ruffle, he never gets bad-tempered, the sort of person you know that you can ring up, erm, late at night and is, and just sort of, you know, pour your heart out to him, he's, he's a great bloke.

B So, is he your best friend, then?

S Yeah, I suppose so. He's certainly one of my oldest friends and I suppose if I … it's not quite the same when … you're older to talk about best friends, but he is a very good friend, yeah, yeah.

B Mmm.

S I mean, just another example. He's, erm, the sort of person, you know, if you, if you break down in your car and you're miles from anywhere and … you can always ring him up and say, you know,

'I'm stuck. Can you help me out? and if he can, you know, if he can he will …
B That's really important, yeah.
S Yeah, yeah.
B Yeah, it's funny, isn't it, how, you know, some friends are better friends than others. But you know we all look for different … qualities. You know, I mean my best friend, I mean, I don't particularly like sometimes, but she's got lots of things about her that I really admire.
S Mmm. What don't you like about her?
B Well, she's a bit bossy, she's a bit pushy, but then on the other hand that can be quite positive, erm, you know, she's very encouraging and, er, and she'll always stick by you so, you know, if you've got a problem, just like your friend you were saying …
S Yeah …
B … you know you can rely on them …
S Yeah.
B … and I think that's probably one of the most important qualities for a best friend or a …
S Yeah.
B … friend to have really …

11.12 (see p.112)

11.13

1 What do you think of modern pop music?
2 What about classical music?
3 Are you keen on jazz?
4 Do you like traditional folk?
5 What's your favourite kind of music?
6 Is there any kind of music you don't like?

12.1

J   So, what are you going to do after university?
Jen Well, I'd love to work as an interpreter for the United Nations or that kind of organization.
J   That's funny – there was a programme about international relations on TV last night. They interviewed an interpreter. You didn't see it, did you?
Jen No. Who was it?
J   He was American – I can't remember his name.
Jen Was it interesting?
J   Yeah, fascinating. They asked him how he'd become an interpreter in the first place.
Jen What did he say?
J   He said he'd started work at the United Nations.
Jen I wonder how he got into that.
J   He didn't say. Anyway he worked there for five years.
Jen Did he work with anyone famous?
J   Oh yeah, after the UN he worked for the American government – apparently his first job was an official visit to Moscow with – wait for it – the President himself!
Jen Wow! The top job! What did he say about the President?
J   Well, he said he was just a normal person – he claimed they were good friends.
Jen Did he say what it was like in Moscow?
J   Well, he confirmed what everybody thought at the time – you know – the atmosphere at that first meeting had been pretty cool.
Jen Did he say how he felt?
J   Yeah, that was really interesting. He said he was really nervous to start with, but he admitted he felt quite proud of the part he'd played.
Jen I bet he did.
J   Yeah, but he also said it was really hard work – he

did concede that interpreting at that level takes incredible concentration.
Jen I can imagine. It's such an enormous responsibility. If you don't get it quite right, you could mess everything up – possibly even cause an international crisis. What else did he say?
J   Oh, it was funny, they asked him if he tried to copy the President's manner when he interpreted – you know all the gestures and things.
Jen What did he say?
J   Well, he said his interpretation was usually neutral. He explained that the speakers themselves can use body language and facial expressions to get their message over – so, he just provides the words.
Jen Hmm – I'd never thought of that. What else did he say?
J   Erm, oh yeah, at one point he implied that the President really loved the show-biz side of the job.
Jen That was pretty obvious, though, wasn't it?
J   True, but he also thought that the President had made a real contribution to world peace – and he felt he'd been really lucky to be part of that process.
Jen Great job!
J   Right, but I just can't imagine the sort of brain you've got to have to be an interpreter. Just imagine it, you're there between two of the most powerful men in the world. They don't speak each other's language. They're completely dependent on you. So what happens? The American president starts talking – you can tell it's going to be a long sentence – the Russian president looks puzzled. The trouble is you probably can't start interpreting until you've heard the whole sentence – and then you haven't really got time to think about the best word to use – you've just got to make an instant decision. Sounds like a nightmare to me!

12.2

Part 1
I Jo, can you speak a foreign language?
J No.
I Why not?
J I don't know. I tried at school. I was taught French. When I was older, I did Spanish for a year and later on, years later when I had left school, uhm, I tried German … Now I start off fine, everything is OK, then I get to a stage when I realize that everyone around me is talking in a language, understanding one another, and I don't know what they're talking about. I can't tell you what stage it is, because I think I'm getting along fine but then suddenly … I don't know, a blank wall seems to set in. I just can't seem to learn a language. I can remember odd phrases, I can speak the odd few sentences in German if I need to, like 'Have a seat' and, you know, 'Would you like a cup of tea?' but that's about as far as it goes and if anyone actually answered me which is what happened to me at work the other week, ooh, I said to this German lady to have a seat and I would bring her a cup of tea and she turned round and said 'Ah', and I got this stream of German and I couldn't understand a word … ooh … I don't know, I haven't got an ear for languages at all.

Part 2
I Do you blame the fact that you haven't got an ear for languages, or is it just because you simply don't have the motivation because you don't have to speak it very often?
J No, I would like very much to learn another language. I love listening to Italian spoken. I think it's an absolutely beautiful language and I would

love to be able to speak it.
I Do you like any other languages?
J Yes, I like German, too. When I tried to learn it I really enjoyed it but I just couldn't make progress.
I Why do you think that was?
J I just seem to have a total blank when it comes to learning languages, but I really have tried.

12.3

1 I've always wanted to be a newspaper reporter.
2 On several occasions I've spent the night in a prison cell.
3 As soon as I saw the newspaper advertisement, I wrote off for further information and a job description.
4 Car drivers should take a test every ten years.
5 Drug addiction is a problem in most countries of the world.

12.4

1 He's a window cleaner.
2 It's a teapot.
3 It's an apple tree.
4 It's a television screen or a TV screen.
5 It's their wedding day.
6 It's a fax machine.

12.5

1 Did you see that strange black bird in the garden last night?
2 My father grows tomatoes in his greenhouse.
3 I've always been athletic. At school I always won the long jump.
4 Your case is a really heavy weight. What have you got in it?
5 I know what to get, I've made a short list.

12.6

Call 1
R Hello, Fringe Benefits. Mandi speaking. How may I help you?
C Good morning. My name's Mrs Davidson. Is Wayne there, please?
R I'm afraid he's not in today. Can I help?
C No, not really, I need to speak to Wayne. It's rather urgent. When will he be in?
R Well, erm, I'm afraid he's on holiday now for two weeks. I could put you through to the manager.
C Yes, please, if you would.
R Sorry to keep you waiting.
M Patrick here. Can I help you?
C Hello. This is Mrs Davidson. I had an appointment with Wayne yesterday afternoon and …
M Oh. hello, Mrs Davidson, yes I remember seeing you in the salon. I'm afraid Wayne's on holiday …
C I know. The thing is I came in yesterday to have highlights put in. And I, well, I washed my hair this morning and, the thing is, it's gone a funny shade of green. I have to have it put right immediately – I've got an important business meeting this afternoon. When can you fit me in?
M Well …
C I won't take no for an answer. I hold your salon to blame for this.
M Let me see. How about midday?
C Not soon enough I'm afraid. My meeting starts at one o'clock.
M Erm. Eleven-thirty?
C I have contacted my solicitor.
M Come in straight away, Mrs Davidson. We'll see what we can do.

Call 2

W Hello.

C Oh, hello. I'm ringing about the advert in the paper.

W Oh, yes. You need to talk to my son. I'm afraid he's out at the moment.

C Erm. Do you know when he'll be back?

W Well, he usually gets home about six o'clock.

C Can I leave a message?

W Yes, of course, hang on a minute, I'll just get a pen. OK.

C My name's Ed North and I'm interested in the motorbike. My number's 986402.

W OK, dear. I'll get him to ring you when he comes in.

C Thanks a lot. Bye bye.

Call 3

R Hello. The surgery. How can I help you?

C Oh, good morning. Yes. I'd like to make an appointment with Mr Barbury.

R Certainly, sir. Can I take your name, please?

C Yes, it's Paul Collins.

R Let me see. The first appointment I've got with Mr Barbury is September the twenty-third.

C What? That's six weeks away. I need to see him before that. I'm not sleeping and eating is very painful.

R I see, well, if you need an emergency appointment, Mr Collins, I could fit you in at half-past three tomorrow afternoon.

C That's better.

R But I'm afraid you'll have to pay an emergency supplement.

C That's OK.

12.7

Conversation 1

J ... rather ill, erm, and I'd like to make a personal complaint to him.

H I see. If you'd like to hold on just one moment, I'll put you through to his secretary.

J Thank you.

Ju Hello. Can I help you?

J Yes, as I've just explained to your colleague, I'd like to speak to Mr James, please, urgently.

Ju Oh, I'm afraid he's not in today. Can I help you?

J No, you can't. I want to speak to Mr James, the Chairman of the company, please. It's rather urgent. I've been taken ill on one of your airlines and I believe I've had food poisoning. Now, can I speak to Mr James in person, please?

Ju Well, I'm very sorry, he's not in today. Maybe someone else can help you if I can't, but I'm sure if you give me all the details, I'll be able to help you.

J Well, there's nothing more that I can say, other than I've been to my doctor and the tests have shown that I have had food poisoning on your airline. I'd like to speak to Mr James in person and nobody else. Thank you.

Ju Oh, well, I see. I'm very sorry, but erm, I'm afraid you just can't. I can put you through to his Personal Assistant if you really insist.

J Yes, I do. Thank you.

Ju OK, well, if you'd like to hold on.

Conversation 2

K ... and I really want to talk to somebody about it.

H I see. Can you tell me when you wrote to us?

K Er, it was, er, it was two weeks ago. And the bill came yesterday, so really you should have, er, you know, sorted it out by now. Er, is it possible to talk to somebody?

H No, I'm afraid not at the moment. Erm, can you tell me how much the bill was for?

K Well, er, er, well it was for twenty-eight pounds thirty, but I, I really need to speak to somebody, erm, who can do something about this, erm. I'm

going to be going away for a week, erm, and I don't want you to invoice me again.

H I see. And you say that you've paid this twice?

K No, I've paid it once but you're, you're invoicing me twice and I can't afford to pay it twice.

H Well, what I can do for you is I can leave a message with the person concerned and make sure that they don't invoice you again. And that the money isn't taken from your account.

K Well ...

H Would that be all right?

K Well, that, that seems fine, but I mean, will somebody get back to me and let me know that, ... will confirm that with me?

H Yes, certainly, but it won't be today.

K When will it be?

12.8

1 Can I help you?
  Can I help you?

2 Could you hold the line a minute, please?
  Could you hold the line a minute, please?

3 I'm afraid he's not here at the moment.
  I'm afraid he's not here at the moment.

4 I'll put you through to his secretary.
  I'll put you through to his secretary.

5 Sorry to keep you waiting.
  Sorry to keep you waiting.

12.9

1 Can I help you?
2 Could you hold the line a minute, please?
3 I'm afraid he's not here at the moment.
4 I'll put you through to his secretary.
5 Sorry to keep you waiting.

12.10

1 Can I speak to Mr Gray, please?
  Can I speak to Mr Gray, please?

2 I'd like to speak to Mr Gray.
  I'd like to speak to Mr Gray.

3 Is it possible to talk to somebody about my holiday?
  Is it possible to talk to somebody about my holiday?

4 I need to talk to someone about my holiday.
  I need to talk to someone about my holiday.

12.11

Call 1

A Good morning, Hopkins Engineering.

B Oh, good morning, could I speak to Mr North, please?

A I'm afraid he's not here at the moment. Can I take a message?

B Yes, thank you. Could you tell Mr North that Jenny phoned and ...

A Jenny?

B Yes, that's right, Jenny Staples. And could you say I'm really sorry but I can't make our meeting this evening. Problems at home, I'm afraid. I'll ring him tomorrow. OK?

A You can't make this evening's meeting.

B That's right. Thanks, and don't forget to say how sorry I am.

Call 2

A Hello. TVs Direct. Sarah speaking.

B Hell. I'd like to speak to Mr Flag, please.

A I'm sorry, but he's out of the office at the moment. Can I help?

B No, I don't think so, but I would like to leave a message for Mr Flag.

A Yes, certainly.

B Right. My name's Boycott, Tim Boycott, and I'm calling about the TV I ordered from your shop three weeks ago.

A Did you say Boycott?

B Yes, that's right. That's B–O–Y–C–O double T. It's about the TV I ordered three weeks ago. I'd like you to let Jerry Flag know that I am cancelling my order because I am fed up with waiting.

A I see. You wish to cancel.

B That's right. Oh, and incidentally, tell Mr Flag that Price-Savers have the same TV in stock at a lower price. Goodbye.

Call 3

A Hello, City Bank. How can I help?

B Hello, this is Elaine Barker. I really wanted to speak to my sister, Helena, but she's probably out at the moment.

A Erm, yes, I'm afraid she is.

B OK. Could you to ask her to ring me back as soon as she gets in, please? Just say that Elaine rang. It's about our party on Saturday.

A The party?

B Yes, I'm going to get the food and drink this afternoon and I really need to know how many people have told her they're coming.

Call 4

A Hello.

B Oh, good morning. I'd like to speak to Mr Collins, please.

A I'm sorry, but he's at work today. Can I take a message?

B Yes, if you wouldn't mind. This is the Wheels Insurance Company claims department. My name's Paul Baker.

A Wheels Insurance, yes, and what was your name again?

B Paul Baker.

A Paul Baker.

B Yes, could you let Mr Collins know that we have still not received his completed claims form and that until we do we cannot deal with his claim.

A Oh, yes, I'll tell him as soon as he gets in. Has he got your number?

B I don't know, but tell him he can phone me on 327859 or simply post or fax us his form in the next day or two.

Writing guidelines

Formal letters
Units 1, 3, 6, 8, 10

There are different degrees of formality in letter writing, from old-fashioned legal style letters to a friendly, but careful style of a job application or a simple request for information.

For most everyday situations you need only to be able to write in a polite style which is not too familiar.

Note These notes apply equally to other types of correspondence, like faxes and e-mails.

Important features

1 Use full, uncontracted verb forms.
   We are looking forward to hearing your news.

2 Link clauses to make longer sentences.
   As we pointed out previously, all payments are due by the end of the month.

3 Choose formal words and phrases rather than slang or colloquialisms.
   We are most grateful for all your help last weekend.
   NOT *Thanks a million for giving us a hand last weekend.*

4 Use single-word verbs in preference to phrasal verbs – as long as you can do this without altering what you want to say.
   *I am **returning** the form which I have **completed** fully.*
   The writer uses *returning* (not *sending back*) and *completed* (not *filled in*).

5 Avoid the over-use of the personal pronouns *I* and *we*, which make writing sound too personal.
   ***It would be of interest** to know if other customers feel the same.*
   NOT ***I would be interested** to know …*

6 Use passive verbs to make what you write sound more formal or less personal.
   *Payments **will be made** to you twice a year.*
   NOT ***We will make** …*

   Which of the features **1–6**, can you find in this letter?

Dear Parents

You are welcome to make an appointment to see your child's teacher to discuss the report on either 23rd April between 3.10 and 5.00 or 24th April between 6 p.m. and 8.30 p.m.

Please complete the reply slip and return it to us no later than 14th April, so that staff can arrange the timetable of appointments.

Every effort will be made to see you on the day you would prefer, but we are sure you will understand that it may not be possible for everyone to have the time of their choice.

Making notes
Units 2, 3, 10

If you have to give a talk, speech or presentation, it is important to prepare what you are going to say. Written notes will help to remind you about important information, ideas and opinions you want to express. They can also make you feel more confident.

Making notes can be a helpful when you are preparing to write a report or a letter. They provide a simple way of organising your ideas.

Important features

1 Notes should be brief and to the point. They are intended to help you remember the main points, so don't write more than is necessary.

2 Write only important topic words. Leave out unimportant grammar words, like articles, auxiliary verbs, pronouns, etc.

3 Use numbers, letters or symbols to make your sequence of ideas clear.

4 Use CAPITAL LETTERS, and underline or highlight particular words and phrases to make your notes clear to read and understand at a glance.

   Read these notes for a short speech or for a written report on the reasons for moving the head office of a company from a city centre to a new small town location. Which of the features can you find?

Why move?

1 **MONEY** – higher rent
2 **STAFF comfort** – city / stress
3 **TRAVEL** – shorter journeys to work
4 **CONVENIENCE** – on motorway / near airport

Practicalities
1 **WHEN to move?** Next year– May –> July
2 **Staff EXPENSES** – £1000 each
3 **JOBS** – no redundancies / 50 – 60 MORE

Next steps
1 Regular meetings – weekly until move
2 Choose new site – by October
3 Building work – select architects and builders
4 Moving arrangements

The style of informal letters is similar to that of everyday speech. The better you know the person you are writing to, the more informal your language can be.

Note These notes apply equally to other forms of correspondence, like faxes and e-mails. E-mails are often written in very informal language.

Important features

1 Use contracted verb forms.
   ***You'll** probably think **it's** strange that **I'm** writing again so soon.*

2 Leave out certain words, for example pronouns and auxiliary verbs.
   *(**I'm**) Looking forward to seeing you. / (**I'll**) See you soon.*

3 Write in short sentences. This makes writing sound more like speech.
   We went to Paris for the weekend. It's a great city. Have you ever been there?

4 Choose slang or colloquial words and phrases.
   *I can't **get enough telly. Watching** a **corny soap** is my way of **unwinding**.*
   NOT *I really enjoy watching television. My favourite method of relaxing is to watch an unoriginal soap opera.*

5 Do not deliberately avoid using phrasal verbs in preference to single-word verbs.
   *I can't **get through to** her any more.*
   NOT *I cannot make her understand any more.*

6 Choose active rather than passive verbs.
   ***We all agreed** that …*
   NOT ***It was agreed** that …*

7 Include conversational questions.
   What do you think? Don't you agree?

8 Include dashes (–) and exclamation marks (!!).
   You'll never guess what's happened – I've passed my test!!

9 Write in a personal tone.
   I'm glad you're getting on OK in your new job. Is it well paid?

Which of the features you can find in this letter?

Dear Jo,

Thanks for phoning this morning. Sorry I was in such a hurry – but you know what it's like when you're worried about being late. Tried to get back to you at lunchtime but there was no reply. Where were you ? – Anyway, I thought I'd write instead. If there'd been time this morning I'd have told you the great news. You've probably guessed already – I'm expecting a baby! Due in April !

Often when we write, we include narratives or 'stories' – descriptions of things that happened to us or to people we know. We tell the stories for interest or to provide explanations or background information.

Probably the most important part of a narrative, whether it is factual or imaginary, is the beginning. In the opening paragraph of a novel, a short story or an anecdote in a letter, for example, the writer tries to capture readers' interest and set the scene for what follows.

Important features

1 First paragraphs
   a Describe the background to the main event. This will probably include saying something about where and when the event takes place and will probably involve a combination of the Past simple, Past continuous and Past perfect.
   b Introduce the main 'characters' in your story. Mention their personality, appearance and behaviour. If you (the writer) are/were personally involved with the events and the characters, make this clear.
   c Start the sequence of events which make up the story itself. End the paragraph leaving the reader wanting to know the rest of the story. Remember to use appropriate sequence words like *First, Later, Then, Afterwards* etc.

2 General
   a Think carefully about the beginning, middle and ending of your story and the links between them.
   b Create an appropriate mood or atmosphere. Describe sounds, smells, the time of day, the surroundings and 'your' feelings.
   c Use a variety of adjectives and adverbs to make the narrative 'come alive' for the reader.
   d Remember to use appropriate narrative tenses.
   e Include 'direct speech' if it is appropriate.

Which of the features can you find in this first paragraph?

It was late by the time we left the house-warming party. Frost sparkled on the grass as Mary and I slowly strolled towards the front gate. It was nearly a quarter past twelve and there was no sign of the taxi we had booked for midnight. We chatted about the party, about the old friends we'd talked to and the people we'd met for the first time. We were tired but it had been a great evening and we were feeling very relaxed. Suddenly, we heard a loud crack and, when we turned round, we saw smoke pouring from the upstairs window of the house we'd just left.

'Oh no!' I screamed. 'My Letters!'

Whenever you write a set of instructions telling someone you know well how to do something, or more formal instructions like rules, (e.g. for a club, or organisation or for a game), clarity and accuracy are important.

Important features

1 Use direct, recognisable language structures to express what the reader should and should not do. Imperatives are a useful way of doing this.
Do this! / You've got to … / You should … / Remember to …
Don't do this! / You shouldn't … / Don't forget to …
Make sure you … / don't …

2 Avoid indirect forms of instruction which may hide important information or confuse the reader.
I wonder if you could possibly …
If you wouldn't mind etc.

3 Break up complex instructions into several stages to keep your writing simple.

4 Order instructions in the correct sequence if this is appropriate (for using electrical equipment, or playing a game etc.). You can use numbers to emphasize the sequence.

Which of the features can you find in these instructions?

1
John, Sorry to hear about your camera. Of course you can borrow mine, but the only thing is I've lost the booklet that came with it. Don't worry, it's pretty simple.

Check the battery — I haven't used it for a couple of months.
Make sure you use the right kind of film — it works best on a 200.

Choose the shape of picture you want — you can have a normal square picture or wide landscape view.

When you're ready to take the photo, press the button quite hard — it sticks sometimes. Don't press it too hard — it sometimes jams.

Good luck Sean

2
To reply to an e-mail you've been sent, display the original e-mail then follow these steps:
1 Click the Reply button.
2 Type the text of your message in the box in the bottom half of the dialogue box.
3 To send the message click the Send icon.

Radio adverts are expensive, so concise writing is important. The main advantage they have over printed adverts is that voices, sound effects and music can be used.

Important features

1 The words must be clearly audible, especially if there is background noise, or if a conversation is included.

2 The language must be easy to understand at first hearing as you don't know who the audience is.

3 In commercials, the important points are often repeated two or three times to be more memorable.

4 Use words which sound interesting when they are spoken.
Alliteration *It's **n**ew. It's **n**atural. It's **N**ovamatic.*
Rhyme *If you're feeling **sickly**, or your throat's sore and **tickly**, for a fast recovery. take Medi**quickly**.*
Onomatopoeia **KERPOW! PRANG! SMASH!** – *Relax your car's insured with The Crashfree Insurance Company.*

5 Use a wide range of tones and styles – from serious and informative to light or humorous.

6 The context or situation should be clear, include information which helps listeners to visualize the scene.

Which of the features can you find in these commercials?

1
We interrupt this programme to bring you an important announcement from Star TV and Audio. You could be paying too much for your TV and video. Find out how much you could save every month by calling in to any Star TV and Audio store. For more details phone us on Freephone 0880 484437. There's a Star store near you.

2
Attention! Thinking of selling or trading in your car? Call us first. Call Deals on Wheels on 081 899768, that's 081 899768. At Deals on Wheels, we'll give you a good deal on your wheels. Call Now!

3
Noise of car driving along, music in background. Then sound of mobile phone numbers being dialled. Music is turned down.
Man Hi, Mandy.
Woman John. What a surprise!
Man I couldn't wait to phone you.
Woman I've been hoping you'd ring.
Man Can I see you tonight? I thought… **(Screeching noise)**
Oh no! **(Crashing noise)**
Woman What is it? John, are you OK? John?
(Ambulance siren)
Serious voice Don't dial and drive if you want to hear someone's voice again. Hang up now! Remember
Don't dial and drive.

Note Script 3 is a public information announcement rather than a commercial.

Reviews of books, films, plays, live concerts or recorded music appear regularly in newspapers and magazines. A good review may persuade us to buy a new CD, go to see a particular film or change our opinion. Although people who are not professional critics are more used to *talking* about films, books and CDs, the ability to express opinions in writing is a skill which you may be able to use in many types of writing, from personal letters to home-produced newsletters and magazines, or on Internet websites.

Important features

1 Include factual information about the thing you are reviewing.
The new CD from Bass Instincts, 'Dance Instinct', has 17 tracks and lasts 56 minutes.

2 Give readers an idea of the subject matter and some background information as well as saying who the film / book is for.

3 Include your own opinions and the reasons or explanations for these opinions.
I must admit, I found this film rather boring. For a start it lasted nearly three hours – and for at least half this time we were simply watching people having conversations which were difficult to hear clearly.

4 Choose an informal or a more formal style of writing depending on who the review is for.

5 End your review with a definite recommendation to the reader.
You'll be sorry if you miss this film.
Unless you enjoy feeling suicidal, resist the temptation to buy this novel.

Which of the features can you find in this film review?

Nell, starring Jodie Foster and Liam Neeson is a wonderful film. It's the fascinating story of a young woman who has grown up in complete isolation in a remote part of America's deep south. An anthropologist and a doctor discover Nell and study the way she lives. They have to decide whether she can continue to live alone or whether she needs to be looked after. The close relationship which develops between the doctor and Nell is sympathetically portrayed by Neeson and Foster. For me this was the most interesting aspect of this film which gripped me from beginning to end.

Don't miss **Nell** if it comes to a cinema or video shop near you.

Taking phone messages is something many people do on a regular basis at home and at work. At home, we usually simply write a few notes on a scrap of paper, whereas in work contexts, specific information and details may have to be written on printed forms.

Important features

1 Messages should be clear, simple and easy to understand without further explanation from the writer of the message.

2 Write down only the most important information. Don't try to write down everything the caller says unless a particular form of words is important. In this case, ask the caller to dictate the message slowly to you.

3 Use abbreviations to help you to write more quickly.

4 Make a note of these details.
  a Who the message is for.
  b Who the call is from – include a phone, fax or e-mail number where this person can be contacted.
  c Who has taken the message.
  d The subject or purpose of the call.
  e Any specific instructions from the caller.
    Please return call after 3.00pm.
    Will call again this evening.
  f The time of the call.

5 Mention the attitude of the speaker or add a personal opinion to the message if this is helpful or appropriate.
The caller was very annoyed. I think a quick response would be a good idea.

Which of the features can you find in these messages?

1 Message

Karen Your Mum rang this morning. Going home for dinner? Ring her before 6.
                                         C.

2 Telephone Message

FOR		*Penny Holton*
CALLER	name	*Jeremy Gratton*
	company	*City Exports*
	tel.	*231 9786 Ext. 87*
	fax	*231 9889*
MESSAGE		*Today's meeting cancelled. Next Monday OK instead –8.30 in morning? Ring to confirm a.s.a.p. Mr Gratton really sorry – don't think it was excuse.*
DATE		*17 Jan*
TIME		*10.05 am*
		Message taken by Paul Nixon

Interaction and check

From Unit 5 p.44/45

Lucie and Matthew Moss   Nelson Fuller and Ruth Praill   Pip and Helen Rook

From Unit 10 p.97

Student A

Read these statements, then report them to your partner using passive constructions to show that you do not know whether the information you are passing on is true.

- Elephants and lions lived in Alaska 12,000 years ago.
- In 1956 an iceburg larger than Belgium was seen in the South Pacific.
- The greatest number of UFO sightings happen when Mars is at it's closest point to Earth.
- The average person can tell the difference between 2,000 smells.
- In California it is against the law to kill a butterfly.

From Unit 10 p.97

Student B

Read these statements, then report them to your partner using passive constructions to show that you do not know whether the information you are passing on is true.

- When it is born, a panda is smaller than a mouse.
- No piece of paper can be folded more than seven times.
- Forty-six countries in the world don't have a coastline.
- A mosquito has 47 teeth.
- 99 percent of all forms of life that have existed on Earth are now extinct.

From Unit 10 p.98

The Kennel of confusion is, of course, an optical illusion – not a mind-bending reality. The pieces that make up the frame contain sawn-out gaps. Photographed from just the right angle they are filled in by those behind – which appear to be in front. To further confuse the eye, clever shaping means that some of the pieces of wood are wider in places, and so you believe them to be closer. The apparently horizontal piece of

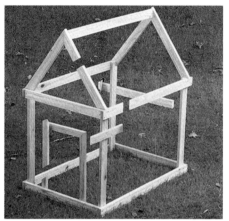

wood on which a puppy seems to be climbing in the original trick shot is actually a separate piece of wood on the ground behind the kennel.

OXFORD
UNIVERSITY PRESS

Great Clarendon Street, Oxford OX2 6DP

Oxford University Press is a department of the University of Oxford.

It furthers the University's objective of excellence in research, scholarship,and education by publishing worldwide in

Oxford New York

Athens Auckland Bangkok Bogotá Buenos Aires Calcutta Cape Town Chennai Dar es Salaam Delhi Florence Hong Kong Istanbul Karachi Kuala Lumpur Madrid Melbourne Mexico City Mumbai Nairobi Paris São Paulo Singapore Taipei Tokyo Toronto Warsaw
with associated companies in Berlin Ibadan

Oxford and Oxford English are registered trade marks of Oxford University Press in the UK and in certain other countries

ISBN 0194330850

(2000) Impression

Printing ref (last digit) 6 5 4 3 2 1

Printed in Hong Kong

Acknowledgements

The authors would like to thank the following people for their help and advice: Jill Coleman, Roger Steel, Heather Barton, Tony Kidd, Julie Peirson, Hannah Piper, Daniela Santos.

The publishers and authors are very grateful to the following teachers and organizations for reading, and/or piloting the manuscript, and for giving invaluable feedback: David Barnes, Peter Beswick, Martine Braekman, Brian Brennan, Fiona Campbell, Patrick Creed, Malcolm Cook, David Doyle, Jackie Halsall, Felicity Harwood, Tim Herdon, Forrest Hobbs, Jane Hudson, Amanda Jeffries, Marina Lambrou, David Massey, Paul Meehan, John Mullarkey, Dennis O'Neill, Penny North, Teresa Pelc, Christina Ruse, Nick Sheard, Yolanda Scott–Tennent, Academia Cambridge House, Madrid, Spain; C.I.E.L, Strasbourg, France; City College, English Language School, Radom, Poland; Diamond School, Paris; EFL Department, Hampstead Garden Suburb Institute, London; PHTI –OSP, Gent, Belgium; Regent Godmer House, Oxford; Teach-in, Rome, Italy; The British Council, Budapest; The British Institute of Florence, Italy; The English School of Communication Skills, Kraków, Poland; EOI Tarragona, Spain

The authors and publisher are grateful to those who have given permission to reproduce the following extracts and adaptations of copyright material: p.6 'An easy, risky way to get around' by Alison O'Connor. Appeared in *The Irish Times* 18 November 1995, and reproduced with their permission; p.6 'Out of Japan: A restaurant dish to die for' by Terry McCarthy. Appeared in *The Independent* 26 April 1993, and reproduced with their permission; p.6 'The dangerous games our children play' by Sally Williams. Appeared in *The Independent* 27 May 1996, and reproduced with their permission; p.16 'Hidden Talents' by Anne Harries, 4 May 1994 © *The Guardian*; p.18 'The happiest day of my life' by Germaine Greer first appeared in *The Guardian* 21 January 1994. Reproduced by permission of Gillon Aitken Associates Ltd; p.24 'How a changing globe reinvents it's wildlife as it rolls along'

by Dougal Dixon appeared in *Focus* January 1994 edition, and reproduced by permission of Gruner & Jahr (U.K.) Partners; p.25 'Futuropolis' by Fergus Flemming appeared in *Focus* January 1995 edition, and reproduced by permission of Gruner & Jahr (U.K.) Partners; p.30 Oxford Advanced Learner's Dictionary (5th edition) © Oxford University Press 1995; p.38 'Life in a frozen land' appeared in *Focus* January 1995 edition, and reproduced by permission of Gruner & Jahr (U.K.) Partners; p.44 'Couple Matching' March 1995 © *She Magazine* / Sally Brown; The National Magazine Company; p.48 'Brainy apes make a show of themselves' by Anthony Georgieff, reproduced with his permission. Appeared in *The European Magazine* 5-11 September 1996; p.54 Lark Rise to Candleford: Candleford Green by Flora Thompson (Oxford University Press 1945) by permission of Oxford University Press; p.54 'The day that changed my life', 1 February 1996 © *The Guardian*; p.54 Reproduced from 35 Up by Claire Lewis and Kelly Davis with permission of BBC Worldwide Limited; p.55 'The day that changed my life' by Ute Lemperer, 2 November 1995 © *The Guardian*; p.56 'Hilltop hideaway of longevity: Campodimele' by Rossella Lorenzi, reproduced with her permission. Appeared in *The European Magazine* 6-12 January 1995; p.58 Extracts from BBC Radio 4's 'The Afternoon Shift' 1 July 1997. Reproduced by permission of the BBC; p.65 Extracts from Issue Brief summarising CAEPR Discussion Paper No. 109, 'The economic status of Indigenous Australian households: a statistical and ethnographic analysis' by D. E. Smith and A. E. Daly published in July 1996 © CAEPR; p.65 Extracts from 'Traditional Aboriginal Culture'. Copyright © Grolier Incorporated; p.66 'My terrifying journey through hotel inferno' by Ruth Fisher, 4 October 1990 © *The Observer*; p.66 'Man falls from jet and lives', 4 April 1994 © *Daily Mail*; p.68 'Paradise? No, but one of the world's greenest cities' by Jan Rocha, 5 June 1996 © *The Guardian*; p.69 'Driven to distraction' appeared in *Focus* September 1994 edition, and reproduced by permission of Gruner & Jahr (U.K.) Partners; p.75 Extracts from 'Kennedy Family' and 'Fonda Family'. Copyright © Grolier Incorporated; p.76 'Keeping it in the family' by Dalbert Hallenstein, reproduced with his permission. Appeared in *The European Magazine* 18-24 April 1996; p.78 'How the family pecking order affects you' by Elizabeth Udall. Appeared in *The Independent* 16 September 1996, and reproduced with their permission; p.84 'Have school, will travel' by Reva Klein, reproduced with her permission. Appeared in the *Times Educational Supplement* 8 August 1997; p.86 'Tourists move in as city locals flee the big heat' by Samantha King, reproduced with her permission. Appeared in *The European Magazine* 15-21 August 1996; p.87 'Chapter of accidents from a public safety ad', 15 September 1984 © *The Guardian*; p.94 'Bogus schoolboy stuns pupils', 20 September 1994 © *The Guardian*; p.96 'Virtual pets live virtual lives to the full' by Jack Scholfield, May 1995 © *The Guardian*; p.98 'Don't believe your eyes' appeared in *Focus* December 1994 edition, and reproduced by permission of Gruner & Jahr (U.K.) Partners; p.105 'The Sean Penn Syndrome' by Ursula Kenny appeared in *Options* October 1996 edition. Reproduced by permission of Robert Harding Syndication; p.105 Channel 4 Hard News Special (September 1997) by permission of Channel Four Television Corporation; p.106 Savage Skies, Granada Television booklet published by Granada Television Ltd; p.108 'He that hath no fans', 1992 © *Daily Mail You* Magazine; p.115 'Conversations with my fridge' by Tim Nott, 23 March 1995 © *The Guardian*; p.115 'Chattering Glasses' by Robin Dunbar from Madame Figaro, March 1996 © *The Guardian*; p.118 'Did you hear about yer wan?' by Arminta Wallace. Appeared in *The Irish Times* 23 March 1996, and reproduced with their permission.

Although every effort has been made to trace and contact copyright holders before publication, this has not always been possible. We apologize for any apparent infringement of copyright and if notified, the publisher will be pleased to rectify any errors or omissions at the earliest opportunity.

The publishers would like to thank the following for their kind permission to reproduce photographs and other copyright material: p.46 Advertising Archives (Volvo logo); p.76 (Benetton adverts), Ivan Allen (Inkshed/cartoon); p.46 Apple Computers (logo); p.6 Ardea London (puffer fish); p.46 BMW (logo); p.46 The Body Shop (logo); p.54 Bridgeman Art Library (A Sprig of Heather, Cheltenham Art Gallery & Museums, Gloucester, UK / Lady Pansy Pakenham, Christies, London / Nun, City of Bristol Museum & Art Gallery / wedding, Musee des Beaux-Arts Rennes, France / H Cordier,

Towner Art Gallery, Eastbourne / First Steps), p.99 (painting of plane); p.52 Camera Press Ltd (W Conran / lap top); p.64 Colorific! (P Tweedie / Aboriginal art); p.108 (R Open / Elvis memorabilia); p.34 Comstock Photo Library (father and son); p.39 Corbis UK Ltd; p.4 (P Corrall V / speaker); p.6 (T Shreshinsky / hitchhiker); p.18 (Bettmann / woman); p.49 (Humphrey Bogart); p.74 (Bettmann / Peter Fonda, UPI / Edward & Rose Kennedy); p.104 (Bettmann / Reuter / Princess Diana), p.116; p.96 Cyberlife; p.24 Mary Evans Picture Library; (aerotaxi), p.58 (wedding), p.114 (proposal cartoon); p.46 Ford (logo); p.114 Jason Ford (cartoon); p.48 Anthony Georgieff (Copenhagen Zoo); p.46 Haagen Daazs (logo); p.16 Robert Harding Picture Library (J Baldwin), (T Demin / Int'l Stock), p.64 (Rainbird / Aboriginal art), p.90, p.106 (tornado); p.46 Harrods (logo); p.14 The Image Bank (White / Packert / man); p.46 KFC (logo); p.6 Katz Pictures (M L Fairbanks / train surfing); p.4 S Starr / snake owner); p.104 (R Baker / paparazzi); p.74 The Kobal Collection (Bridget Fonda, Jane Fonda); p.46 Levi Strauss (logo); p.77 London Features International (P Loftus); p.104 (Celebrity Photo / Madonna); p.94 Murdo MacLeod (Brandon Lee, schoolchildren); p.46 McDonalds Restaurants Ltd (logo); p.4 Magnum Photos (C S Perkins / firewalker); p.9 (S Franklin); p.64 (T Hoepker / Aboriginal art); p.84 (G Mendel / Romanian Gypsies); p.44 NMC Enterprises (men and women), p.159 (men and women); p.5 Network Photographers (M Power / divers), p.108 (L Celano / Saba / Elvis impersonators); p.56 Antonello Nusca; p.94 PA News (Brandon Lee with schoolgirls); p.68 Panos Pictures (P Smith / Curitiba); p.112 Pictor International Ltd (cocktail); p.49 Pictorial Press (Brief Encounter); p.74 (J. F. Kennedy, Robert Kennedy); p.104 (Sean Penn); p.5 Planet Earth Pictures (stars); p.19 Rex Features Ltd (D Cole); p.58 (Eva Magazine / old man); p.66 (T Anderson / hotel fire); p.74 (Henry Fonda, The Kennedy's); p.76 (K Harvey / Luciano Benetton); p.84 (New Age Travellers); p.88 (G Bednarev / elderly driver, Chat Magazine / road accident); p.104 (P Mowatt / paparazzi); p.107 (flood); p.4 Science Photolibrary (NASA / space rescue); p.52 Sony UK Ltd (camera, mobile phone); p.24 Frank Spooner Picture Library (Marinopolis); The Stock Market, p.13, p.34 (family), p.36, p.52 (D Mason / fax); p.23 Tony Stone Images (J Darrell / woman, D Durfee / man, C Ford / woman), p.34 (J Gray / supermarket, T Shonnard / tired boy), p.62 (E Pritchard), p.64 (P Chesley / Aborigine boy, O Strewe / Aborigine man, P Tweedie / bark painting / Aboriginal dancers); p.67 (P Harris); p.68 (P Chesley / Bangkok, Lineka / Paris); p.74 (E Bernager / single parent family); p.78 M Dovet / mixed race family, p.78 D Madison / runner, p.78 D Young Wolff / large family), p.84 (L Resnick / Bedouins, P Tweedie / Berbers), p.86 (L Munneret / family, S Nuber / Rome); p.88 (young people), p.106 (A R Moller / tornado), p.112 (A Marsh / popcorn), p.114 (B Ayres / couple), p.118 (gossiping), p.23 Telegraph Colour Library (L Bray / man), p.26 (Masterfile), p.66 (VCL / parachutist), p.88 (passing test), p.112 (glitter ball); p.118 (FPG / S Osolunski / baboons); p.24 Vintage Magazines (car park, house); p.46 Virgin (logo).

We are unable to trace the copyright holders of p.98 and p.159 (Kennel of confusion) and would be grateful for any information which would enable us do so.

Illustrations by: Aldo Balding / Allied Artists p.38; Jon Berkeley pp.8, 24 (night stalker), 69, 89; Francis Blake / Three in a Box Inc. pp.47, 59, 108, 109; Phil Disley p.10, 50, 53, 80, 93, 110; Mark Duffin p.25 (future city underground); Emma Dodd / Black Hat Ltd pp.30, 60, 82, 83, 120; Spike Gerrell pp.63, 114 (chattering); Madeleine Hardie pp.20, 40, 70, 100, 117; Sarah Jones / Debut Art pp.11, 51, 71, 91, 121; Beverly Levy p.37; Anne Magill / The Inkshed pp.31, 61, 101; Kevin O'Keefe / Black Hat Ltd pp.73, 123; Dettmer Otto pp.21, 41, 81, 111; David Semple pp.17, 87; Cover image Dettmer Otto

Commissioned photography by: Mark Mason pp.12, 22, 32, 42, 43, 52 (mugshots / camera), 58, 62, 72, 79, 82, 92, 96, 102, 105, 112 (mugshots / menu / tickets / magazine), 122; Haddon Davies p.16